MO MOWLAM

MO MOWLAM

Julia Langdon

LITTLE, BROWN AND COMPANY

500 611 612

A *Little, Brown* Book

First published in Great Britain by
Little, Brown and Company in 2000

Copyright © 2000 Julia Langdon

Family photographs all reproduced with permission from
the Mowlam family. Photograph of Mo Mowlam's sculpture
provided by Shenda Amery.

A CIP catalogue record for this book
is available from the British Library.

ISBN: 0 316 85304 6

Typeset in Berkeley Book by M Rules
Printed in England by
Clays Ltd, St Ives plc

Little, Brown and Company (UK)
Brettenham House
Lancaster Place
London WC2E 7EN

Contents

Contents

Acknowledgements

This is not an authorised biography. I did not interview Mo Mowlam for this book, nor has she personally contributed to it. But she allowed me to talk to anybody who was prepared to spare me the time and it is her family and friends who really make sense of her story. I am grateful to Mo Mowlam herself for opening this door and, of course, to all of those whom I have interviewed: those whose contributions are acknowledged in the notes and those whom, for one reason or another, I cannot identify. I have interviewed at least 200 people in the course of my research – although there were as many again to whom I might usefully have spoken. I very much want to thank everyone who helped me, dug out their memories and their memorabilia and felt able to talk to me. I owe a particular debt to Tina Mowlam, who was one of the first to suggest that I wrote her daughter's life story. I am so sorry that she did not live to see it published.

A few notes on the text:

References to interviews between me and Mo Mowlam were mostly in 1998 and relate to my research at that time for an in-depth profile published in the *Guardian* newspaper.

Mo Mowlam was known as 'Marjorie' at home as a child and throughout her teens before she went to university. She became widely known as 'Mo' in her late teens, but many of her early friends still continue to refer to her as Marjorie. I have tried to use the name by which she was known at the relevant time.

There are many references to Mo Mowlam's language and her familiarity with the Anglo-Saxon. I have not used the vernacular in the text, not out of prudishness but from a desire not to weary the reader from repetition.

I owe many friends for help. Thank you so much to everyone who responded to my many pleas for assistance. But, in particular, my thanks for help beyond the call of friendship, are due to Lenka Adamova, David Alden, Lara Alden, Sarah Barlow, John Benton, Jeff Boyling, Liz Boyling, Rhidian Bridge, Alyson Corner, Peter Dobbie, Meg Fisher, Frank Glanville, Richard Hoggart, Karen James, Linda McDougall and Igbala Jovelic. Thank you, above all, to Celia Edwards. And finally my heartfelt thanks to Alan Samson and Becky Quintavalle at Little, Brown and Bill Hamilton at A.M. Heath.

Julia Langdon, August 2000

For Georgia and Edward and
in loving memory of Geoffrey

Author's Note

Mo Mowlam decided to stand down as an MP and leave the front-line of British politics within weeks of losing her post as the Secretary of State for Northern Ireland. In the course of the winter of 1999, she discussed the matter privately with her husband and with one or two close friends – including other ministers with similar views. She wanted to leave the government with which she felt increasingly out of sympathy and she contemplated resigning from Parliament with immediate effect. She was prevented from doing so by her profound loyalty to the Labour Party. She told one particular friend on several occasions that she wanted to resign but recognised her potential for irretrievably damaging the standing of Tony Blair's 'new' Labour government. 'I don't want to be the focus for a huge division in the party,' she told him.

She was reselected as the prospective parliamentary candidate to fight the next general election for her constituency of Redcar in early 1999. By the following spring of 2000 it was clear to those who knew her best that she was not intending to contest the election. She visited the constituency far less frequently than she had throughout her previous twelve years as the MP and this was widely remarked within the local Labour Party. 'Her Redcar days are done and gone,' one party member said in the early summer. It led to a direct challenge at a party meeting in the constituency in May when she was handed a letter asking what her intentions were at the next election. She did not respond directly, but was clearly angered. She engaged in a bitter series of exchanges about Government policy in which she strenuously defended the record of the administration and then she swept out of the meeting.

When it was disclosed in early September 2000 that she intended to stand down as an MP she was initially greatly dismayed. She had hoped to keep her plans private until nearer the date of the election. But it was also, in a way, a relief. She put on a new dress and jacket and faced the cameras, insisting that she had not been forced into this position by her demotion in the Cabinet ranks and that she had made this decision herself. She said she wanted 'to achieve something more in the life I have left'. It was true. The irony was that it was a decision she was obliged to take not because she had been a failure as a minister but because she had proved to be too popular.

CHAPTER 1

'There's room at the top they are telling you still'

Belfast and London 1998–2000

When Mo Mowlam was the guest on the BBC radio programme *Desert Island Discs* in March 1999 a political friend of hers rang her at home as soon as the broadcast finished. The Secretary of State was in the bath and her husband, Jon Norton, took the telephone call. 'I gather we could be in trouble,' Jon Norton said to the caller. 'They won't like "Working-Class Hero".' It was a joke but he was almost certainly right. John Lennon's lyrics don't really chime with the ideology of the 'new' Labour Party. Just like Mo Mowlam's politics.

Her life has not been an easy one, which is maybe why she doesn't make things easy for herself. She has always challenged herself and others, and she has continued to do so since she left her job as Secretary of State for Northern Ireland, the post in which she came to prominence as perhaps the most unusual and exceptionally popular politician of her generation.

Since then, as the Minister for the Cabinet Office, she has been in almost constant political difficulty, much of it brought upon herself. In June 2000 she even reheated her own hot water before plunging in, reiterating controversial remarks first made six years earlier about re-housing the royal family. It was almost as if, this time, she was challenging the Prime Minister to sack her from his Cabinet, in the knowledge that her personal standing gave her a political strength that rendered her inviolate. The Downing Street press office secured a transcript of the interview she had given to *Saga* magazine and then adopted an officially 'relaxed' response, on the grounds that the worst thing would be to do anything. The Queen, meanwhile, let it be known that she was staying put.

It was an odd episode for a Cabinet minister whose responsibilities still officially included the effective co-ordination and presentation of the Government's policies. It was odder still because Mo Mowlam occupied the job known unofficially as 'Minister for the *Today* Programme' and yet one of the tests one young journalistic applicant eager to join the programme staff in the summer of 2000 was set was: 'We are on air and we've just heard Mo Mowlam has been sacked. Who would you get on the programme?'

Her present political difficulties started some time before she left Belfast, involuntarily, to come back to Britain. Many attributed the trouble she encountered to her public success, to a political process that breeds envy among those with lofty ambitions and low motives, but it was more complicated than that and the roots lay much further back in her past. She had a sense of unfulfilled ambition and the public opinion polls justified her belief that somehow she had missed out.

She had decided in the autumn of 1998, after an extraordinary public display of affection for her at the Labour Party conference in Blackpool in October when she was given a standing ovation in the course of the Prime Minister's speech, that she would like to be Foreign Secretary. It was a post which looked then as if it might possibly become available because the incumbent, Robin Cook, was not having a happy time. She told a number of her political friends and journalistic contacts that this was the job she would like. During October she told one journalist that she would like Peter Mandelson as her deputy, as Minister for Europe. To most people who heard this, the Foreign Office seemed a fanciful choice for her and, besides, there wasn't a vacancy. Identifying Peter Mandelson as her potential number two seemed odd. It seems even more so now, in retrospect.

The first job that did come up, however, was one for which there was a big empty space marked 'Vacant' in large letters. It was the Labour candidacy for Mayor of London or, more specifically, to ensure that Ken Livingstone didn't get the party's nomination for that post. This was the beginning of an extremely ill-managed and ultimately unsuccessful exercise on the part of the Labour Party, which culminated in the triumphant election of the 'People's Ken' as an Independent. The name of Mo Mowlam, as someone who was popular enough to beat him, was first mentioned in early December 1998 and it was discussed with her on a semi-official basis by the Chairman of the Parliamentary Labour Party, Clive Soley, before the turn of the year. Her response was calculated. She knew that Frank Dobson, the Health Secretary, was the favoured choice, but even so she didn't rule herself out. She told Soley that she didn't think Tony Blair would be very happy about her occupying a high-powered, publicly visible job like that, as he was already rather worried that she was more popular than he was, as demonstrated by the opinion polls and at the party conference that had only recently been held.

And that was that – or it would have been if Dobson had agreed. In early 1999 he told Labour Party officials that he was unable to accept the candidacy. 'He said he didn't want to run because he was worried that his family would be dragged through it,' according to one of those involved. Party officials started looking elsewhere. One of those approached was the former party leader Neil Kinnock. He was delicately asked if he would consider chucking in the baubles of a life in Brussels, but he felt that he had done his duty by his party with nine years thankless leadership in Opposition and was not prepared to pass up the cushioned comforts of the Commission for a job which anyone could see had neither power nor a meaningful budget.

At Labour's Local Government conference in February 1999, Kinnock bumped into Dobson in a corridor and greeted him affectionately with the jocular cry 'My Lord Mayor! How are you?' Dobson replied with a short and repeated exhortation. They discussed the post and it was plain that Dobson had reached an identical conclusion to Kinnock. By this time, Mo Mowlam had also decided that the mayoralty was not a job that matched her expectations and she told friends that she had no intention of being drafted. 'Are you going to do this Mayor of London thing?' one friend asked. 'Oh good God, no,' she replied. Even so, her possible candidacy didn't hit the newspapers until March, when Michael White reported it in the *Guardian*.[1] Although she had ruled it out for herself by then, she didn't know if she was still on the Downing Street list of possible starters. She telephoned a number of journalist friends the day this story appeared and casually inquired, laughing, 'Did it come from Number 10?'

She tried to make it even more plain. She had been friends with Ken Livingstone since she had been the Shadow spokeswoman on Northern Ireland and she had used him as a go-between with Sinn Fein in the run-up to the 1997 general election. Livingstone was trusted by the leadership of Sinn Fein and he passed messages in both directions. He explained: 'Once I'd been briefed by Sinn Fein I'd go and tell Mo what they'd been doing. She would say what she was doing and I'd pass that back. If Sinn Fein was about to do something they might use me to tip her off. Both sides were trying to work out how they were going to work together after the election. She was clearly taking risks being seen talking to me when Sinn Fein were in the building.' On one occasion Livingstone even shuttled between Mo Mowlam sitting on the front bench in the House of Commons and the leadership of Sinn Fein in an interview room. 'By the time she came to the election, I think she had no doubt she could deal with Gerry Adams and, if he gave his word, it would happen,' he said.[2] Livingstone was also aware that she was lobbying Tony Blair – unsuccessfully as it turned out – to appoint him to the Northern Ireland team as a minister.

That had not happened when Labour won the election, but there was nevertheless trust and friendship between them. Livingstone boasts that she is the only Cabinet minister ever to dine in his house. It was no surprise that Mo should be the first Cabinet minister to urge his readmission to the Labour Party after he eventually won the contest for London Mayor as an Independent. So when her name was floated as the one Labour politician who might beat him, he knew she didn't want to do it. She confirmed this when, coincidentally, the suggestion of her candidacy appeared in March 1999 on the day of a publishing party to launch the paperback edition of Livingstone's biography. That afternoon Mo Mowlam's office contacted his; the Northern Ireland Secretary had regrettably mislaid her invitation to the party but would very much like to attend. Where was it being held? 'She turned up and told every journalist she could get hold of: "I'm not running for Mayor. Ken is",' Livingstone recalled. Unfortunately for Mo, who was trying to put over a more serious political message, her efforts made only one small paragraph in a gossip column.

She was in a very anomalous political position in the spring of 1999. She had become very famous. She continued to command a largely adulatory press and was in demand throughout the media. She was a natural performer and the public liked her. Everyone fell for her charm. When she appeared on *Parkinson* with the heart-throb actor Warren Beatty it was evident that he was enchanted by her as she brazenly flirted with him on air. The actor Alan Davies, who was on the same programme, related afterwards that before the programme Mo had somewhat surprised Beatty in the green room. Beatty had just peeled a banana and was about to eat it. Mo took it out of his hand, fed it to Davies, took a mouthful herself and handed Beatty back the remains.[3] Hollywood actors aren't used to politicians who steal your banana and of course he loved her for it.

She had collected honorary degrees and won awards – although she was particular about accepting such things only from places with which she had a connection. She was granted the Freedom of the City

5

of Coventry where she had grown up. She was awarded the Freedom of the Borough of Redcar and Cleveland which she represents in Parliament, the only person other than the footballer the late Wilf Mannion. She had a sheaf of honorary degrees from universities where she had studied or taught. She had become a politician of distinction and international renown. The Prime Minister recognised how useful she was to the image of the Labour Government and deployed her. According to her constituency agent in Redcar, Keith Legg, every time she appeared on a Party Political Broadcast the applications for membership of the Labour Party would be double those on other occasions. One appearance resulted in a record number of applications to join. Tony Blair was 'more than happy to play the Mo card', according to several ministers. So when, for example, the Government was in trouble with the nurses about the National Health Service, it was the Northern Ireland Secretary who went to speak to the Royal College of Nursing and who was cheered in a manner no other member of the Government could possibly have achieved.[4] She was pragmatic about it: 'I always say yes, but the party only ever ask me to do the most difficult jobs,' she complained to a friend. 'At the first bad news that breaks, it's always: "Oh, send for Mo!"'

She knew it gave her an independent and powerful standing within the Government, but not everybody was happy with this. One friend, another minister, said that she developed an inflated view of both her popularity and her power and she did not work out what he called her 'exit strategy'. Some of her friends, particularly those who had known her from years before, were uneasy and warned her. Neil Kinnock told people that he was worried about her. Tony Blair had 'a lack of diamonds in the crown' the former Labour leader said, referring to members of the Cabinet. A former member of Kinnock's retinue reported that the view from Brussels was that Mo should tread carefully. Professor Tim Gray, her former colleague from her days teaching politics in Newcastle-upon-Tyne, put it succinctly: 'I think she is quite a unique personality in politics. I'd like that uniqueness to be cherished and not damaged.'[5]

Another professor and old friend, Laurie Taylor, feared that the damage was already being done. 'I feel that her success in political life has meant that what was her essence has been turned into a commodity that has to be curbed,' he said. He compared the woman he used to know with Polly Garter from *Under Milk Wood*. 'She had a terribly happy, loving, embracing view of the world and she's had to try and curb it – and it's a bit sad.' He described the poignancy of watching her at Hillsborough, when he and his partner went to stay for the weekend: 'There was this thoroughly good person embroiled in a political machine which no amount of her bonhomie and goodness was sufficient against. People say her open-hearted, generous, emotionalism could be turned against her. It's always distressing to see the intrinsic part of someone's character being turned into something that everyone can comment on and turn against them. It was all just so dreadfully sad.'[6]

The Good Friday Agreement was signed at Easter in 1998. Mo Mowlam's public popularity continued to grow but was also attended by the inevitable problems of what became known as 'delivering the peace'. By the spring of 1999, it was obvious that she would have to move from Northern Ireland before long. Even had there not been evident political problems, her two years in office had been gruelling. It is a job that takes a toll, it burns you up, whoever you are and whatever your energy levels. Tony Blair knew that she was an asset, but she was also a problem – because she wanted to leave Northern Ireland under her own terms.

The first time Peter Mandelson's name had been publicly mentioned as her possible successor in Northern Ireland was in the autumn of 1998. The idea was floated in a political column in the *Independent*,[7] by his biographer, Donald Macintyre, giving some clue as to the authority which might have informed this thinking. Although the biography was not authorised as such, Mandelson was known to have talked freely to Macintyre for the purposes of the book. Northern Ireland was a subject in which Mandelson had been interested since his time as a researcher on the television programme *Weekend World*, where, according to Macintyre, he had become something of an expert on Northern Ireland. Later, as the Cabinet Office Minister without Portfolio, he kept an eye on what was going on in Belfast, too. He visited Northern Ireland in the summer of 1997, an event that gave rise to some comment. According to one report it suggested 'that Downing Street might be seeking to assert a more central control'.[8] It was certainly the case that, having won the election, the Prime Minister already sensed the importance of Northern Ireland. He would have wanted to know the views of his most trusted adviser on Northern Ireland and the Secretary of State. 'Tony *always* listens to what Peter says,' said one minister. Mandelson had been friends with Mowlam years before, but he had long since held the view that she was 'terminally undisciplined'.[9] This was not something that he kept to himself. Mandelson may well have formed the view then that Northern Ireland was a job with personal political potential for him: he must have been struck by the Gallup Poll in the *Daily Telegraph* on the first anniversary of the Labour Government's election, which gave Mo Mowlam first position with an 86 per cent public approval rating and put him last with 34 per cent.[10]

But at Christmas 1998, Peter Mandelson was obliged to resign from the Government, over the disclosure of his home loan from his Cabinet colleague Geoffrey Robinson. The prospect of him securing an early return to office seemed highly improbable. When one Irish journalist first heard his name linked with the Northern Ireland portfolio in the late spring of 1999 he didn't believe it. 'I dismissed it with incredulity,' he said. 'Then in June, Peter Mandelson – who hadn't bothered to speak to me for months – smiled and said: "How are you?" and I thought, "Christ! It's true!"'

There were many confusing and conflicting stories circulating about Mo Mowlam's future by the early summer of 1999. Mandelson felt it was too early for him to return to Government and that he could not expect to be politically rehabilitated until after the 1999 party conference. He complained to friends that he was 'alarmed' and even 'slightly upset' at being dragged into the ongoing discussion about what to do with Mo. 'So-called "friends" of hers – even if they exist – were saying I was trying to push her out because I wanted her job. I wasn't and I didn't. I couldn't have,' he protested privately.

Things came to a head when relations between Mo Mowlam and David Trimble broke down completely and he demanded publicly that she should be sacked as Secretary of State. It was the eve of a crucial round of talks and he was later asked, off the record, with whom she should be replaced. It was reported that 'senior Unionist sources' had said that there was only one person of substance available 'who gets things done' and that this person was 'currently unemployed'. After delivering this bombshell, Trimble went off to lunch with his friend the newspaper executive David Montgomery, who he had known since they were children growing up in Bangor, County Down. Montgomery was at this point acting as a go-between with the Unionists for the Government. The Unionist leader apparently made no reference to these exchanges when the two men met, because later that day Montgomery rang Mo Mowlam – with whom he had become a personal friend – on routine business. He is said to have been greeted by an incandescent Secretary of State who, almost speechless with fury, put the telephone down on him. She apparently believed Montgomery knew about Trimble's demand for her replacement – and that Mandelson's name had been mentioned – and that he had therefore colluded in what had taken place.[11] From that day onwards, as she must have realised, Mo Mowlam was profoundly damaged as Secretary of State for Northern Ireland.

The run-up to the expected Cabinet reshuffle in July 1999 was punctuated with press speculation about what was going on. It would have made sense for Mo Mowlam to have accepted another portfolio at this time because, despite her professed wish to stay in office in Northern Ireland during the tricky period of negotiation that was then under way, she had in a way lost the moral authority of her position because her political authority had been removed. She had achieved

more as Secretary of State for Northern Ireland than any of her predecessors, but politically she was seen as having run her course. And
she was too popular for her own good. Her enemies within a highly
competitive administration didn't like that one bit. So while the
circumstances may have been unkind, unfair and unjustified – that
didn't really matter if her authority wasn't there any more. Between
them, she and Frank Dobson, quite possibly in collusion, rendered the
reshuffle inoperable. He didn't want to be the stop-Ken candidate for
the London Mayor and she didn't want to be anything less than
Foreign Secretary. They both made public pronouncements, suitably
coded for consumption both by Number 10 and the political lobby,
and thus effectively limited the Prime Minister's ability to operate. The
reshuffle was restricted but the headlines, which had read, typically,
'Mo pleads: Let me finish my job as minister for peace',[12] were soon
replaced with the alternative 'Blair's "revenge" on Mo deepens Ulster
crisis'.[13] Many of her friends were convinced that she had made a profound mistake.

She was offered the job of Secretary of State for Health. It was an
idea that was first kicked around in the spring. She told some friends
then that it was a job she would have liked. Yet she also let it be known
to one journalist when it was all over that it was not a job she could
accept because the historic antagonism between her and the
Chancellor, Gordon Brown, would be used to ensure that she wouldn't
get the money she would need to do the job and the National
Health Service wouldn't get the money it deserved. At least one of her
ministerial friends tried to persuade her that it was a very important
Government position, that it concerned matters of serious political
policy, that it would be at the centre of public debate, that there was so
much to be done that would need somebody with her skills at embracing people and politics. And, most interesting of all to a politician, that,
because of the cyclical nature of these things, there was bound to be
another crisis in Health politics soon which she could help resolve. 'She
said she didn't want it. She wasn't interested,' said this friend. 'She

always says very disarmingly: "I've been away from the whole domestic political agenda for five years." She said that she didn't know about the politics of health. But it's very odd for somebody who is so politically brilliant and so in touch that she didn't stay sufficiently integrated in domestic policy things. What *they* say now is that she was frightened.' *They*, in this context of course, are the members of the apparat.[14]

Mo Mowlam finally turned down the appointment as Health Secretary in the autumn, when Frank Dobson was eventually obliged to vacate it. Politics can come down to basics and it did in this case: Dobson was given the choice of resigning as Health Secretary in order to run as the officially approved Labour candidate in a rigged selection process against Ken Livingstone – or simply to resign as Health Secretary. Number 10 pushed Dobson into what was always a hopeless contest.

The inevitable second reshuffle when it came on 11 October 1999 saw Mo Mowlam appointed to the Cabinet Office as Chancellor of the Duchy of Lancaster and confirmed Peter Mandelson as the new Secretary of State for Northern Ireland. They went together to Buckingham Palace when he was sworn in as her successor. The Queen was late, presumably a prerogative, but Mo and her one-time friend passed the time amicably enough as the flunkeys fluttered around them in the anteroom. The occasion was all very dignified. Then they flew to Belfast together and Mo said her farewells. At the brisk little photo call they took together, sounding pretty choked, she said of Mandelson's appointment that she was pleased the job was going to someone with his ability, skills and commitment. It sounded like the acceptable minimum she could say.

What has not previously been disclosed is that Mo Mowlam speculated privately in her office some months beforehand that she might be prepared to accept Peter Mandelson as her deputy in Northern Ireland. Initially she told several colleagues that while she didn't want him to have her job because he would be 'hopeless', she would be prepared to accept him as her second in command and then move on and leave him to inherit the post from her. In the course of the summer of 1999, however, having made what was such a bad call in July, by stopping her own move at that time, it was nevertheless obvious that she could not remain in her post and she discussed with the Prime Minister who her successor should be. At some point she put in writing to the Prime Minister that she would be content with the appointment of Peter Mandelson.[15] Her thinking was maliciously interpreted by one colleague as being possibly prompted by the suspicion that Northern Ireland would keep Mandelson so busy he might leave the rest of the Cabinet on the mainland to get on with their jobs without his interference. Whatever her motivation, Mandelson did not appear to be either grateful or appreciative, above the minimal courtesies. He told one friend at one of the soirées he introduced into the Hillsborough social calendar, 'I've had to repair such damage caused by that woman.'[16]

When she had gone to Northern Ireland as Secretary of State Mo Mowlam had drawn up a private programme for her First 100 Days. She had no such agenda for the Cabinet Office and the first 100 days were horrid. Everything seemed to go wrong at once. Her mother, Tina, died shortly before Christmas. Her husband, Jon Norton, had lost his job with the Australian and New Zealand Banking Group earlier in 1999 and she was very upset about that. That led in turn to anxiety about their future finances and they decided to put their house in Islington up for sale. They moved to an official apartment in Whitehall, but when it emerged that Mo had been negotiating with publishers to write her memoirs, there was inevitable speculation that she was planning to leave the Government. She engendered some unfortunate publicity by then appearing on Graham Norton's television programme. It was disclosed that her security coverage had been removed – a remarkable enough event for a minister so recently in such an exposed position, but even odder that it was revealed at all. She suffered greatly at the hands of the press, with much cruel and unkind speculation about her state of health. Each separate incident must have caused her more emotional anxiety. And besides all of that she was missing Northern Ireland. She had a chessboard in her office in which one set of pawns was fashioned into 'terrorists' and the other set into 'RUC officers'. It wasn't quite the same. She resented her exclusion from what was happening in Northern Ireland, too. At one point in late February 2000 she passed the Prime Minister in a corridor and he spoke of events there. She told a friend bitterly afterwards that it was the first time anyone in the leadership of the Government had used the words 'Northern' and 'Ireland' in the same sentence to her since she left the post.

It would have been hard to find any job that suited her. The Cabinet Secretary, Sir Richard Wilson, had been instructed to make her new post meaningful, which led to much trouble behind the Whitehall arras. Should she have Rural Policy? Women's issues? Drugs? John Prescott didn't want her to have the first, she didn't want the second and the Prime Minister meant to relieve her of the third – although it slipped past. She picked up a rag-bag of policies, which also included the modernisation of Parliament, machinery of government and genetic modification of foods. Really, though, it didn't matter what her brief was, because she didn't seem to be interested. To the astonishment of her friends, at this point in the spring of 2000 when Frank Dobson's campaign for Mayor of London was going disastrously wrong, she proposed herself as a last-minute substitute official candidate to rescue the ill-fated election on behalf of the party. The idea was floated in the press but was not taken seriously. It was highly impractical, in any case, and would have been quite undemocratic. She had to content herself instead as a member of fourteen Cabinet committees and all that really meant was more meetings. The Cabinet Office has been described by one of its previous ministers – Peter Mandelson, no less – as 'a cross between Waterloo Station and a telephone exchange'. She could easily have made the job matter, but she repeatedly told friends: 'I don't need this. I can do something else.'

It nearly all went wrong when she first took the Cabinet Office job.

She was physically exhausted after relinquishing the responsibilities of Northern Ireland. She had had enough. She said to one friend: 'What am I going to do? I can't take any more of this. Talk me out of it.' 'Out of what?' he asked. 'Cutting losses,' she said. This friend reminded her about swings and roundabouts in politics. It was odd that he needed to do so, because it is something of which she has spoken often when privately discussing her own public standing. A wise politician – particularly in Northern Ireland – knows that you can be popular only so long as things are going well. But even though her political life was not an unqualified success and she found herself increasingly out of sympathy with the whole 'new' Labour operation, she was still seen by the public as the epitome of the perfect politician. Her tragedy was that she had become a prisoner of her own popularity.

At a supper party in the Speaker's House in the early summer of 2000, she was talking quietly in a corner to another friend. 'I can't! I can't resign!' she told him. 'It would cause such a tremendous split and it wouldn't be understood in the right way.' She was almost certainly right about this.

Mo Mowlam sat for a sculptor during this period of her political career. Her university in Durham had commissioned Shenda Amery to sculpt their distinguished former student. The result is delightful. Because artists can sometimes see things in people's faces that others cannot see or are not seeking, her assessment seemed valuable. The sculptor, unprompted, said: 'There's a courage there that's really quite profound. There's a determined energy. I would say she was a driven woman.'

CHAPTER 2

'You could tell by her little face that she was going to win'

Moulham, Watford and Southall 1066–1962

Mowlam, however you spell it, is an old and distinguished name. It even boasts a coat of arms: 'A. a Chevron G. between 3 square Marbill Stones B.' William the Conqueror gave his carpenter, Durandus, the manor of Moulham, near Swanage in Dorset, whereupon the grateful recipient changed his name. One suggestion is that he had accompanied William to England from Normandy and certainly he called himself De Moulham originally. The manor was an area of land which at one time comprised quite an extensive property and it was a handsome gift. Three thanes had held it before the Conquest. When the Domesday Book was compiled on William's orders in 1086 – the year before his own death – 'Durandus Carpentarius' was the 'tenant incapacite' of Moleham. He was taxed for one hide, had enough land for one plough and also had one acre of meadow and a mill. By the second half of the nineteenth century, however, Hutchins' *History of Dorset* observes that the name 'Moulham . . . though anciently used to designate a more extensive property, now only survives in a parcel of ground adjoining the south side of Godlingston farm.' Today, in the way of these things, it is a caravan site.

Durandus was actually rather more of a master builder – or an architect even – than a mere carpenter and he received this reward for his work on the great tower of Corfe Castle, the mediaeval fortress commanding a cleft of the Purbeck Hills which remains grimly impressive, even in ruins. The work, however, was to be ongoing. The Moleham property was granted in exchange for a contract to clear the gutters or as the local records relate: 'That hee should repaire the Timber Work of the great Tower of Corfe Castell, and cleanse the Gutters as often as neede required.' Durandus was clearly happy enough with this. He also received some other property nearby and he founded a dynasty. As the Rev. Mr Coker of Mapowder records in *A Survey of Dorsetshire* in 1732: 'The posterity of this Durand were, from the Place, named de Moulham, and lived there untill King Henry the Fifts tyme.' And beyond. Mowlam and Mowlem are now the most common spellings, but throughout the last millennium the descendants of Durandus have peopled Dorset, particularly the Isle of Purbeck around Swanage, spelling their names in a huge variety of ways because of their illiteracy; some couples often changing the spelling with the registration of the birth of each child.

One such couple in the late eighteenth century, John, a marbler, who married Hannah Froom and had six children, managed to spell their name Mowlam, Moulham, Moulim, Mowlim, Mowlham and Mowlem on various visits to the parish registrar between 1782 and 1797. But they were the people who were first to ensure that their name became well known. It was their third child and first son, John Mowlem, born in 1788 – and baptised Mowlim, as it happens – who made the name famous, founding the construction company which still bears his name. He left Swanage in 1805, the year of the Battle of Trafalgar, going by sea on one of the heavily loaded vessels carrying Purbeck stone to London. He was 17 years old and he went to seek his fortune. It took a bit of time but he made it. His first big contract was in 1839 and it was to pave Blackfriars Bridge in London. They were proud of him back home in Dorset: he was known as 'London John' in Swanage and he was to reciprocate the affection in which he was held. He became a considerable philanthropist in his later years, founding the Mowlem Trust in 1863 'to afford moral and intellectual improvement and gratification to the inhabitants of Swanage' and his name is still everywhere in the town. The Mowlem Theatre stands now on the site of what was previously a reading room called the Mowlem Institute ('for the Benefit and Mutual Improvement of the Working Classes') and there was a De Moulham Road – built by John, of course – although it was later renamed Victoria Avenue in honour of the Queen.

At about the time John Mowlem was building this fortune, one James Moulan, rank and profession cowman, was quietly earning his living in a rather less dramatic fashion on an agricultural estate at Batchworth Heath high on a hill above the hamlet of Rickmansworth in Hertfordshire. His father had left Swanage some time before, or so the family believe. James had married Catherine Maria Saunders and their son, the splendidly named Harry Percy Mowlam, was born in Batchworth Heath in 1888. There is the usual muddle about how the name is spelt, but on Harry Percy's birth certificate his father is clearly identified as James Moulan. It was Catherine who had registered the birth, also spelling her own name as 'C.M. Moulan' and it seems, in keeping with family tradition, she spelt it wrong. Interestingly, however, in 1914 James Moulan took the trouble to make a statutory declaration to the Registrar amending his son's birth certificate. 'For Moulan read Mowlam' reads the signed and dated correction.

Harry Percy Mowlam grew up to be a postman. He didn't move far from Rickmansworth, just down the road to Watford, where he met and married Hilda Alice Filby and where he was to spend the rest of his very long life. It was there, in Abbots Langley, just to the north of the town, that their son Frank William Mowlam was born on 22 March 1916. Frank was to be an only child who was doted upon by his mother, who 'spoiled him rotten',[1] while his father over-compensated for this by being excessively strict.

Harry and Hilda were a kindly couple, particularly in due course to

17

their grandchildren, yet there was little laughter in their house. Hilda was a stickler for detail. The chairs in the living room were covered by sheets to preserve them, even while people were sitting on them. Pets were not allowed in the house; friends were not encouraged to visit. She counted the sticks used to light the fire – no more than five were ever allowed – and it was a source of challenge to her to see how far she could stretch a casserole of meat and carrots. 'By the fourth day you were only eating carrots,' her daughter-in-law Tina remembered. 'Wartime cooking was her joy. They hadn't had much, everything they had, they'd earned and saved for – so they were incredibly mean.' She had a few challenging run-ins with Hilda in the early days: 'She said that I never got up and lay in bed all day.' On one occasion when Tina was staying overnight and lit the fire first thing in the morning, her mother-in-law pulled it out on to the grate and made her light it again, this time using no more than five sticks.

Perhaps the central tragedy of Frank's life – his descent into alcoholism – is rooted in this repression at home. That was certainly the view of the woman he loved and married. He was a thwarted man and his wife lay part of the blame with his parents. As a boy, Frank had passed the examination for the grammar school but his father wouldn't allow him to take up the place. Harry believed that what had been good enough for him would be good enough for his son and that was that. So Frank left school at fourteen and became a telegraph boy in Watford. He was, however – like father, like son – very stubborn and determined to better himself and do well. 'I'll do it, even if you don't help me do it,' he said to his father, and indeed he swiftly impressed his employers with his potential.

Frank was an attractive personality. He wasn't particularly tall, nor even good-looking, but he was outgoing and friendly and charming. He was one of those people who is always at the centre of what is going on. This was a characteristic he would certainly pass on: all her life, from long before she was famous, his second child, Marjorie, was often described in exactly the same terms. In Frank's case it was because he had a compelling presence that others gravitated towards. As a young man he could win girls' hearts, too: he was thoughtful and kind and soft-hearted. When the Second World War started he was 23 and he joined up in the 3rd First London Signals as soon as he could. He had became engaged to one Peggy Watson and had it not been for a chance encounter, when he popped in to visit his friends still working in the Watford Post Office, perhaps he would have married her. As it was he met Tina.

Bettina Mary Rogers narrowly missed being christened Sally Polly Rogers. Her mother, born Maud Ethel Mary Renshaw, had been a lady's maid as a girl to a Lady Margaret Hamilton-Russell and while in service in London from her native Rugby had made friends with another maid, an Italian girl named Bettina. Maud did well for herself, marrying Charles Rogers, a civil servant, an executive officer with the Board of Education, and settling with him at Oxhey, Watford Heath, on the outskirts of the developing Hertfordshire suburb of Watford. They couldn't afford to live in London itself, but the electric railway had been built and Charles could get to the ministry easily enough. He became a commuter, setting off for the train in the morning from their home with the requisite hat and umbrella. They had two sons, Jack and Ken, with a gap of three years between them, and then after twelve years, there was the surprise arrival of a daughter, born on 6 October 1920 when Maud was 40. When the time to christen this infant arrived, it was ordained that she was to be named after two godmothers who were present to be so honoured. Maud, however, was clearly an admirably independent-minded woman; when the moment came she named the baby girl after her old friend instead. Sally and Polly walked out of the ceremony and Bettina ended up without godmothers.

After this somewhat ill-starred overture, Tina – as she was known throughout her life – had some difficult years ahead. She was perpetually ill, with a tendency to catch colds and suffer chest infections. She didn't have a Christmas out of bed, she used to say, until she was 16. As a consequence her parents were very protective, ensuring she had a very sheltered childhood. But she was a survivor, she had lots of fight in her – which she was going to need later in her life.

Tina and Frank were brought together, somewhat improbably, by kippers. Tina was working as a telephonist at Watford Post Office. Things like kippers were, of course, in short supply in wartime, but there was someone in the office who sometimes had things to sell that would supplement the ration book. As Tina was leaving after work she went to see if there were any kippers that day, and as she put her head round the door of the office there was Frank Mowlam. She had known him slightly for years but here he was, home on leave in his uniform, a survivor of Dunkirk, an impossibly romantic figure. Despite his engagement to poor forgotten Peggy Watson, they went out together and then, in a whirl, they were married: his regiment was being sent overseas, it was wartime, there seemed little choice.

Tina and her cousin Jean Allford had also joined up by this time. Tina had wanted to join the Royal Air Force, possibly because her elder brother Ken was in the RAF, while Jean wanted to join the Royal Navy. They agreed to join the Auxiliary Territorial Service, the ATS, and signed up together in Northampton in the autumn of 1941 when they both celebrated their 21st birthday. They spent six weeks in Northampton and were grateful for each other's company, as they were relentlessly teased for being better-to-do than many of the other women volunteers. 'We wore pyjamas and had writing paper,' is how Jean remembers the distinction.[2] They were both selected to work in radar and sent to Oswestry for an intensive course of training; it was during this time that Tina took leave to marry Frank.

Neither set of parents was delighted about this union. Tina's parents were a little better off than the Mowlams and marrying Frank was 'a step down' for their daughter. They were also worried because it was so hurried. The Mowlams for their part were a bit dubious about a family whose members appeared to have had the benefit of some education yet had no money. But whatever any of them thought made not a scrap of difference to the young couple. On 25 April 1942, Frank and Tina were married. They went from the church in Watford to the pub and from there to the London train and the Cumberland Hotel in Oxford Street, where they had a few short days together before Frank went away for three years. They went to a few London pubs. Frank was a social drinker but it was some time yet before his mother-in-law was to catch him putting water in the gin bottle.

Back in Oswestry both Tina and Jean were selected for the Officer Cadet Training Unit and Tina made a significant decision. Jean went away on leave and when she came back she was surprised to find that her cousin had already been posted – to the 498 Battery of the 144 Regiment in Nottingham. Tina had left her a rather poignant letter explaining that she could not accept officer training. 'She had decided not to go to OCTU because it would upset Frank; because he wasn't commissioned, he would find it unacceptable if she was,' Jean said. In Jean's view, Frank Mowlam always had a chip on his shoulder because of his lack of formal education. It shouldn't have mattered, but it did to him and Tina had obviously correctly interpreted how he might have responded if she had accepted training as an officer. Despite their separate decisions, however, the cousins' military lives continued intertwined: Jean completed her officer training and was then sent on an artillery course, coincidentally to the same regiment as Tina – and where the man who was to become Jean's husband, Frank Hughes, was the second in command. In the meantime, Tina had been promoted and was a Company Sergeant Major. She still had to call Jean 'Ma'am', but it didn't matter and they both had a great deal of fun.

When the war ended and Frank Mowlam returned from his years abroad – re-grouping after Dunkirk in Ireland, then out to the Middle-East, then chasing the Germans up the Greek peninsula – the young couple were able at last to start their married life together. They lived in two rooms in the house next door to Tina's parents in the Old School House on Watford Heath and while they were here their first child, Jean Caroline, was born in 1946. Eileen Theobald, who owned the house they lived in and who was friends with Tina's parents, was

Jean's godmother. The lodgings were convenient, it was handy for Tina to be living next door to her parents and it was a friendly arrangement. But Frank was an ambitious man and the object now in his sights was to purchase his own house. Just over two years after Jean's birth, Tina was pregnant with their second child and while it was going to be expensive and difficult to afford, they had decided to buy 28 Richmond Drive, a new three-bedroomed detached house in an area of north-west Watford called Cassiobury Park. It was a very handsome piece of property for a relatively poorly paid postal worker. 'He so wanted his own home,' Tina said, 'and in the end, of course, it paid off.'

Tina's cousin Jean had her doubts. Everyone was short of money after the war but in her view Frank and Tina made life more difficult for themselves than perhaps it need have been. They didn't just buy a new house, but also furniture from Heals and ready-made curtains. Such things were untold luxuries at that time. Jean watched her cousin's lifestyle with a degree of envy tinged with worry and slight disapproval. Although she liked Frank, she thought he was a bit pretentious. When something went wrong between Frank and Tina, he would make it up to her with an extravagant present, a lovely nightdress, something Tina would appreciate but didn't actually need. When money was so short, gestures like that, although charming, were to Jean rather reckless. They were going to have to be paid for and, in their different ways, in the years ahead both Frank and Tina were to pay the price.

Their second child, another girl, arrived on 18 September 1949, shortly before they moved into the new house. She was born weighing 7 lbs 7 oz in a nursing home in King Street, Watford. When Frank went to register his daughter's birth, by the time he arrived at the register office he couldn't remember the second name that Tina had chosen for her. So she was just Marjorie Mowlam. When she was a little girl she would be angry that she only had one name while both her siblings had two. But for all that, it was a good strong name. Presumably she was named after her godmother, Marjorie Cooley, whose husband Reg worked with Frank at the Post Office. Little Jean remembers wearing a blue frock on the day the baby came home from hospital. She recalls being horrified at 'this thing' arriving and being fed and then realising that she was here to stay.[3]

It was a bit of a squash for the four of them in the two rooms next door to Tina's parents while they waited for the new house to be completed. But Tina had reason to be grateful that her mother was nearby that winter. The new baby caught pneumonia in December and was very ill. With Maud's help, an anxious Tina nursed little Marjorie through the illness. 'Granny and I had to keep you in a basket on the kitchen table to keep you warm,' she told her daughter later.[4] The baby also had constant attention for months in consequence. 'She's convinced that's why I've been demanding attention ever since,' Marjorie would say.[5]

Two years after Marjorie's birth, Tina had a third child, a boy named James George, known throughout his childhood as Jimmy. These were carefree times and the three children lacked for little in their early years. They maybe didn't have much materially, but as they got bigger, there were bikes, a sandpit in the garden, and they had plenty of little friends to play with. They went fishing in Cassiobury Park, near the watercress beds, walking down with their jam jars and fishing in the shallow bit. They played hopscotch on the side of the road, marking the pitch up on the pavement and then being made to clean it off later by Tina. She was always particular about the need for a clean and tidy everything. The girls went to a little acting class in a neighbour's front room and put on a play. And there was the first family dog, a cocker spaniel named Billy, who was very temperamental, thumped his feet together like a rabbit and, according to Tina, was frightened of life. He used to walk between Tina and the pram and given half a chance would try to get into the pram. Tina and Frank decided it was safer to have the animal put down. It was Tina who had to take him to the vet; Frank refused. He walked away from awkward situations.

The growing family saw a fair bit of both sets of grandparents. They went to tea with Hilda and Harry; Poppy Gran, as Hilda was known, named after a stuffed doll called Poppy which she had given the children, would make a beautiful tea. But there was a formality about these occasions that made the children uncomfortable. 'It was like a party tea, with jellies and cakes, but we were never happy there,' Jean explained. 'We hated going. I used to sit and watch the test-card'. They were much more at ease with Tina's parents. Little Granny, as Maud was dubbed, was more homely. She was handy with a needle and she made dressing-up clothes for the children which they appreciated, although she also knitted socks which they didn't. While everyone else had proper white socks, the Mowlams had to wear grey knitted ones. 'Horrendous!' is how Jean remembered them. 'Aunty' Eileen, next door back at Watford Heath, made clothes for Rosebud and Pearl, Jean and Marjorie's dolls. Marjorie was never really interested in Pearl, who was her doll, and Jean used to dress it for her and try to force her, unsuccessfully, to play with it.

Tina kept the doll – and all the clothes – in case Marjorie's own children might like it one day. 'Had she gone a different road, she would have had children,' her sister Jean said years afterwards.[6] But also Tina had learned never to throw away anything of Marjorie's. As a little girl Marjorie insisted on keeping everything and even once she had grown up, if she found her mother had been having a clear-out she would be out at the dustbins retrieving all her stuff. Jean took after her mother in that she was tidy. Little Marjorie was never tidy. Her mother tried to inculcate this virtue and failed from the first. 'Pick that up!' she would instruct the child. 'No!' Marjorie would reply and that would be that. She would stick out her lip, Tina recalled. 'She wouldn't answer. She wouldn't cry. She wouldn't do anything. She'd just be determined.'

In addition to determination, she was forceful. Marjorie remembered when, aged three, in 'a moment of pique' she pulled the tablecloth off a table while everything was on it, including a teapot full of hot water. 'I can still remember the screams and the carry-on. I don't think anyone got burned but it was rather a shock,' she said.[7] Tina thought that both her daughters took after their father rather than her. They were more self-confident than she was, and Marjorie, in particular, inherited her father's approach of making the most of something even if it had gone wrong. Another characteristic Marjorie showed from an early age was her ability to get on with anybody. She treated everybody, including children, in the same fashion: she dealt with them completely naturally. It was a considerable gift.

A short walk away from their home was Cassiobury Park School and both Jean and Marjorie started their education here. It was a very new school, with an impressively progressive headmaster. But school for the children brought new problems for Frank and Tina. The pupils were required to wear uniform and this introduced another strain on the already stretched family budget. 'We were so hard up, we didn't have tuppence to rub together,' Tina recalled. She used to save money by walking into Watford where she would buy a pound of mince for the family's meal. She served the meat to the children and to Frank, who used to cycle home for lunch, and then after he had returned to work she would have the gravy and potatoes that remained. It was a matter of necessity rather than martyrdom and the sacrifices were not all hers. In order to help make ends meet Frank took a second job, helping out in a club in the evenings. It was perhaps an ill-judged choice of work given Frank's future problems with alcohol. According to Tina's cousin Jean, who watched the couple's problems developing, it was actually the pressure of two jobs, the strain of the shortage of money and the very opportunity provided by his evening work that led Frank to drink more than he should have done.

Things were still happy enough, however, when the family moved to west London in 1955 as a result of Frank's promotion to Assistant Head Postmaster at Southall Post Office. He was doing well. He was known within the organisation as somebody who was not only honest and trusted, but always very good with people. He was a man who never shut his office door and was always available to his colleagues.

The family moved to a three-bedroomed house in Shaftesbury Avenue, Norwood Green, on the outskirts of west London. It is a pleasant area on the northern fringes of Osterley Park, with lots of open space and trees and a feel of the country nearby, which in those days would have been regarded as a decent, respectable neighbourhood for the upwardly-mobile middle class. Today it is still a quiet backwater but the culture of the area has changed significantly in the interim. Despite being on the doorstep of the nation's capital, it is now more a residential suburb of the thriving Asian community which has made Southall its centre, rather than the London dormitory it was then. One Mowlam family photograph from those days marks the passage of the years in more ways than one. It shows the children in costume for a fancy dress event at their school: Marjorie, aged eight or nine, is dressed as Little Bo Peep; Jimmy is blacked up from the waist upwards as an 'Indian'.

The Mowlam children went first to the George Tomlinson Primary School in Melbury Avenue, a few minutes' walk away. Today the memory of George Tomlinson, who was briefly the Minister of Education in the post-war Labour Government, has been obliterated, a victim of political in-fighting in the London Borough of Ealing during the 1990s. The council was briefly under Conservative control then, during which time an attempt was made to rename all schools that previous Labour councils had named after socialist politicians; George Tomlinson was one victim and was renamed the Three Bridges Primary School.

The semi-detached house had a small lawn in the front garden and a larger one at the back with fruit trees and enough space for games for the imaginative. The real charm for the children, though, was that the property backed on to the Grand Union Canal. For safety's sake, Frank and Tina immediately had a tall fence erected at the bottom of the garden, but as the years passed adventures on The Cut were to be an important part of Marjorie's childhood. The children made a tree house in the apple tree, overhanging the water, from which Jean remembers watching the horse-drawn barges that still worked the canal slowly trudging past. Swans nested on the canal bank, and there was plenty of interest. While they were all still at primary school, the children called themselves 'The Black Mac Gang' – this garment being the only one the three of them had in common. As the oldest Jean was the undisputed boss. She made horse jumps out of flower pots in the garden and Marjorie and little Jimmy were obliged to be the horses. Jean was also stoic. She and Marjorie had a three-legged race home from school one day and fell over. Marjorie ran home screaming. Jean, who was rather more badly hurt, just held her nose and tried not to cry. She was left with a lump on her nose for life.

Sometimes the children were allowed to light fires on the canal bank. One favoured pastime was wrapping potatoes in copious layers of newspaper, setting fire to the newspaper and eating what ensued: usually raw potatoes with charred skins. They also used to hold 78 rpm vinyl records over the heat of the fire and mould them into bowls. They organised a fête once, posting notices advertising the event on nearby lampposts, but nobody came except the next-door neighbours, the Baldwins, who gamely pretended to be the local Mayor and Mayoress. The children charged 1d. for the programme of events and until her death Tina kept her copy. It was a memory of the good times.

Money was increasingly a source of argument between Frank and Tina. At this time the bills were still being paid and there was enough to keep a car and for holidays and school trips. But things were tight. The dreadful day had not yet arrived when one of Frank's friends came to see Tina to say that he was sorry, he hated doing this, but he had to tell her that the mortgage was not being paid. Now though there were still outings and picnics, day trips for birthdays, or even on Sundays sometimes.

The family car was a blue Ford Consul with a sofa seat at the front and a column gear change; later it was replaced with a black Morris Minor with a split screen. Frank wouldn't let Tina learn to drive in those years so he did the driving and she sat, front or back, nursing the potty. 'Marjorie could go for 60 miles, or one hour – and then she was sick.' They would picnic in Bushey Park or drive out to Burnham Beeches and march through the woods. Frank and Tina would lay paper trails and give the children Biros as prizes; they were allowed to take friends sometimes. The family would go and stay at Oxford with Tina's cousin Jean and her husband Frank and their two children, Bridget and Michael (their third child, Richard, was born ten years after Michael). Holidays were usually spent at Mevagissey in Cornwall. One year, however, with the entire family wearing borrowed Post Office macs, they went by boat to St Agnes Island in the Scillies – everyone was sick that time.

It was a comfortable childhood and the children did all the usual sorts of things. The girls joined the Guides which they enjoyed. Marjorie went away to camp once, somewhere on the edge of the New Forest in Hampshire. A furniture van was procured, and was driven to the chosen spot with the bell tents, the equipment and the girls. Some of the parents accompanied them to help set up camp. Hilda and Harry had gone along as well on this occasion and there is a photo of all the family having a picnic tea in front of one of the tents. It was after the parents had packed up and gone home and the girls were chopping wood for their camp fire that Marjorie, with an already irrepressible sense of fun, got a couple of the others to help her back to the tent with what looked like a ghastly wound on her leg. It proved to be strawberry jam – but not until after it had given Brown Owl a nasty shock.

Marjorie also pulled a fast one on her mother when she was about nine and for some reason didn't want to go to school. She powdered her face to look poorly and when her mother took her temperature, she slipped the thermometer on to a hot water bottle. It worked a treat – and more than once. But despite this, she was in fact already doing well at school in her primary years. Jean, however, was not doing well. She did not like school and it was little surprise to anyone that she failed the Eleven Plus and went on to Heston Secondary Modern. She was much more interested in clothes and records and, in due course, boys. It was the time of winklepicker shoes and Cliff Richards' 'Living Doll'. The girls were allowed to go into Southall shopping as they got older and they bought their first record together – the Kaylin Twins' 'Three o'Clock Thrill'. Jim remembered that when Jean was a teenager she was going out with a boy who had a bike with 'Jean' written on the frame. She got a Saturday job with EMI at a bonded warehouse.

While all this was going on Marjorie was working at her school books. She passed her Eleven Plus and in the autumn of 1961 went to Chiswick Girls' Grammar School. It was a good school with an excellent reputation and accessible by train, and the grammar school girl embarked on the daily journey cheerfully enough. The school had good sports grounds, too, which was important. Marjorie had grown long legs and she was always very keen on games. She had a sharp competitive edge. 'She was very determined and very good at sports. You could tell by her little face when she was running in a race that she was going to win,' Jean recalls.[8] She and Jean had started to grow apart, but that was predictable given their age difference. 'We didn't really argue much until we were teenagers,' Jean said. 'Then she borrowed my prize pair of boots.'[9] Marjorie was still up for pranks, however, even though she was working hard. Jim remembered getting sent with her to school for some reason once and it was her idea – of course – that they should climb up and lie in the netted luggage racks on either side of the railway carriage.

As it was to turn out, Marjorie spent only a couple of terms at the grammar school. Frank was moved on once again, this time to Coventry, where he was to be Assistant Postmaster. Tina knew the city a little from having visited her grandparents in Rugby when she was a girl, but the children didn't know it at all and they were horrified at the prospect of moving to 'the North'. When they were adults, looking back, those years in west London seemed like happy times. It was before they were aware of their father's problem, before the troubles started. The photographs, small and out of focus as they are, nevertheless illustrate a traditional, secure family growing up in relative comfort and tranquillity. It was not to last.

CHAPTER 3

'An alcoholic father is a family legacy'

Coventry in the 1960s

T he Mowlam family moved to 63 Styvechale Avenue in the Earlsdon area of Coventry within weeks of the consecration of the new cathedral in the city in May 1962. The house was a good find. It was a solid, comfortable semi-detached in what Tina described as a 'nice' area. There was a garden at the back and there were shops nearby in Earlsdon, known locally as 'the village'. The girls were to go to Coundon Court, the pioneer comprehensive school in a city which was at the forefront of the introduction of the new secondary school system. It was a single sex school at the time which had, until very recently, been a girls' grammar. Jim went for a time to a boarding school at Broadway in Worcestershire and then to a local boys' school. The children were relieved to find that there was plenty going on in the city when they arrived: there was much excitement surrounding the new cathedral in particular, lots of artistic events – ballet and dancing and plays designed to involve the entire community. They maybe appealed rather more to adults than to children aged between 10 and 16, but even so the Mowlam children quickly felt better about the move. It was

Tina's life which was to be marked by the most distinct change when the family arrived in Coventry.

There was no defining moment at which it was recognised that Frank was an alcoholic, but it quickly became apparent that they didn't have enough money. Such as they had just disappeared. It went because he was drinking it away of course and Tina was naturally aware of that, yet the circumstances were unpredictable. It now became impossible to plan anything. Engagements would be made, bookings arranged for family outings or a visit and then there would be no money – or no Frank. 'There was always a disaster waiting round the corner,' Tina said. 'You'd think you were OK – and then even the mortgage wouldn't have been paid.'[1] Tina recalled one occasion when Jean was due to go on a school outing. It had already been booked and organised but Tina couldn't let Jean go because 'suddenly there was no money. I had to stop her going because I hadn't got the last eight pounds.' It was a frightening burden for her and although she had made lots of new friends in the area, she felt the responsibility very keenly.

She had started to pick up the reins of the family finances a few years beforehand; she got her name on the bank account and wrote her first cheque at the age of 36. But now she was confronted with the reality that she needed to return to work. It was a horrid prospect, but nothing like as bad as not being able to pay the bills. She hadn't worked for seventeen years, not since she left the army, but in Earlsdon one day she saw an advertisement for a telephonist at Owen Owens, the Coventry department store, at eight pounds a week. She decided that the time had come for her to ensure that there was at least some money coming in to keep the family afloat. She applied and got the job. She was well qualified, after all, from her days with the Post Office in Watford before the war and within a year of joining, she was in charge. She was employed there for most of the rest of the children's school years, moving in 1966 to work for the local authority at Coventry's new swimming baths where she ran the reception and took the bookings.

Tina did something about her social life on arrival in Coventry as well – because, as she said, she 'wouldn't have got out much' if she hadn't. She joined the local Business and Professional Women's Club, an organisation which in some ways could be seen as a precursory women's lib group and which certainly assisted her in finding a bit of independence. Best of all, she learned to drive.

When they lived in Southall Frank used to throw his empty bottles in the Grand Union Canal. By this time in Coventry he was going to bed early, just in order to drink. It had taken a little time for Tina to accept what was happening, but she knew now. 'He was a flamboyant character and I just don't think Tina realised,' said her cousin Jean, who witnessed all this.[2] In the past, when the two couples had met up, Jean and Frank Hughes had known that there was a problem and used to hide the bottles of alcohol in their own house in a vain attempt to try to help. They knew that he was drinking more than he could afford.

In some ways circumstances became easier when it was recognised that something was actually wrong. Frank started going for treatment. Frank and Tina had no money for this, but his parents, Hilda and Harry, helped to pay for his drying-out sessions as, it turned out, they had been helping him over the years. 'For many years he had obviously been getting extra money from his parents,' Jean Hughes said. 'He could do no wrong so far as his mother was concerned.' It must have seemed oddly ironic to Tina that all Hilda's carefulness with money over the years would eventually come to such ignominious use.

He was a patient at several establishments: notably in the alcohol abuse unit at St Andrew's Hospital, Northampton, and at a clinic in Dumfries in Scotland. The children noticed how quiet it was when he was away. Frank was approaching 50 by this time and, according to Tina, he really did want to do something that might help him stop drinking. He tried hard enough, she said, but it was too late. One of the doctors told her: 'If we'd had him before he was 25, we might have done something.' The drinking patterns of alcoholics are set early in their lives, she learned – but by the time she knew about it, this wasn't a terribly helpful piece of information. He was 26 when they married, after all. But she remembered then that when she had first known Frank, he had told her how he joined the tennis club in Watford by pretending that he was older than he was – and that he enjoyed going there for a drink. And she remembered too how he used to go to the Watford Palace Theatre every Saturday night – and then for a drink afterwards. 'It may even have started during the war – at Dunkirk . . .' she said, hopelessly seeking an explanation, years afterwards.

It was horribly difficult for her. She used to ring her cousin Jean Hughes often for a comforting chat on the telephone. One of the sad things was that with all his charm Frank would try to pin the blame on Tina for his problems when he was discussing them with his medical advisers. 'She felt completely on her own,' said her cousin. 'She expected support from the people who were trying to help him and she felt very put down.'[3]

The three children handled their father's 'problem' in different ways. It affected them, of course. They were kept short of money. When Jean wanted to get married in the early 1970s, she had to work for a year to save up the money to pay for her own wedding. Earlier, when they were all still children, they were embarrassed and ashamed and didn't very often invite anybody to the house. Marjorie said: 'Of course there were times when I was ashamed of my father. Anybody would be. At that age you're very easily socially embarrassed . . . I rarely took friends home because I was worried he'd slur his words and be drunk. It was as simple as that. Drink is one of the hidden sufferings in families.'[4] Jean said: 'You never knew whether he'd be drunk, sober or walking round half-dressed.'[5] Jim remembered what must have been a humiliating experience for a teenage boy: walking home down the road to their house and seeing his own father staggering from side to side on the pavement.[6]

The circumstances were not ones to which any teenage children would readily expose their friends. But, for all that, when Marjorie in later years used the word 'dysfunctional' about her family she didn't get it quite right. She told the journalist Lynn Barber in 1997[7] that the family was dysfunctional, but she was seeking to make the point – one that she would make repeatedly – that having an alcoholic parent need not make the child dysfunctional as well. Shortly after this interview appeared, Tina reported that her cousin Jean Hughes was furious about this remark. 'You weren't a dysfunctional family. You were very close,' she told Tina. Her namesake Jean agreed with this. 'I don't think we were dysfunctional. It was something that you coped with . . . It was just there and we coped with it.'[8]

Or not. Marjorie's chosen means of 'coping' was by working, although the rest of the family agreed that this in fact enabled her to escape. There were some arguments in the household between the siblings about the preferential arrangements for Marjorie and Tina said often that it was 'Jean and Jimmy who got the rough bits' – partly because Marjorie was in her room working when she was a schoolgirl and then she left home to go to university and never really returned. She came home often, of course, and became very close to her mother as an adult but she never lived permanently at home again. 'Mo wasn't the one that coped,' Jean said, without any bitterness or resentment. 'She wouldn't be there. She was always academic.'

There were difficult times, though, within the family. One school-friend, Stephanie Oyama, even remembered Marjorie talking about it: 'It did create tensions at home. She got out of the washing-up because of her work and it was very very difficult I think growing up with her brother and sister.'[9] They obviously had periodic rows. Stephanie recalled Marjorie referring to times when they weren't on speaking terms and Jean once related how, while she was still at school, the two sisters would cycle the three miles to Coundon 'when we were speaking'. She also had a strained relationship with her mother, perhaps not untypically, throughout her teenage years. 'It was always fairly strained,' one close friend remembered. Their relationship after Marjorie went into politics was 'hugely different'.[10]

Their mother painted a telling verbal picture: 'I'd come in from work and Marjorie would have the kettle on. She'd have one hand on the kettle and she'd be standing on one leg, twisting her hair with her other hand and then when the kettle boiled she'd go and do her homework. Jean would come in and do everything and lay the table and we used to say: "Don't disturb Marjorie – she's doing her homework."' Jean added, knowingly: 'I don't know whether she used to work to get out of doing things, or whether we just accepted it.' The reality is that both were true, although her results proved that she did work hard.

Jim had a personal interest in how much she worked. He would normally go out and play with his chums after school. He wasn't much interested in doing things with his sisters after they reached their teens and this feeling was entirely mutual. There was an occasion when Marjorie was instructed to take him with her to an event she was attending, to which she strongly objected. 'Why should I? He's a social liability,' she complained to her mother. But Jim also had a domestic hobby: he used to enjoy shooting blackbirds on the back lawn. He would scatter so much bread in the garden to attract them that it would look as if it had snowed. The best place from which to engage in this sport was out of Marjorie's back bedroom window but, alas for him, he didn't often get the chance because it seemed as if the occupant was invariably there. Only very occasionally would she vacate the room and then for a strictly limited and arranged period. He remembered because when he did get a chance to get into her room he saw all her timetables spread out on her desk. He looked at them of course. They detailed her programme of revision, but all the other things that she had to do would also be scheduled like 'wash hair' and 'have a bath'. One night a week or so she would permit herself to go out for a couple of hours and see her friends and that, too, was strictly timetabled.

Marjorie carried this discipline into adulthood. In one newspaper profile she was teased about how everything was, in her words, 'factored in' to her diary. In this particular interview, in 1996, she had talked to Noreen Taylor about factoring in time with both her mother and her husband, making them sound like just another appointment.[11] What Noreen Taylor didn't realise was that she had been factoring things in to her diary since her early teens. It developed into list-making. 'She wakes up at night and writes lists,' her mother said. When she became a minister she would have three running lists, 'Today', 'Pending' and 'Action', which would be carried over from day to day.

In contrast with their sister, Jean and Jim left school as soon as they could. Jean was into boys – there was someone called Jeremy who had a scooter. Jim was into laddish things and he got a job at the first opportunity so *he* could save up for a scooter. Meanwhile, Marjorie was in her room, largely unseen – except from the garden when it was hot, when she would put her feet out of the window as she worked.

She never used to talk about her childhood or, more specifically, about being the child of an alcoholic, on the grounds that she didn't wish to embarrass her mother or the rest of the family. Quite under-standably she would say that her siblings did not deserve to have their lives dissected when they had not themselves chosen to be in the public eye. But after her mother had herself spoken of her husband's problems in an interview,[12] Marjorie would refer to it occasionally. It turned out that she had wrongly thought her mother would mind. She told Michael Parkinson on television in the autumn of 1998 that when her mother had learned she was to be on this programme 'she phoned me up and said: "Now, if he asks you about your father . . . I don't mind you talking about it."'[13] In this interview she was actually, at times, quite amusing about her own reaction to the domestic circumstances. Referring to her family's rejection of the idea that they were dysfunc-tional, she admitted that since she had said that, she had been obliged to reconsider. 'I'm not sure what a functional background is any more,' she said, securing a hearty laugh from the audience. She also acknowl-edged – as her siblings had suspected – 'I used to go up to my bedroom and do my homework because it got me out of the washing-up *and* having to deal with the problems.' That got a sympathetic laugh.

One of her teenage friends recalled, however, that it was Marjorie on whom responsibility would sometimes fall when her father was drunk at night: 'She would get up and shut him up and close him down when he was screaming at all of them that he was going to kill them. Jean hid under the bedclothes, Jimmy was too young and the mother couldn't cope. That's why I think Marjorie was so much older than her years.'[14] This account may have been elaborated in the telling because Frank Mowlam did not hit his wife or children, but it implies that Marjorie, who did not often let down her guard to reveal details of this nature, may have done so on this occasion at least.

She has only ever talked or written in public about the matter in very limited terms, however, and she has used the same phrase or descriptive circumstance time and again. It's always about 'coping'. For example, in the foreword of the 1999 annual report of the National Association for Children of Alcoholics (NACOA), an organisation of which she is patron, she seemed to be surprisingly revealing about her feelings, describing the tensions of her childhood. She wrote: 'I know what it's like to have to bottle up everything and feel you're the only one with this problem. I used to shut myself away in my room, concentrating on homework. Getting good exam results was my way of coping, my way out into the world.' Her contribution to the leaflet was obviously heartfelt. She went on: 'Of course there was the shame, anger and bitterness and money problems that every family in that situation lives through as a consequence of alcoholism. It was difficult. There was a lot of shouting. There were raised voices constantly.'

These precise words were repeated from an interview she had given in July 1998 to Lynda Lee-Potter.[15] It also turned out that she had used almost exactly these same words before in her interview more than two years earlier with Noreen Taylor.[16] The interesting point here is not that she repeats herself, for which any politician who has given as many interviews as she has could be forgiven, but that she appears to use a rehearsed formula as a protection so as not to give away too much of herself. Although she gives precisely the opposite impression, she does not disclose much about herself to others – however close they may feel they are to her, or however well the journalist may think the interview has gone. She is candid in interviews and says what she thinks. But she actually appears much more forthright than she is in reality. When she is talking to people she always asks far more questions than she ever answers. 'If you're not careful you end up speaking about yourself all the time,' said Stephanie Oyama. One of her friends, the MP Hilary Armstrong, said: 'That has always meant she can weave her way through things.'[17] She asks questions and gets people engaged in the conversation so that they feel flattered that their views are being sought. It is only later, added Hilary Armstrong – who believes that this tactic must have helped her immensely in Northern Ireland – that one finds oneself thinking: 'She's never actually ever told me what *she* thinks.' It is another of her many personal skills in communication: the intimacy she establishes with people lulls her audience – whether it's a friend or a journalist, a public meeting or the nation in front of their television sets – into believing that they are privy to personal disclosures. Yet such private information as she does reveal comes usually from within very narrow boundaries that she has carefully drawn for herself.

Unwittingly, perhaps, she shows another facet of her character in this repetition – and that is how very casual she can be about things. Her biographical profiles are studded with countless factual inaccuracies about her life, which she happily repeats. For example, she is very arbitrary about dates and places in family history. She will often tell interviewers that she was born in Southall, when she was actually born in Watford. Asked specifically about how she could get this fact wrong, she said once: 'probably because I'm not sure. I was born . . . oh I don't know, I went to primary school in Southall . . .'[18] A psychiatrist might conclude that this displayed a lack of self-confidence yet the simple reality seems to be that she very easily gets bored with endlessly rehearsing biographical details and just can't be bothered with minutiae that doesn't seem to matter.

It can lead to some oddities, however. When talking about the family rows in the interview with the *Daily Mail* in July 1998, she evoked a poem by T.S. Eliot 'about branches hitting against the window'. It always reminded her of those days, she said, and she has used the same reference several times. It is a typical tactic of hers – but her allusion is muddled. 'There are plenty of branches and windows in Eliot's poems, but your quotation is not taken directly from anything of his that I can think of,' said an Eliot expert at Faber and Faber, the poet's publishers. It is not a deliberate mistake or a pretension, just an inaccuracy which no one bothers to check and is therefore taken at face value.

However optimistic the message which Mo Mowlam has tried to convey as an adult, the effects of alcoholism on families *is* sad. Her laudable intention is to try to help others who may be in miserable situations and, quite simply, to give them hope. 'If I can do this [her political career] and get through it, so can they,' she said on *Parkinson* in 1998, speaking when she was Northern Ireland Secretary and addressing those whose childhood circumstances are similar to her own. Interestingly, this concern reflects one of the established effects on a child of having an alcoholic parent, which is it gives them a sense of responsibility for others and leads them to adopt a 'caring' role.

'I don't believe I have suffered as a result,' she told Noreen Taylor. 'I don't see or feel the scars.' She was not being brave when she said this, nor attempting to disguise reality. Nevertheless the circumstances that prevailed in her home – notably the lack of money, the arguments, the tensions and stress within the family – were all entirely typical of what professionals term 'an alcoholic household' and it is difficult not to conclude that many of the classic characteristics of children from alcoholic households that she exhibits were a direct result of that. Many of these characteristics are actually very positive. The NACOA has done a considerable amount of work which shows, for example, that children from alcoholic homes are more likely to see themselves as 'achieving', 'charming' and 'successful'.[19] Nobody would deny that all of these adjectives could be used to describe Mo Mowlam.

Another study reveals that children of alcoholics develop what are known as 'resiliences' to protect themselves, which help them to become healthy, competent adults.[20] Mo Mowlam has said many times in interviews that she and her siblings all developed as 'toughies' – which is certainly some sort of resilient response. And it is very easy, according to one psychiatrist who specialises in this field, to analyse the behaviour of people with alcoholic parents in a facile fashion.[21] It is also simple to make false assumptions. 'It is very hard to say: "because this is a child of an alcoholic, this is likely to happen",' he said. 'It is not just one entity. There are many factors involved.'

The same doctor said that in his view there are three possible routes for the children of alcoholics. The first is 'to shut the door, escape at the earliest opportunity and put a lot of distance behind themselves'. The second is for the individual to take refuge in drink themselves when he or she grows up because of the degree of damage inflicted in child-hood. The third is a positive rejection of the drinking parent – 'so you're not just as horrible as your parent was.' This psychiatrist had no doubt that 'the healthy response is to shut it off and get on with it.' This is clearly what Mo Mowlam did. It also perhaps explains her years living in the United States.

The psychiatrist, who acknowledged that others in his profession would take a different view, added: 'I don't think there is a simple answer. One thing can mean almost anything. Something can happen and it can either affect you positively or negatively, depending on how you want to see it. Everything is open to interpretation, but from my point of view, I think things happen and we choose to rationalise them afterwards. Yes, of course things do fit together – but it's not a = b = c.'

'Codependency' is another technical term that describes how a family adapts its behaviour as a result of alcoholism (among other things) and here, too, it is possible to find an echo in how Mo Mowlam has organised her life: according to the research published by NACOA, codependents tend to be people who ensure that they are always in control of their lives, who care for others to the exclusion of their own needs and who are anxious about intimacy.[22] All these would seem to apply to Mo Mowlam. It is also recognised that, as adults, codependents may develop in a way that hides their private anxieties, but that the adult can still remain vulnerable.[23]

Virginia Ironside, the journalist and agony aunt whose own mother was an alcoholic, has a specific expertise in these matters. She does not believe that alcoholism is a disease, nor that there is something genetic which produces alcoholic children from alcoholic parents (a widely recurring incidence), but she does believe that the issue of self-control is vital. She said: 'You do become very adept at control. If a parent is out of control, someone has to take control and that is often *you* – and this can be an enormous strength.'[24]

The writer Jessica Berens, describing the alcoholism of her father, the journalist Richard Berens, has also written publicly about the subject: 'All that is said about alcoholism being a family illness is true. The effects are passed on, as surely as blue eyes and knobbly knees . . . a father's chronic unavailability leads to an unspoken and long-term feeling of loss. The daughter of the alcoholic man looks like a fairly normal person, but something is not there. She has an idea of how things should be, but no psychic facility to realise them.

'One part of the grown-up woman wants a hero with a shiny sword, kind heart and brave outlook, while the other part – the dark, damaged part – is attracted to emotionally retarded twits who can serve up only the same old experiences.' The extent of the incidence of this doesn't minimise the effects on the family and on society, she wrote. 'A drunk dad is a drunk dad is a drunk dad. The legacy is eternal.'[25]

Mo Mowlam lost respect for her father. 'I ended up feeling more sorry and sad for him, a competent man who ruined his life through drink,' she said.[26] 'It's an addiction. Addictions destroy people's lives. They lose a sense of pride in themselves, they lose friends, they lose jobs . . . It's an internal stress in the family, whatever that family unit is.

It's not like a physical disability – that's something that you have to live with – because you never know when it will surface. It's that sort of strong pressure and stress that alcoholic families go through. When you're a kid it's not easy because . . . it's not a socially acceptable problem, like blindness or deafness, those *are* socially acceptable.' She said that their problems were not as bad as those suffered by some families because their mother's strength kept the family together. But, even so, 'it wasn't easy at times'.

She has never spoken publicly in any detail about her feelings for her father, but according to Martin Pumphrey, her first serious boyfriend with whom she had a relationship for seven years, the experience naturally had a sizeable effect upon her. 'An alcoholic father is a family legacy and a difficult thing not to carry with you – that's her narrative about herself,' he said. 'We all of us have bits of our families that have left their marks and that could never have done anything but leave a mark. I think it gave her a complex sympathy for people who may not have been so well off. She loved her father; there's no question of that.' While it was not difficult to despise an alcoholic in some guises, in his view, that apparently was not her response. He described as 'her great virtue' the emotional complexity she has and which he partly attributes to growing up with a father who was 'a difficult figure'. He went on: 'Mo has very sterling qualities in terms of wanting to do things that improve things.'

All the Mowlam children admit to having blocked out some of the painful times. Even so, it is clear that many of the memories are not buried very deep. There were all those Sunday lunches, which would start normally enough and then career downhill; there was the time Frank was drunk on Christmas Day; there was the dreadful day when he deliberately broke all Tina's teacups, which her mother had given her. 'The next day he gave me fifty pounds,' Tina recalled. 'I didn't spend it because I knew there would be no money at the end of the week.'

There was the night when Jim, aged 17, hit his father when he had cornered their mother. 'I pinned him down on the floor and smacked him,' Jim said, simply. 'He was still quite strong but I wasn't having that.' Frank didn't use physical force against his wife or children, but he abused them mentally. 'He liked to manage me,' Tina said. 'Most alcoholics manipulate people.' She acknowledged that, 'It changed a bit, the time [Jim] hit him.'

And amidst this weary catalogue of misery, there was the night Tina actually fled the house to escape one of her husband's drunken rages. Not wanting to go anywhere else, she stood outside in the dark, waiting for the lights to go out, waiting for Frank to either go to bed or pass out. Some time later, while she was still standing there, waiting in the dark, Marjorie arrived home. She would have been in her middle teens at the time. They stood there together, waiting until the coast was clear, but after a while Marjorie said, bitterly, to her mother, referring both to what lay immediately ahead and the future: 'If you don't go, I shall.'

It was a momentous statement, reflected in her subsequent decision to go to a university that was as far away as possible. It is hard to imagine how much sadness such a bleak declaration of intent must have engendered in her mother's heart, but it was enough for Tina to have retained the recollection of the precise words her daughter had used some thirty-five years later.[27]

Even so, they didn't avoid further trouble that night. When the house had been in darkness for long enough and they thought it was 'safe', they went in – only to find Frank sitting in the breakfast room, with all the lights out, waiting for Tina.

Yet despite all this – and his absences when he was away seeking treatment – Frank did play a role in the raising of his children. There was no question about how much he loved them. Marjorie's favourite toy as a child was a bear called Growler. She had wanted a teddy bear for Christmas, but for some reason she didn't get it. Her father went to a newsagent's on Christmas Day and bought Growler for her – it cost a scandalous twenty pounds, a fortune at the time – but his daughter must have appreciated it as Growler was never thrown away.

Frank was also involved at a functional level in Marjorie's schooling. One of her teachers, Margaret Morley, described him as very support-ive. He came to parents' meetings – she remembered smelling the drink on his breath – and she was aware of what a charming man he was. 'Mo has got some of that charm. The easiness she has with every-one – you could see that her father had that. He disappeared for a long time, drying out somewhere, but it was very sad: you could see his attractive personality. When they were young she must have been very fond of him I should think. I sensed a tenseness because she didn't talk about him.'[28]

In her teacher's opinion, the young girl was torn between her par-ents in a mixture of loyalty and shame – loyalty to her mother and shame about her father – but she didn't talk about her domestic prob-lems at school, not to her teachers and scarcely ever to her friends. It was far simpler for her not to do so, to shut away the pain and shame, to try to concentrate on her school books and pretend to the outside world that she was unaffected by the misery at home. It was not so, of course. It had a lifelong effect upon her. One or two of her friends did go to the Mowlam home on occasion and they were aware of doors being closed, of people being on edge. One said: 'I didn't go very often, but one particular occasion I can remember seeing her father sitting in the chair and her shutting the door so I didn't have to go and say hello to him. We had scrambled eggs for tea and I was left to scrub the pan. She didn't actually confide in me. I don't think she confided in many people.'[29]

Marjorie was quite specific about it with her girlfriend Anne Bailey: 'She talked to me about her father's problems and said that she didn't want it to be discussed.' Anne was part of a circle of friends that Marjorie had joined in Earlsdon when she was 15 in the spring of 1965 and the word was passed around the group that alcoholism was not a topic to raise. 'There used to be the occasional drama when things would flare up round her father,' Anne said. There was one incident when Marjorie was terribly upset and distraught about something that had happened and was in tears but 'so little was said at the time'. Her teenage friends do remember going round to her house to collect her on Saturday nights and seeing her father shuffling about in slippers in the kitchen or to and fro between home and the off licence, but it was many years before she discussed it with any of them.

She was to remain close to Anne and it was not until she was in her twenties that she talked about how she felt her father's dependency had affected her character. She would also speak of it twenty years later with another member of this group, Martin Drew, with whom she had a relationship in the 1980s. She told him then that she thought her father's problems could partly be blamed on her mother's nagging. For the last eight years of his life Frank Mowlam was not able to work. He had lost his job with the Post Office some time before that, but subsequently had a clerical job for about six months and later worked briefly for an industrial cleaning company. It was not to be for very long: Anne Bailey worked there, too, and remembered that she thought at the time that he wouldn't be able to hold down the job. He was expected to die from cirrhosis, but he was a very strong man and it was cancer that was to kill him eventually in 1980. Tina's cousin, Jean Hughes, remembered sadly that ironically, after all the pain and hurt and humiliation, in the last few years of his life Frank and Tina had been doing things together again. For her part Tina would cry when she spoke of his death but, she insisted, her tears were prompted by her memory of the overwhelming sense of relief that she felt at the time.

One of the ways Marjorie found she could cope was by separating different aspects of her life. Psychoanalysts term this 'splitting'. It is a defence mechanism people use to deal with problems. As far as Marjorie was concerned everything would be neatly put into different boxes and the boxes kept quite separate.

An example that illustrates Marjorie's use of splitting was when, as a teenager, she had the shock of finding her grandmother dead. Tina's mother, Maud, had come to live with the family in Coventry after her husband Charles died. Tina made a bedsitting room for her, which was on the ground floor as she wasn't well, and Marjorie, who was the first home in the afternoon, would make her a cup of tea when she came in from school. One day, she popped her head round the door and Maud was dead. She realised afterwards, she said, that she must have known by the pallor of her skin. She phoned her mother at work and then went out for a very long ride on her bike. She told a newspaper in 1994: 'I didn't want to face all the fuss when everybody came home, so I disappeared and they were all terribly worried.' And revealingly: 'I tend to hide things like that. I came home and acted as normal. It's how I cope.'[30] She told another interviewer in 1998: 'No, I wasn't scared; she looked quite happy. I just didn't want to have to cope with the furore, thought I'd get away from it. I'm not good at public emotion. I didn't go to her funeral.'[31]

Compartmentalising was one way of coping; working hard was another. It was a way through. It was a way to survive, and was, as she has also said, 'my way out into the world'. Marjorie was not, actually, a natural academic. She was driven to it. Her mother said: 'Marjorie isn't that clever. She's just determined, bloody-minded and deter-mined.' This was a point of view that her teachers and contemporaries at school shared. One of the latter said: 'She worked very very hard. I wouldn't actually say she had any great intellect. She would always be checking out whether she had done the right work – "What did you do?" "Could I borrow your notes?" "What books are you reading?" She just worked very very hard.'[32] Stephanie Oyama recalled Marjorie encouraging her to do her own postgraduate work: 'She would say: "You're much cleverer than I am."' Stephanie added: 'She's cleverer than a lot of people think – but she works hard to see what needs to be done and then does it.'

Miss Morley saw it all: 'She was bright but she was slapdash. Her handwriting reveals her character: it is very open – open and scrawled. It's like it was at school, it's no different. I think it would say the same to handwriting experts: this is an open person who is generous in spirit. But it's untidy and she was a *very* untidy schoolgirl. She made an effort – I never saw her without a beret on, she wouldn't set a bad example – she would tidy herself up and put her tie straight when she had to go on the platform with the head. But those things didn't matter to her very much. There were more important things.' She once gave Miss Morley a piece of homework that the teacher returned with a request that it be resubmitted in a legible form if she wished it marked. Characteristically, Marjorie did not object to the reprimand, rewrote the essay and handed it in with an apology.

Coundon Court (known in those days to the boys at the other nearby school as 'the Coundon Cowsheds') was started as a girls' grammar in the early 1950s by the late Miss Florence Foster, who was the headmistress throughout Marjorie's school years.[33] The main building is a handsome redbrick house – once a family home of a member of the Singer manufacturing company – and it is set among fir trees on a hill above Coventry looking down over the surrounding fields. It is a pleasant place and Marjorie was very happy there. Among later pupils to attend the school was Gaynor Regan, who became the second Mrs Robin Cook. At the time Marjorie was a pupil, it was a school that exemplified the best in comprehensive education, which was specifically why Miss Morley had gone to teach there when she joined the staff as head of history in 1962.

Miss Foster was a martinet, very strict, precise and terrifying to some of the girls. According to Miss Morley, who later became her deputy, she was frightened of letting her emotions show, because underneath her steely façade she was a softie. This was not evident to the girls or even to the dinner ladies, most of whom didn't like taking her lunch to her study. She had a traffic light sign on her study door – red to go away; amber to wait; green to enter – and often a duly terrified girl sitting outside. Discipline was very precise and girls were expected to comport themselves in accordance with Miss Foster's view of things. Any girl spotted out of school without her beret on correctly or her socks crinkled at the ankles would be in for it if it came to Miss Foster's attention. Eating in the street was worse: it was 'cheap, common and nasty'. The girls used to laugh about this amongst themselves, saying: 'I'll be cheap, you be common and she can be nasty.' Miss Foster wore pleated suits, always tailored in the same shape, and she had red hair and wore dark glasses. The girls' grey and green uniforms were reputed to have been chosen so as not to clash with her hair. 'She was dramatic, impressive and articulate,' recalls Stephanie Oyama.

The girls were set according to ability, and when Marjorie arrived at the school from Chiswick Girls' Grammar she joined an established group, the top class of bright girls who were among Miss Foster's favourites. She was in Katherine Bailey House: colours yellow and white. She was an outstanding athlete and she would also prove to be a model pupil. Unlike Jean, whose problems with her undiagnosed dyslexia were to be compounded by six months off school with glandular fever, Marjorie must quickly have won the attention of the headmistress. According to Stephanie Oyama, Miss Foster 'thought the world of Marjorie.' It was "grammar school" – and the "others". The "others" went to the school but they did different things and they were treated differently. Miss Foster was very much the Miss Jean Brodie-type. We were "her girls". She liked our year, our class and within that, a few of us particularly. We were not necessarily the most academically able they had had, but certainly the sparkiest.'

Miss Morley felt the same: 'That little group she was in, it was one which we call in the teaching profession "a good year". They were keen, they were hard workers, they were interested, they were good all rounders. They were a group of girls who responded to what you wanted to do with them.' She also said: 'They were a super bag. She was one of them but she stood out – not academically, she wasn't the best but they were all good – it was her personality, I think. She could be serious, but she could be light-hearted and bubbly and see the jolly side of things and see the joke. She was obviously the leader in the group and she was liked by everybody.'[34]

Other members of staff had the same view. Joyce Keil, now Joyce Hamilton, was another of the high-fliers and she organised a reunion of their year in 1991. 'The staff all said they hadn't had a finer year: we wanted to learn and they wanted to teach.' And in this glittering throng, they all agreed, it was the light of Marjorie Mowlam that shone the brightest. 'She was, basically, sick-making,' Joyce said, with considerable affection. 'She was good at everything . . . she could turn her hand to anything and make it work.' Independently, Miss Morley echoed her: 'I felt she could do anything she wanted to do. If she put her mind to it. With her personality, if she put her mind to it she would be able to do it – and in that sense she is not unacademic because if she wanted to do something she would set out to do it.'

So she was clever-ish and athletic. She was a county hockey player – a considerable achievement – and one of her other friends could still picture her 'flying up the wing' she was so fleet of foot. She ran and played netball for the school; she was good at drama – she played the lead in Shaw's *Androcles and the Lion*; she was in the school debating team, sponsored by the city's Junior Chamber of Commerce, and they not only beat the boys of Rugby School and won the cup, but they held it for five years; she was still in the Girl Guides and while at Coventry she became a Queen's Guide; she did the Duke of Edinburgh Award and won the Gold Award. And in due course she was to win the open election of staff and pupils to be head girl.

It was her first election. Miss Morley who was the sixth form mistress had introduced the new idea of General Studies for the sixth formers. The theory was to give the girls a better understanding of the world and to give them self-confidence. This included such revolutionary ideas for the time as a talk on contraception and also the introduction of an election for the post of head girl. Nobody in the staff room or in the sixth form had any doubt who was going to win it the year that Marjorie's class reached the top of the school. Miss Morley: 'She had got it all. She'd got blonde good looks. She encouraged the juniors at sport and coached them. At lunchtimes you would see her walking round the school, chatting here and there with the little ones. She'd always got her eye open for somebody who needed a word or just a loving arm round the shoulders if a little one seemed down. First formers today are a little more sophisticated, but it was a different world thirty years ago and they were still little girls.' Perhaps more importantly, she did not allow her popularity to go to her head. She romped to victory. 'It couldn't have been anybody else, to be honest,' one friend remembered. Eileen Scholes[35] came second and was deputy head girl, and Joyce was third and was rewarded with the post of Mistress of the Lodge, the sixth form quarters located in the school's gatehouse.

And she was an exemplary head girl, too. There was one occasion when a heavy snowfall closed down the Midlands. Even the headmistress failed to get into the school. Many members of staff had not been able to get to work. But half the girls were there and the head girl had made it. Eventually Miss Morley, who had walked five miles from Kenilworth, also got there. 'I was pretty breathless when I walked in the door.' She was greeted by the head girl, who said: '"Oh, everything's under control, come along, have a cup of tea." I said: "No, I must get on," and Mo said: "No, every class has got either a teacher or a sixth former" – and she'd shown her initiative, her positive initiative to do something practical.'

'She was a very purposeful person always,' Eileen Scholes remembered. 'She was one of the very few natural leaders I've ever met in my life. She was absolutely a born leader. Within my definition of what a leader is it includes a very natural charisma and when I arrived at Coundon Court I would say she was almost universally loved. People were fascinated by her, she was a kind of spell-binder. She was a wonderfully independent spirit and was not too afraid to speak her mind. In a brave sort of way – and this was admirable – she would speak out about things that other people feared to speak of.'[36]

Mercifully, this exemplary child did have saving graces. One was that she was friendly with everybody whatever their station, exactly as she still is. She makes friends and doesn't let people go. She must have one of the longest Christmas card lists of any politician anywhere. This isn't to denigrate her attachments – but how many MPs still send cards to their school dinner ladies? Poppy Smallwood, the school cook, was responsible for about 1,000 lunches a day when Marjorie was a pupil and she remembers her well. 'She was a character, you see, wasn't she? She liked her dinners. There were no packed lunches in those days. I was supervisor and although I won't say I formed a special relationship with her, she was interested in what I was doing, always interested. I didn't know much about her life at home or anything like that – just that she loved being at school and couldn't wait for her dinner, always flying in and out, very active.' Mrs Smallwood may not have felt at the time it was a special relationship but more than thirty years later she is still on Mo Mowlam's Christmas card list.

Another relief was that she wasn't a goody-goody but was perfectly capable of being mischievous. She decided that the school fire practices were a waste of time because the teachers knew that they were going to take place and that the real test would be to ring the fire bells unexpectedly. This she organised, with Stephanie's assistance, and successfully secured the evacuation of the school somewhat earlier on the same day of what would have been a scheduled fire drill. 'Her idea was: "Let's have a real one and really test the system", and it did because there was someone left on the top floor who hadn't heard the alarm,' said Eileen Scholes. It did mean, however, that Miss Foster had to call the fire brigade. The girls got a metaphorical slap over the wrist.

Yet it proved to be a worthwhile exercise: during the coming years there were several bomb scares at the school because of an active IRA cell in Coventry. These events were most vividly remembered by Poppy Smallwood – but even the IRA did not scare Poppy. On one of these occasions she had four ovens full of scones for the next day. 'They said: "You'll have to turn the gas off." So I walked out with the girls – but then I went back again. I couldn't leave the scones. I saved the scones – I must have had 500–600 of them in the ovens.'

Another wheeze of Marjorie's was to land her in the pages of the *Coventry Evening Telegraph*. She volunteered to clean the dirty statue of Lady Godiva in the middle of Broadgate in the city centre. She had noticed that the statue of Coventry's most important symbolic figure was covered in verdigris and needed some attention, which she proposed to provide with the help of two schoolfriends. The story was a godsend for the local newspaper. They photographed the girls against the statue and ran a piece suggesting that a bunch of schoolgirls had put the council to shame. As it turned out, health and safety regulations prevented the girls from doing the work, but the statue was duly cleaned and a point was made. Another result.

It was also gratifying that there were some things at which the ineffable Marjorie Mowlam was not adept. One was music. Although she was very briefly in the choir she shows all the signs of being tone deaf. Miss Morley was very pleased that her most famous former pupil didn't pretend that she had classical tastes when she appeared on BBC Radio 4's *Desert Island Discs* years later. Her choice then was eclectic but nobody would have called it musical. Rod Stewart's 'Blondes Have More Fun' was one record and there was probably a previously undisclosed reason for this choice. When she was a teenager and before Rod Stewart became seriously famous, he used to play at the gigs on the university circuit. As the record may suggest he was also somewhat predisposed towards blondes. At a dance at Warwick University in about 1966, Anne Bailey watched as Stewart chatted up Marjorie with great energy and interest 'and she gave him the real push-off.'[37] Another record on the programme was John Lennon's 'Working-Class Hero'. She also had Noel Coward's 'Mad Dogs and Englishmen', Flanders and Swann's 'A Transport of Delight' and Tom Lehrer's 'National Brotherhood Week'.[38]

The other area in which she was not as good as might have been anticipated was more curious, particularly as she would later make her career in public life. It was in the debating team. When it was first established, Marjorie was to lead the five members and speak first.

However, at a practice before the forthcoming competition among all the participating schools of the East Midlands – which they eventually won – they faced an opposing team raised from within the school. Stephanie was chosen to lead this team and at the trial run in front of the sixth form, her team unexpectedly won the debate; in consequence Marjorie was dropped, in favour of her friend. 'I can remember going to her afterwards thinking: "How am I going to handle this? What is she going to think about it?" and she just didn't care. She wasn't being gracious about it. She just totally didn't mind – and I think that's an aspect of her – I can never remember her being irritated or petty about anything. She doesn't get upset by things that other people would.'

She did subsequently play a role in the team, but another friend also recalled her not being particularly good. 'She couldn't think on her feet. She couldn't think off the cuff – not to start with anyway. That ability perhaps developed, but even now when I see her on the television, I'm just waiting for her to make a gaffe.'[39] Mo Mowlam has, in fact, never been a natural public speaker, although she was later to become at least competent. This would presumably not have figured as a factor in her career plans at that stage, anyway. The same friend recalled that careers advice at Coundon Court was practically non-existent. Girls took either two or three A-levels. 'If you said "three A-levels", the careers adviser said "University"; if you said "two A-levels" she said "Training college". Beyond that, if you were going to university I don't think people really knew what they wanted to do.'

Marjorie took three A-levels: History, Geography and English. She would say later that she would have liked to have been a doctor, but took the wrong subjects at school. The reason she felt that was, she said, 'looking back now with a better understanding of myself than I ever had then, it was because it was practical, because it gets results. I like things that are concrete, specific.'[40] When she made this comment she was Secretary of State for Northern Ireland and she went on to illustrate the point: 'When I go home at the weekend and I have a spare couple of hours, I do one of two things: I either put the clothes in the washer or fill the dishwasher. I do it because in an hour I'll have the results.'

The results of her A-levels were to be good, but there was another hurdle to be crossed first. She had been offered several university places, including Durham, which Miss Morley favoured if a girl was not going for Oxford or Cambridge, and Manchester. Miss Morley had got to know Marjorie well, as she would give her a lift to school some-times when Marjorie wanted to be in early (she took her responsibilities as head girl seriously). Marjorie also disclosed in an interview for the BBC in Newcastle-upon-Tyne that 'when it got diffi-cult at exam times' she would stay with Miss Morley.[41] But in the early spring of her last year Miss Morley, with characteristic percep-tion, noticed that her pupil's work had started to go off slightly. 'You get a feel about a person's work and begin to wonder: "Is it boyfriends? Or is it overwork? Or is it underwork? Or is it trouble at home with brothers and sisters?" She suddenly got cold feet about going to uni-versity. She made some sort of remark – she didn't know if she was good enough to go and she didn't know if she should go. I sat her down and talked to her about it and asked: "What's really underneath this? Is it money?" and she said: "Yes, I don't think I can survive" – she meant financially.

'So I said to her: "Well, look, even if you don't go to university you're going to need qualifications. So let's do first things first. You must get the very best A-levels you're capable of and put university aside in your mind. So I left it for a bit and then her work picked up again and I had another chat with her. She said again: "I don't think I could survive with the money situation", and I said, "Well, look, I'm going to ask you to do something – I'm going to ask you to make a def-inite decision that you're going to university and that if you're ever in money difficulties and you don't want to talk to your parents about it, you'll write to me and we will sort it out somehow. There are ways and means to these things that you aren't aware of or experienced with and we'll find a way somehow."' This strong intuitive woman showed what

makes great teachers great. 'I felt,' Miss Morley said with great sim-
plicity, 'she needed an anchor.'

It was in her latter years at secondary school that Marjorie came to
be known as 'Mo'. She had been known for some time as 'Marjorie Mo'
in the staffroom, partly because she was the sort of personality within
the school who earned a pet name. They were not to know that, as it
happened, her father had been known at various times in his life as
'Mo'. Even though the nickname stuck after her schooldays, she has
never been known by this name within her family. Many of her childhood friends from Coventry also still call her Marjorie. As is well
known, at one point later in her political life, when appointed to the
Shadow post with responsibility for the City, she rather suddenly
started being referred to as 'Dr Marjorie' instead of the more familiar
'Mo'. It didn't last, not least because she didn't approve of it. What is
not so well known perhaps is that this was during Peter Mandelson's
time as the Labour Party's Director of Communications and official
wizard in the black arts of personal promotion – and it was his idea. He
said that 'Mo' was a diminutive and therefore did not accord her status
sufficient for her political responsibility. She is said to have replied:
'That's ridiculous. Why don't you get Tony to call himself Anthony?'[42]

There are various versions of how she acquired the name. According
to Miss Morley there was a vogue in girls' schools in the 1960s to call
each other by their surnames. Several of the others agreed with this.
Eileen Lennox, as was, said: 'Mo was Mo and I was Len. I still have the
hockey stick with Len inscribed into it.' Stephanie had another explanation. She and Marjorie used to meet at lunchtime on the first floor of
the old building and sit on a couple of adjacent desks with their feet on
chairs, looking out of the big bay window over the front door. On one
occasion Marjorie was, most untypically, talking miserably about her
difficulties at home, relations within the family and how much her
mother expected of her; Stephanie was shocked by the revelations and
all the unhappiness that they conveyed. She had to find some way to
cheer up her friend. For some reason she resorted to what she called

'World War One pilots' slang'. She said in appropriate hearty tones: 'Come on, Mo, old chap! Snap out of it, Mowlam!' And it did the trick. 'From then on she called me "Steffo" and I called her "Mo".'

In the local newspaper now they call her, rather gratingly: 'Coventry kid Mo Mowlam'. She gets mentioned often, of course, and she has been honoured by the city as its most famous daughter – albeit an adopted one. In 1999 she was the first woman to be granted the honorary Freedom of the City (and there have been only twelve men).[43] In a ceremony at Coventry Cathedral the previous year, she was awarded an honorary degree from Coventry University and afterwards she visited her old school. She told the pupils how Poppy Smallwood had made her eat apple puddings – and she'd never liked apples – and in a typical aside suggested that while Presidents Mandela and Clinton might be in a position to be impressive, there were others who were impressive in their own way, without the status: 'I think Mrs Smallwood is someone who is impressive.' In answer to the question what, in her view, was the most difficult challenge in life, she answered, cycling up the hill to Coundon Court – and keeping her temper in Northern Ireland. And she told the pupils: 'You can do anything you want in life. If I can do it, you can. Determination is what this school gave me.'[44] It wasn't true, of course. She was born with it.

CHAPTER 4

'Her mind was on larger things'

Coventry, Durham and London 1965–1972

O n the evening of Saturday, 3 June 1967, at a party in a house on Middleborough Road in the Coventry suburb of Coundon, a group of three teenagers stood around the record player, which was on the table in the front window. They were singing along with one of the tracks on the new Beatles' album *Sergeant Pepper*, which had been released that day and was on the turntable all night. The song the three of them sang, learning the words and laughing, was 'Lovely Rita Meter Maid'.

One of the three was 17-year-old Marjorie Mowlam and another was her boyfriend, Chris Hutt. The third was another friend called Rod Chaytor who was later to become a journalist and who demonstrated that he had some innate skills in that direction because, a generation later in time, he could still remember almost everything about how Marjorie looked that night, even though he couldn't precisely recall her clothes. The impression that he retained was that she was wearing a tight skimpy top and a short skirt, but what he most vividly captured in his memory was her aura. She had straight, long blonde hair with a centre parting which gave her just a bit of the look of Mary Hopkin. Her eyes were bright and intelligent and direct with just the hint of a question mark at the back of them. She had full lips – what *Private Eye* would later come to describe as 'gorgeous, pouting' – a slim, graceful body and nice legs. She gave the impression of having everything under control in an impressive, relaxed kind of way. Later, as she moved around the party, Chaytor noticed her easy way with people. She wasn't shy, but neither was she pushy or gushing or hearty. She just drifted around, chatting to people, moving in and out of conversations with what looked like a low-key, natural effortlessness.

The blend of inner certainty, social competence, clear intelligence and obvious good looks was a fairly powerful mixture to Chaytor. In 1999 he wrote to Chris Hutt: 'I don't know why this should be, but when I see her now on the telly I wish that people could see her as I saw her. She was stunning, she really was.'[1]

The singer Mary Hopkin had been at the top of the charts with 'Those Were The Days My Friend'. But the comparison that people most frequently made when they met Marjorie Mowlam in those years was, surprisingly, with Mick Jagger. Indeed, one of the group of young people with whom she hung out had actually written in her diary for 10 April 1965, when she first met Marjorie, that someone had produced a new friend who 'looks like M. Jagger'.[2] Her mother preferred to think she looked a little like the actress Hayley Mills.

Marjorie was introduced to an established group of teenagers in the Earlsdon area of Coventry. She was an instant hit with the group. 'She took the crowd by storm. Everyone fell in love with her, including me, the parents, everybody,' said Julia Edwards, one of the group. 'She was dynamic, she was funny – she was hysterical! She was great!' Most of the group had initially been brought together either through school, the cathedral – several of the families had connections with the clergy or staff – or at a more prosaic level by a band called The Rippers in which most of the boys played. So far as any of the group could remember, Marjorie's introduction was through some connection between an athletic organisation, the Coventry Harriers, and Marjorie's sporting prowess. Very few girls were runners then but Marjorie was very fast and ran for her school and also for some outside organisations sometimes. It was quite a different social scene from that of either her home life or her school life. The Mowlams lived in the middle-class Coventry suburb of Earlsdon, but Marjorie was at a comprehensive school; most of those in the group were at grammar schools and were the children of middle-class professionals. At least one of the circle, looking back, wondered whether Marjorie deliberately detached herself from her domestic background to provide herself with an entirely separate social life. If so, it would have been an unusual thing for any teenager to have engineered. It was probably an incidental introduction into a milieu that suited her. Nevertheless she was someone who joined the group from outside.

Marjorie's schoolfriend Stephanie Oyama thought that Tina Mowlam actively encouraged her daughter's social life in this group. Although she went out with them sometimes, Stephanie did not much care for Marjorie's other friends, all of whom she felt made too many demands of Marjorie. Stephanie was one of Marjorie's few school contemporaries that she saw socially and Stephanie believed that one reason they had a particular friendship was because they were both from the south, from London, and that while their families did not have money, they were from a different social background to many of their school contemporaries. Coventry was a city in which many fortunes had been made, if rather swiftly, both in the motor industry and other manufacturing and there was a certain amount of conspicuous wealth in evidence. The phrase 'nouveau riche' captures the Coventry society that Stephanie perceived: there were some people with money but no class and some – as Stephanie certainly saw her family – with class but no money. Many of the other girls at Coundon Court were neither of these, but from working-class families who lived locally, Stephanie explained, whereas she and Marjorie lived in what she called 'the posh part' of the city. Mo Mowlam has frequently acknowledged that she has the social characteristics of a chameleon – perhaps that is how she acquired her ability to be equally at home and welcome at a dinner party or a truckies' diner.

It was at about this time that Marjorie developed an awareness of politics. Her family described themselves as not particularly political – but they were non-political in a conservative-with-a-small-'c' sort of way. Her mother was once a supporter of the Conservatives and her father, according to Tina, 'was a Conservative through and through'. Tina Mowlam was very particular: she had a very strong work ethic – which some of Marjorie's friends were sure she inherited – and was fanatical about keeping the house spotless; it was always being redecorated and looked immaculate and extremely elegant. One of Marjorie's friends described Tina as being like a human tornado around the house and that she set herself extraordinary standards. There was perhaps an element of keeping up appearances here. She was also very careful with money, everything had to be accounted for – quite understandably in the circumstances.

She was a member of the Business and Professional Women's Club and she became interested in politics when her children were at school because she was 'fed up with the Conservatives', who had been in office for thirteen years from 1951. She wrote letters to the local paper – sometimes to the embarrassment of her family. She once wrote to the *Coventry Evening Telegraph* in support of capital punishment, writing that she herself would be prepared to 'pull the lever'. When Marjorie heard about this she was said to have been 'horrified'.[3] After Jean left school she worked as an au pair for the American academic and futurologist Alvin Toffler – establishing what would be a long-standing relationship between the two families – and through him and his contacts in British politics Tina had met the former Liberal Party leader Jeremy Thorpe. This galvanised her to join the Liberals and work for them in Coventry, but it didn't last long. 'It was full of failed Conservatives and failed Labour people,' she said.[4]

Marjorie's first awareness of politics was through sports. As an active athlete who represented her school at a number of other schools in the city and the region, she couldn't help but notice the superiority of the sports facilities at private schools compared with what was available at her own comprehensive. In consequence she has said: 'I understood inequality and unfairness.'[5] There was also a certain amount of discussion about current affairs at school – apparently she got 'angry about South Africa'[6] and, according to her mother, she successfully persuaded her elder sister to lead a Young Socialist march with her in the course of the Cuban missile crisis in the autumn of 1962 – 'banners and all' – through the centre of Coventry. It seems more likely that Jean was able to take the initiative on her own. 'I was CND before Mo was,' she said.[7] In any event, they both incurred parental wrath. Tina remembered: 'Daddy saw you both leading this march and wasn't pleased. He went ballistic.'

But most of Marjorie's time and energy were taken up with school work and an active social life, hanging out with the local crowd she had met. The group did all the usual self-conscious things that teenagers did in the 1960s. Some of them would meet up every day after school at the Edwards' house. Julia's brother, John, played rhythm guitar in The Rippers and was to be one of Marjorie's early squeezes. Chris Hutt, who was to be an object of some ongoing competition between Marjorie and Julia, played lead guitar. Over a period of years a number of the group 'went out' with one another, chopping and changing their emotional loyalties fairly regularly. 'Going out' quite often only lasted for a month or so. The teenagers had parties in each other's houses, particularly when the parents were away. They sometimes played a game called 'Funerals', where one person would lie in the middle pretending to be dead and the others would all discuss what they missed – or otherwise – about the 'departed'. Some functions were organised through the cathedral youth club and Marjorie was among those who went to Sunday school in the early years. 'She was the most Christian atheist I've ever met,' according to Chris Hutt. 'She had no interest in what they were doing, but always came top in the tests.'

As they got older, the group went further afield to parties, out in cars, on holiday to the West Country and the Continent. Like others of their age they went to see the films *West Side Story* and *Dr Zhivago*. In 1967 there was a memorable holiday when five of them met up in Switzerland and went to the Italian Riviera in Chris Hutt's Austin 1100. Marjorie was with Chris, Anne Bailey was with John Edwards and another friend, Chris Dammers, made up the party. They spent one night sleeping on the beach under the boardwalk in Rapallo. When they were on the road Chris Dammers particularly remembered 'Marjorie sitting with her feet on the dashboard attracting whistles from the passing French lorry drivers.'[8] Another time they drove to Cornwall in a van. They went drinking scrumpy in a pub and Marjorie earned herself her first hangover. She remembered Anne Bailey, to whom she was particularly close, standing on a table reciting Shakespeare. 'My last memory is of being helped out of the pub and a woman at the end of the bar saying: "I would never let my daughter get like that."'[9]

They were a very bright bunch of young people, all of them funny, somewhat introspective – exploring together the agonies of growing up – and clever. 'If you were not considered to be sufficiently academic, you were not worthy,' said Anne Bailey. It was to cause several of them problems, however, as they struggled with their various insecurities: one of the group committed suicide in his late twenties, another became an alcoholic. Looking back now, Julia Edwards thinks that they were all unstable. They had been brought together by their intelligence. Perhaps, being introspective and clever also caused the problems that some of them suffered.

Julia had a complicated relationship with Marjorie. She thought Marjorie was very liberating. 'She brought the word "knickers"[10] into my vocabulary and taught me to dance in a particularly sexy way. I really enjoyed the wild, free, let-your-hair-down, raw sexuality of it. I liked it – but it was also incredibly threatening.' Julia and Marjorie were slightly younger than the others in the group and Julia often felt put down by the older members. But, as a grateful Julia recorded in her diary, Marjorie never joined in the put-downs, indeed, she sometimes stopped the others being unkind to her or 'torturing' her. Throughout her life Marjorie has always been immensely kind – those who know her best will always attest to her lack of malice. But while Julia appreciated Marjorie's sensitivity, everything changed for her after the other girl joined the group. Most significantly, she would lose Chris Hutt to Marjorie. 'She nicked my brother, my boyfriend and my everything,' she said with feeling, thirty-five years or so later.

Oddly enough, however, not really knowing why, she was also sorry for Marjorie. Several times she wrote 'poor Margery' (as she used to spell it) in her diary. When the two women met up in 1987 when Marjorie Mowlam was a new Member of Parliament, arguably with the political world at her feet, Julia again found herself feeling particularly sorry for her old teenage companion. 'I felt sorry for her,' said Julia, who has a professional career of her own, 'because we were both 37 and I had a husband and two kids and she didn't.' When they talked about this, Mo responded perceptively about her prospects of finding a partner: 'You have a real problem as an MP – the only people you meet are MPs and journalists.'

Chris Dammers was the same age as Julia and Marjorie and because he was a little younger than the other boys, he was licensed as the joker. But as well as being the official entertainment, his role was to sort out the chord sequences for The Rippers. Chris remembered Marjorie as a much-loved member of their crowd. 'She was very popular and very mature. We were all going through our teenage trials, but despite her family background – which I knew very little about myself – she seems to have been one of the calmer and most mature and stable of all of us.' He remembers being the 'baby' of the group, younger and spottier than everybody – always 'the gooseberry' – and yet, despite her ascendant position in the hierarchy – 'She was the top of the tree as the most desirable person to go out with' – she still found time to be kind to the youngest kid on the block. There was something else too: 'Most girls felt you couldn't be too nice without it getting complicated. She wasn't like that. She had a maturity that sticks in the memory.'

They had regular outings supporting The Rippers on gigs, usually when they played at local parties. But for two years running, in 1965 and 1966, they competed in a national competition, of which the finals were held in London's Trafalgar Square. All the group travelled down in a coach. Mary Edwards, mother of the Edwards children, wrote a song called 'Hanging on a Tree' – it was a time for making religion relevant – for them and The Rippers were among the winners. They came third in the first competition and seventh when they competed the following year.

There was, of course, lots of discussion about sex, but teenagers in the 1960s were much less forward than they were to become in the next generation. Anne Bailey remembered that one of her schoolfriends was conducting a survey in her class at school about which girls had had sex with their boyfriends. 'Have you done it yet?' Marjorie was asked. 'Done what?' she said. 'Oh don't worry – I'll put you down as a No.'

Marjorie didn't take a great deal of care of her appearance. If she was going out she would wash her hair – she needed to wash it every day if it was to look nice and sometimes she just didn't bother. 'Most of the rest of the time it was rats' tails,' said Stephanie Oyama. All her teenage friends agreed that she was extraordinarily attractive, but that it was due to her personality and bounce rather than because she was classically pretty. She wasn't beautiful, she was sexy, they all agreed. She didn't wear make-up and because she was sporty she was always in and out of her clothes. She didn't wear a bra either – except when she was being 'posh' – but as Martin Drew, one of the Rippers crowd, remembered 'she had all the working parts and she moved them'.

Marjorie and Stephanie soon made an important discovery – that attractive young women are able to manipulate impressionable young men if they want to do so. One of their classmates, a buxom and attractive girl, brought a magazine full of photographs of women in filmy lingerie into school. All the girls, fifth-formers at the time and lumpy teenagers as they mostly were in their regulation school uniforms, were looking at these pictures when the girl who had produced the magazine said she liked underwear like that. Stephanie recalled: 'We said: "We're not those sort of women – and neither are you."' But it had started Marjorie and Stephanie thinking and when they went to a party with this girl shortly afterwards and watched her flirting with all the boys, 'turning it on and off', the two of them decided to conduct an experiment.

Stephanie explains: 'We decided to see how it worked, doing that sort of thing – looking boys in the eyes and saying "Oh that's really interesting!" – and to meet back in the kitchen in twenty minutes. So off we went and we came back so confident and cocky. I got back to the kitchen first and was helping myself to some cider and I remember her face as she walked in. We were both so shocked at how well it worked! I've an idea we didn't try it again because we were so shocked.'

Another charming insight into how Marjorie felt about life in general and boys in particular is provided by letters she wrote to Chris Hutt in the summer of 1966 when he was on holiday in the United States. They had started 'going out' in June of that year, when Marjorie was nearly 17 and after Chris had ended an eighteen-month attachment to Julia Edwards. There was much teenage angst on Marjorie's part about all of this. She wrote a twenty-page letter, much of it late at night, after endlessly chewing over with Julia the situation and how it should be handled – plus their mutual depression at Chris's absence:

I am trying to get this horrible empty feeling out of me by writing, it will probably be such drivel I will never send it to you. Julia and myself are now on the best of terms, that sounds very sarcastic now I've written it but it's true. We talk about a great variety of topics, usually you because that's what we have in common. The conversation is pointless really because we both miss you and therefore are extremely nice about you.

Tellingly, she then disclosed how she managed her own feelings. 'I just keep to myself that I am unhappy which gives everyone the wrong impression, but is better for everyone all round.' After a few more pages of analysis of the tortuous relationships between the three of them, she promised not to mention Julia again and described the sort of teenage feelings that any young girl – and her parents – would recognise:

I don't know whats got into me recently I have just gone off everybody! I have argued with my mother solidly since last Friday, I am just down right rude to girls and staff and school and the rest of the group, – well I just treat them like dirt. Anne said that she went like this for a couple of weeks and couldn't stand anybody especially boys but all of sudden the mood just passed. I feel exactly the same as her so the mood shouldn't last that long. Lucky your not here otherwise we would probably 'picker (?)' all the time.

There then follows a passage which may well have caused a few missed heartbeats on the other side of the Atlantic:

I have just stop writing for ten minutes because I saw the new slip I brought this afternoon on my bed and I tried it on. It is a gorgeous light blue colour with panties to match and fits perfectly. My mother fell for the colour before I did! God knows what the people in Warwick road[11] must think, prancing about in a slip at 12.30 p.m. because I forgot to close the curtains.

Oh . . . KNICKERS! While I've been writing this I've worked my way through a bag of humbugs, my latest craze and have got a sore mouth from eating too many. I have just dropped my last precious goody on the carpet half sucked, but I had to have it back in my mouth hairs and all because it's too good to lose . . .

She clearly wrote in a stream of consciousness, partly because it was always late at night.

> I was going to read over what I wrote last night, but bum, I
> can't be bothered. I just skimmed through because half of it was
> illegible. I think I will send it to you because apart from
> anything else it will be a great waste of paper. Just take all I said
> with a pinch of salt . . .

She went on to describe various outings with The Rippers – at one of which she felt bored stiff and 'sat and smoked most of the evening', and how she had run a stall at a garden fête, taking money from people to throw balls at cracked crockery to free themselves of their inhibitions. This was apparently such a great success that she got her photograph in the local newspaper – which was really rather unfortunate as she had pleaded illness to take time off from her summer job![12]

Marjorie – or 'Marge' as she signed herself – always worked in the holidays because of the family finances. She had done some Saturday work as a telephonist at the department store, Owen Owens, where her mother worked, but this summer she was on the switchboard for three firms involved in advertising and sales. She was paid seven pounds a week 'which is jolly good for a sixteen-year-old' as she wrote to Chris from work in a nine-page A4 letter, started just a little over a week after her first epistle.

She wrote that there were 'a lot of old men' in the offices.

> I have a little office to myself which is glass and they all come
> and peer at me, so I just smile sweetly and carry on with what
> I'm doing. They are all over nice, but I get cups of milk by the
> score, sweets, cigs (which I am trying to give up but not
> succeeding), cakes, sausage rolls and lifts home the last I
> decline gracefully because I wouldn't trust any of them an inch.

She described the view of a busy junction from her window:

> I could watch people all day they really fascinate me. There are
> so many different types and I love imagining what they do.
> Yesterday morning was quite eventful, two crashes and a queer
> man who sat in the middle of the road until a policeman picked
> him up and sat him on the pavement! This morning I was really
> bored not through lack of work, but due to it all being the same
> so I started counting the number of times the traffic lights were
> red, I gave up at some number in the early hundreds . . .

She went on to discuss what the group was up to – there were two lost
virginities and a breaking-up to report, a detailed analysis of which parents were away ('there are so many houses to go to its hard to decide
where to go, a change from a month ago!'), and gossip about who had
said what to whom. She described one evening when she had been
babysitting and the group of friends arrived somewhat unexpectedly:

> She (the mother) settled me down with 20 cigs, a raido [sic],
> record player, television, paper, books the lot, and left me eggs
> and bacon to cook. She also left me 10/-. I was settled down for
> a lovely evening, but about 20 mins after she had gone they all
> turned up. God knows how they found out, but I ended up by
> cooking bacon and eggs for all and making the beds when they
> had finished at 11.30.
>
> I really must apologize about this letter, apart from it being a
> mess it only seems to be about sex, I wonder why.
>
> It may sound as though we are having a good time, but I
> assure you we are not. Apart from it being hopeless without
> you, everyone is getting on each others nerves . . . They still
> enjoy mucking me about, about you. If I don't say anything for
> five minutes or so they all start at once 'unhappy Marge' 'cry on
> my shoulder' 'pining poor girl'.

She wrote this letter, she told him, lying on her stomach on a garden chair in the spare bedroom, with a fan on the floor blowing hot air on her stomach because it was so cold and with the Animals' LP 'going very loud driving my mother mad'. The previous week she had been 'really mean' to her mother, but regretted it now and was trying to be extra nice. The weather was wet, but she had rejected the use of a contemporary product called 'tanfastic' to go brown overnight because she knew somebody who had come out a revolting shade of yellow. She planned to get her hair cut and in the event did so twice – shorter than she had intended as she had inadvertently set it alight when lighting the gas fire and needed to have the singed bits trimmed. She signed off, perhaps somewhat confusingly for her poor boyfriend: 'Have a good time won't you (no doubt about that with all those girls, but mind you I don't blame you in the same position I would not hesitate.) All my love Marge.'[13]

Her next letter recorded a visit to stay with her cousin Bridget, the daughter of Jean and Frank Hughes, who at this time lived in Horsham in Sussex. This 'girl cousin', as she carefully described her to Chris,[14] was a year older than Marjorie and was about to go to Durham University, as she would herself two years afterwards. The cousins exchanged visits from time to time – 'in my mother's eyes relations come first' she told Chris – and this may have been the occasion when, Jean Hughes later remembered, Marjorie left her mark. The Hughes lived in a large, creeper-covered Victorian house and Marjorie was by this stage an ardent member of CND. Years later, when the Hughes cut back the jasmine, they discovered the slogan 'CND' painted in large letters on the wall of the house – and they knew who was responsible.

The rest of the Hughes family was away for at least part of the visit so the girls had lots of freedom. They were obviously growing up because Marjorie wrote to Chris, with an evident degree of surprise as she reported this, 'we found that when we were not restricted we still came in at the same hour.' They didn't bother to cook as they both hated it – 'most of the time we starved or went Chinese'. When she returned home to Coventry her mother went away for a weekend and she described with some distaste having to cook, iron and do housework in consequence: 'Ugh! I quite enjoy it when I'm doing it, but the thought of it, – if I get married I would have to have a housekeeper.'

She signed off with some more news of how other members of the group had passed the summer and how she had not spent the money she had earned. 'I was going to have a nice long spend with my earnings but I think I am going to be tactfully forced to bank it for my needs after school, it seems a little distant, but that's the way the cookie crumbles.' Before she ended, in a very teenage fashion, 'see you in about 22 days or 528 hours or 31680 minutes', she told him not to bring her letters home because his mother would read them in the distant future and 'hold and [sic] even worse opinion of me yet'.[15] There was something about the letters, or about their friendship, that made Chris ignore this instruction, however. They continued to go out together for another year until November 1967, when, in the parlance of the time, Marjorie chucked him.

As is often the nature of teenage relationships, there doesn't seem to have been a particular reason. Although they had been together for eighteen months, Marjorie doesn't seem to have taken it very seriously and the teenagers hadn't become lovers. All her school friends felt that at that stage boys didn't matter to her much. One of them remembered that she had a lot of boys who were friends, as opposed to boyfriends, but made the point that the culture was different. 'The last couple of years there were boyfriends floating around – and she had more boyfriends at school than I did – but it wasn't like it is for 16- and 17-year-olds today.'[16] Her schoolfriend Joyce Hamilton said: 'Mo just wasn't interested in any of that. We never sat about discussing make-up and things – we had higher things to discuss. Everybody was working. We took it all very seriously. Everybody wanted to get their grades and do well.' And they were competitive. They didn't want to do worse than the others in the grades they achieved.

And perhaps she had a lucky escape as well. Marjorie always used to travel in the front seat of Chris Hutt's car with her feet on the dashboard. A week after the pair broke up, Chris took out Marjorie's friend from Coundon Court, Heather Gardner.[17] On 11 November 1967, driving his mother's car and with Heather in the passenger seat, Chris lost control of the car when it skidded on a wet road and finished upside down in a ditch. 'Heather was wearing a seat belt but still bruised her head on the roof when the car flipped over,' Chris recorded. 'Marjorie never wore a seat belt.'[18]

Her last year at school was devoted to a great deal of work and it was rewarded. Her results meant that she could take up the place she had been offered at Durham University. Before the dreaded day when the results were due to arrive, she whiled away the time – and helped finance her future – by taking a job as a cleaner and, as she wrote to Chris Dammers in August 1968, the consequence was that she was both tired and bored. But by the time she wrote she was able to address herself to the main point of that summer: 'I passed my exams and am going to Durham . . . I'm still a cleaner but retire soon.'[19] It seemed that she had taken Miss Morley's advice and decided that even if she couldn't quite see how she was going to survive, she would take up the place she had been offered to read Sociology and Anthropology at Trevelyan College. She was the first member of her family to go to university.

There is one more snapshot of those years. It was taken when Marjorie was still going out with Chris Hutt and he called for her one Saturday afternoon. Her father, Frank, was unexpectedly in evidence. It was in fact the only time Chris Hutt remembered ever having any kind of conversation with him. Frank Mowlam was sober, he was animated and he was very proud of his popular daughter, whom this young man had come to take out. It was evident to Chris Hutt how much her father loved her and how he recognised that she was what Hutt described as 'star material'. Frank stood there, beside Marjorie, and said, 'Maggie's going to be the first woman Prime Minister of England', and then he put his arm around her. He called his daughter Maggie. She cannot have been more than 17 at the time and it was, in its way, a remark of really astonishing perspicacity. She didn't become the first woman Prime Minister but she became perhaps the most popular politician the country has known in the post-war period.

Marjorie continued to work and play hard when she arrived at Durham. She started her university career living in at her college for the first two years and she made a considerable and immediate impact. Trevelyan College was a brand-new women's college which had won awards for its architecture and was much prized by the university. It was actually a nightmare to live in, designed rather like a spider's web with mysterious corridors leading who knew where; it could take for ever to make a short journey within its precincts. One of Mo's first contacts was with her college tutor, Barbara Dennis, who was responsible for her welfare and moral well-being. She remembered 'a very independent kind of person' who had strong views on everything. An English teacher, now at Lampeter University, Dr Dennis kept a detailed record of their contacts.

'Marjorie Mowlam. Sociology/Anthropology (1st year Joint Honours)', the first entry is headed. 'Comes from Coventry', Dr Dennis wrote in her notes for 21 October 1968. 'Very self-possessed and articulate.' This was days after Mo arrived at university, yet according to Dr Dennis's notes she was already holding forth about departmental policy and demonstrating the extent to which she would get involved in everything during her scholastic career in Durham. A few weeks later, even more of this particular student's personality shines out from the page.

'15 January <u>Never</u> stopped talking! Looked a wreck – on principle or defiance? v. enthusiastic, mixture of blasee and naïve . . . plays hockey, but also stays with student revolutionaries.'

She got quite respectable marks in her first year exams, didn't turn up for a couple of meetings when she was due to see Dr Dennis, but they took sherry together at the end of the academic year. They often shared a glass of sherry and sometimes she and other students would go to breakfast with Dr Dennis in her flat within the college on a

Sunday morning. Being Mo, she also reciprocated the entertainment. Her tutor noted on 28 May 1969: 'v. happy, professes total unconcern with usual worries!' And she was into everything: she was the Trevelyan College representative on the University's Student Representative Council; she was organising the Freshers' Conference for the next year's students; she was rowing for the university; and she was going to work in New York for three months in the summer, helping out the Mowlam's family friend, Alvin Toffler for whom her sister Jean had lately been an au pair.

Admittedly, there had been a run-in about her room. She had initially been obliged to share a room with another student, to which she objected. She got into trouble with the principal, Joan Bernard, who solved the dispute by moving Mo to a single room but simultaneously admonishing her about her 'callous attitude'. Dr Dennis noted: 'Hard boiled character.'

As the founding principal of a new college in an ancient university, Joan Bernard wanted students with, as she said, 'a bit of oomph' and she personally interviewed and chose all the candidates for places as undergraduates. She had no problems with Marjorie Mowlam lacking oomph. 'She was an outstanding personality,' she said. Her abiding memory is of an unusually pale-faced girl, who exuded spontaneity and warmth and 'a sort of bubblingness – she was so full of life and energy'. Not surprisingly the former principal no longer remembered the disagreement about sharing rooms, but even before the college opened she had herself expressed the view that it was unreasonable to expect students not to have a room to themselves. Perceptively, she thought that she might have the first woman Prime Minister among her students that year. 'I suppose the timing was a bit wrong but I really did think that. One thought she would go into politics most likely, rather than anything else because that seemed where her heart lay,' she said. She was also aware of the direction of Marjorie's political interest – 'I didn't expect her to join the Conservative Party' she said drily – and finds today's politician a very recognisable individual, very much the same personality. 'She was not the sort of person you forget and I've really been terribly proud of what she's been achieving.'

In her second year, Mo had branched out and was even more involved in multitudinous activities. 'Her mind was on larger things than just college life,' Dr Dennis said.[20] She noted, with mild acerbity, in her records for 1 November: 'Saw briefly, for a few minutes of her precious time. Very collected. On every committee in Durham . . .' At the end of that month she was elected as the first ever woman vice president of the SRC of the University of Durham and she was involved in everything that moved in terms of student politics. It was a very political time for students; there was a strike in the Sociology department and Mo, being attractive and opinionated, appeared on television. She was 'a moderate militant student', Dr Dennis noted. Later in the year she was organising the Beer Race for the student Rag Week and told her college tutor that she was resigned to getting only a 2:2 in her end-of-year exams, although she felt capable of a 2:1. She was planning to live out of college in her third year.

She had also made friends with Ann Moss, who was a resident tutor; Ann lived in a house on the college site and was responsible for administration and admissions and pastoral work with the students. She remembered how Mo made something of a name for herself by decorating her room in college in an outrageous fashion. The most notorious was when she lined the walls of the room with tinfoil and pictures of Jimi Hendrix. The college was possibly quite relieved when in her third year she was allowed to live out, not least because it meant that during vacations when students' rooms are let to visitors, there was an additional room that people might actually want to rent. Hers had been a room that habitually went unrented as nobody wanted it.

Durham is quite a small university and at this time the students divided themselves up by their interests. There was, for example, a strong contingent whose interests were centred on athletics; there was a social crowd and a Christian crowd and people who were interested in politics. Mo quite naturally had several overlapping interests: she rowed for the Women's Eight for her college; she had a very active social life; and she had joined the Labour Party during her first year. She enjoyed life, but she did admit that she behaved in a somewhat outrageous fashion and that her behaviour was a little disruptive.[21] Formal dinners were held at the college at which the students were expected to wear their gowns and Mo added to this ensemble a pair of boots – a very new high-fashion item then, of course – and also bunny ears and a tail which rather reduced the dignity of the event. Later, a touch defensively, she drew attention to the fact that while she was active in politics, joining the college coach to go to London to join demonstrations and marches, at the same time she did also accept the orthodoxy of university life by representing the college as a rower. 'I was always a contradiction,' she said. 'I will object, but I don't reject the system as a whole because you've got to function within it if you're going to change it. I was accepted as vaguely off-beat, but not totally out of the ball-park.'[22] When the time came to graduate she was still not conforming: at the ceremony she wore boots, hot-pants – another seriously fashionable item of clothing for young, slim women – and took as her guest the nanny who looked after Ann Moss's children.

She did work hard, for which she must have been forgiven quite a lot by her teachers. She chose the subjects for her degree deliberately because they were different to what she had done at school, but not with an end in sight. Others saw things for her, however. Her tutors had a view of what might lie ahead. Barbara Dennis wrote in her notes in Mo's final year, 1970–1971: 'Everyone says "the first woman Prime Minister" – Principal, Resident Tutors, etc. Hm.' The eloquent 'Hm' that Dr Dennis added was, she explained, because of the very individual and independent line that Mo struck on everything. Her tutors seem to have been ahead of Mo's own thinking, because when she left Durham she had no idea what she wanted to do. She said later that she would have liked to have been a doctor of medicine but took the wrong subjects at school; at university she applied herself to her books with the purpose of securing her degree rather than applying it. Her friend

Chris Pye, who was a year ahead of her, remembered how diligent she was – while he, as he said, was busy scraping by. He was entranced by her.

Chris was a considerable figure in student circles because he ran the jukebox in the Students' Union, housed in a building beside the river called Dunelm, the old name for the city. There were no clubs in Durham at the time so the entire social life of the university revolved around this hub. It was here that people sat around in coffee bars doing all the things that students do: complaining about their workload and putting the world to rights. It was in this large building that the dances and the drama festivals and all the other less obviously cultural college activities – like alerting people to demos – were organised.

Chris was reading Politics and remembers being more interested in its theoretical study than in its practical application; he doesn't have any particular memory of Mo being politically motivated at that time: 'I don't recall ever having a conversation with her about a deep political issue.' This seems surprising, both because she clearly had a profound and developing interest in all political issues at this time and was very motivated as a member of CND and, increasingly, as a Labour activist, but also because another boyfriend, Laurie Taylor, was to echo almost exactly that phrase in a later interview. Even so, as far as Chris recalls 'we didn't sit around on beanbags talking about politics.' In fact, perhaps not surprisingly after more than thirty years, he found it difficult to remember much of what they did do. They did read, he recalled, and they played table tennis and she worked. What he does remember is being in love with her.

He repeats the familiar adjectives that people use to describe Mo: fun, interested, lovable, bright, forceful, energetic, charismatic, magnetic. She wasn't beautiful, not obviously so, although he thought she was, with her strong cheekbones, slightly protruding chin and very fine hair. She was thin as a stick insect, and she was straightforward and enthusiastic about everything. She bowled him over, she bowled everybody over with what she wanted to do. 'There was no: "Oh, what do you want to do? Oh, I'm not sure." It was: "All right! Let's do that tonight! Right! I want to do that! Let's have a Chinese meal! Now!" And because she had an enormous capacity for enjoyment, when you actually did it – you didn't sit there thinking "bloody hell, why are we doing this?" because she was enjoying it – and if she enjoyed it, you enjoyed it.'

Although still resident in her college, Mo moved in with Chris for a spell in her second year at university. He was writing his dissertation and had rented a damp, terraced house in a village called Pity Me, just outside the city of Durham, and they lived there happily, surviving on beans and toast and with their teenage love to keep them warm. Not for ever after, but for a few contented months at least. It was, of course, cold, as Mo's houses often were. Her sister Jean remembered visiting one place she lived in Durham where there was a pile of coal actually in the middle of the floor. Another place at which she lived at during this time was so cold she habitually went to bed in a hat and gloves. Pity Me had a telling ring to its name, but Chris remembered happy times. Mo was not the sort of person who sat around and analysed a relationship and assessed her degrees of contentment. She lived it.

Yet there was a cloud on Chris Pye's horizon and it was a rival called Martin Pumphrey. None of them could have known at the time that this was the man who would dominate Mo's emotional life for much of the next decade. She had actually met Martin before starting her relationship with Chris, but at the time he was just a friend. When she started going out with Martin it was obvious, even to Chris, that there was something very strong between them. Yet even so, Martin and Mo were initially reluctant to commit completely to each other; they were students and having fun and they all had a variety of partners. Chris and Mo still rubbed along together for a bit. 'Martin was probably a better person,' he said. 'At that age I'm sure I lay in bed and cried and thought: "Oh, effing Martin" – but it wasn't aggression, I never really knew him. At one or two stages it was probably either me or him in a flimsy sort of way, but ultimately when she went off with him that was that, that was fine, that was the way life was going to be – and I didn't wander around distraught.'

Chris believes that he and Mo cared for each other, but retrospect has lent him an oversight. 'Ultimately, if I were honest about it, I think being with Mo would be a major struggle because she's terribly forceful and she is – in the nicest possible sense, as they say – a control freak. She wants to do things her way, not because she's right but because that's what she thinks. I am also a control freak, but much more calm and much more dull than she is. I like doing the same things every day. I like routine in my life. Mo likes things being exciting and she likes things being exciting all the time and I quite like life not being exciting – so even back then I'd probably worked this out in some way.'

What interests him particularly looking back is the extent to which he underestimated both her political commitment and her passion. Even now he finds it quite extraordinary that she secured such a powerful political career because then he would not have seen it as either possible or likely. 'I wouldn't have thought she had the intellectual capability for doing that or handling that. She was a fun-loving, energetic, active, persuasive person and I never got the impression back then of the depth of her intellectual feelings. I understood the depth of her personal feelings, because she was good with people – so if you'd said to me: "Could she be a politician?" I would have said, even back then: "Absolutely, she could be a politician." She could also be a personnel officer or a probation officer. She can handle people beautifully – she really is persuasive and caring. But if you said: "Is this a person who should go and have a chat with the President of the United States?" I'd have said: "This seems unlikely." If you had said: "Should she be involved in negotiating World War III?", well – I think I would rather do that myself actually.' She was not irresponsible or thoughtless, but it never struck him that she had such a strong sense of responsibility towards society.

Chris Pye is now a distinguished executive in broadcasting and he and Mo have remained good friends. He described how they recently had a discussion about broadcasting policy, during which he explained some aspects of the industry about which she had been uninformed. 'We sat down and talked it through and she absorbed it – and then she'd be fine. Her instinctive intellectual grasp is not as strong as it might possibly be but if you sit down and say to her: "Right, the reasons are this and this" her personality is so strong she'll get it right. But there were five people at Durham University I can think of who were far more likely to govern the country than Mo.'

He described how, over the years of their friendship, their lives diverged: 'I was a kind of shallow media person and she was increasingly becoming a person who cared about issues.' He had no doubt that she was not in any way motivated by self-interest and that her pursuit of a political career sprang from a genuine belief that it was possible to do something. She was always ambitious and energetic and forceful and he had no doubt she would have pursued a successful, high-profile career but, as he described her, he was still struggling with his difficulty in reconciling the girl he knew at 18 with 'the most famous, loved and respected politician in Britain.' He went on: 'She's not shallow in terms of politics with a small "p", not shallow in terms of her understanding of people, not shallow in terms of caring. I think she may be a touch shallow intellectually. But not that badly. Given the choice I think I'm more intellectually equipped to be Prime Minister than she is, so part of what I say is mirrored by my own sense of self-worth which I can't help. Is she brighter than me? No. Is she better with people than I am? Just about.'[23]

In fact she was becoming increasingly good at winning people over. In adult life, in politics, Mo Mowlam would admit that she could be more difficult to deal with than people might imagine from her public profile. She has always been intolerant of inefficiency and laziness. She always wants solutions, answers, immediate results. But she also wants very much to be liked and in her late teens she shrewdly learned how to treat people in a way to which they responded. At school several of her peers remember that she could be rather too forceful, tending to impose her will regardless of others' points of view. 'That's why she didn't have many close friends because she didn't spend her time with us, she had the bigger picture,' said Stephanie Oyama. 'So some of our contemporaries – most – had mixed feelings about her, I think, and I remember spending quite a bit of time explaining what Mo was doing. She can appear to sort of drop in and announce things – "This is going to happen! This is a good idea!" – instead of doing the legwork and getting people on side. It could appear arrogant.'

Before long, though, she was giving Stephanie advice which brought back to her mind the girl in the fifth form who had flirted with the boys at a party. Stephanie said: 'That girl was right! You could pretend to be whatever you wanted to be, certainly as a woman. Marjorie gave me that advice. She said: "Start by agreeing with people." Marjorie's take on it was that you want them to change their point of view and you want them to listen to you and you want to get somewhere – so start with thanking them, or agreeing with part of what they've said, or whatever, and that way you'll take them with you.' It was a very perspicacious piece of advice. Stephanie was to become an academic, and knowing how to make friends and influence people is something that teachers need as well as politicians. The interesting thing is that some politicians never understand this – yet it was a lesson that Mo Mowlam had learned before she was out of her teens.

Joyce Hamilton identified something of what this has meant. 'One thing that people say about Mo and I would say it, too, is that she is just as she was; she hasn't changed. I find that a bit worrying – a brush with death and a Cabinet minister, she *should* have changed. I think she's always been profoundly different underneath. You always think with Mo that what you see is what you get, but I don't think that is so.'

Martin Pumphrey, like Chris Pye, was a year ahead of Mo at Durham and was reading Language and Literature. He was taught by Barbara Dennis. He was a popular man and very attractive to women. At least one of Mo's girlfriends remembered what a magnet he was for women at parties. Stephanie knew him well and saw a great deal of the pair of them when they were together. She thought him vain and self-centred, although at the same time she didn't think that he tried to exploit his good looks. 'I don't think he's happy being as pretty as he is,' she said.

Stephanie thought that the relationship between Mo and Martin was particularly strong, but that they were like two very separate people who happened to be going out. It was very different in comparison with, for example, the relationship which Mo would later find with Jon Norton. In Stephanie's view the photographs of Mo and her husband show a couple – but if photographs of Mo and Martin existed they would show two very separate individuals. She thought Mo and Martin, having established their relationship and its mutual benefits, both then felt that they could get on with the rest of their lives and didn't need to deal with emotional issues. 'I'm sure he wasn't too demanding in terms of closeness, emotional closeness . . . It was very different from relationships that I'm used to. I thought it suited them both fine.'

When Martin graduated he went to Leicester University to do a Masters degree in Modern English and American Literature. Mo was still at Durham, until the summer of 1971, but spent as much time as was feasible in Leicester. Stephanie saw the couple there, too. They had a house and at one point, while Martin was working at home, Mo helped support him by working in an old people's home. It was an extremely unpleasant job because one of her responsibilities was dealing with corpses, cleaning them and attending to the other various unsavoury necessities. Stephanie was very unhappy about her friend's situation: 'It was grim and the house they were in was really grim. I cared about her and I didn't like this – but I didn't comment because I never understood the relationship so it wasn't for me to do so. She wouldn't do anything she wouldn't want to do, but she was finding it very hard, very sapping.'

Fortunately it wasn't for long. Mo graduated shortly before Martin secured his second degree and they then went to live in London for the greater part of a year, living at one stage with Stephanie and her boyfriend. Martin got a job teaching in Tulse Hill and they both did what jobs they could find to get the money they needed to live on. One unexpected source of help was the American Alvin Toffler. Mo had met the Tofflers when her sister Jean worked for them and had visited them in New York fairly regularly from 1968. 'She came back and forth and lived with us off and on for a period of years,' says Heidi Toffler.[24] 'She became a part of the family.' 'She was a kid when we first knew her,' Alvin Toffler remembers. 'She was very bright and alert and eager to be involved with the world.' He noticed, however, that there was something different about her, as a result of her problems at home. 'She always struck me as somebody who had some adversity in the family when she was very young and that it made her smarter and more mature.' She met them in London in the spring of 1969 while she was still at Durham and because of her interest in politics they intro-duced her to some of the British politicians they had come into contact with as a result of their research work. Mo happened to be staying with the Tofflers, on holiday from Durham, in April 1969, when Bernadette Devlin was elected as the youngest Member of the House of Commons.[25] 'I said to Mo that if she can be elected to the House of Commons at 21 – so can you,' says Alvin. Two years later, in the spring of 1971, he introduced Mo to Tony Benn. That summer, after she graduated, she looked after the Tofflers' house in London's Mayfair (which Alvin had purchased after the successful publication of his and Heidi's ground-breaking book *Future Shock*, which anticipated the 'knowledge' revolution and argued that information would become more highly prized than material resources). The house was the very model of American luxury – notably possessing an extraordinary shower that distributed water at different temperatures in waves. The only trouble was that Mo had failed to get the electricity turned on and here she was, installed amid this unaccustomed comfort, with a portable gas camping stove as the sole means of cooking and lighting.

Despite their different political views – the Tofflers are declared lib-erals, with a small 'l', but these days are closely allied with the right-wing Republican Speaker of the House Newt Gingrich – they have taken some pride in Mo's career. Later they sponsored her to study in Iowa and retain very fond memories of the enthusiastic woman they knew so well.

In the spring of the following year, Mo went to work for Tony Benn in his famous basement office beneath his home in Holland Park. He realised that she was very interested in British politics and that, financially, she was badly off. So he put her to work on a research project in his then Bristol constituency, compiling what he described as 'a very early form of a new Labour data base'. The object of the exercise was to draw up a list of all the main services in his constituency – schools, doctors, pubs, hairdressers, hospitals – anything that might be remotely relevant to his ability to represent the area. According to Benn she sent out about 40,000 questionnaires, generating a huge postbag. She was extremely conscientious, competent and a lot of fun, he recalls. She worked in the office until June 1972, returning, with Martin Pumphrey, to do some more work on the project later that year. It was all invaluable experience, although she and Benn would never be natural political allies. He knew that she was ambitious, but even now he is surprised by her success. 'You don't expect somebody working in your basement as a student to end up in the Cabinet,' he said.[26]

Mo had also worked for Alvin Toffler in New York that summer, doing some precis of several books for him. She spent the time contemplating whether she would return to the United States on a full-time basis with Martin, who had decided to study for a doctorate in American Studies at the University of Iowa. Now she was really getting out into the world.

CHAPTER 5

'America makes all sorts of things possible'

United States 1973–1979

I t was the cold which, in later years, Mo would always remember about Iowa. The Midwest state has a continental climate and while the summers are very hot, in winter there is always at least one week when the temperature never goes above freezing, falls to 30 degrees below at night and with the windchill factor blown in can go down to minus 70. It freezes the lipstick on a woman's lips or, in Mo's case, the stockings on her legs. When she first arrived she didn't realise it was necessary to wear thick woolly things to stay warm and walking in the city, her tights froze onto her body.

Iowa City, in the eastern part of the state of Iowa, is a small place. In the early 1970s when Martin Pumphrey and Mo Mowlam went to study there it had a population of about 35,000. It is essentially a university town with a large attractive campus downtown, adjacent to the commercial area. One campus building boasts the earliest capitol constructed in the state: it was started in 1840, which makes it seriously old for modern America. It is a comfortable place to live. The fertile countryside is pretty, the people are open and friendly and the society is an egalitarian one. The University of Iowa is an important academic institution, numbered among the 'big ten' of the public universities in the United States, albeit the smallest. It also has a distinguished Department of Political Science, rated in the top twenty-five such departments in this huge country. It was here that Mo Mowlam was taken on as a graduate student in the fall of 1973.

Martin Pumphrey remembers their time there as good years and very happy ones. 'America makes all sorts of things possible,' he says. 'I think what America offers us in Europe is not its money but a sense of possibility. It's one of the things you take away.'[1] It is an important point because, as he says, Mo with her upbeat personality is a very can-do person and these innate personal skills were clearly refined by the experience of living in the States. Philip Lader, the American Ambassador in London when Mo was Secretary of State for Northern Ireland, was always very aware of the American influence on her personality and believes she displays what he calls 'American qualities – a directness, an ability to relate to people of very diverse backgrounds and persuasions and a relatively casual approach.'[2]

She is remembered now, nearly thirty years later, with immense affection and admiration by everyone whose lives she touched then. Her teachers, her fellow graduate students, the friends she made in the United States all speak of an attractive, energetic, funny, hard-working and committed person. Several remember how inclusive she was and how she was always aware of what was going on around her. While she enjoyed being the centre of attention, as she often was because she was so lively and charismatic, she would sense if someone was being excluded from a group and would draw that person in to what was going on. 'She always wants to include people,' says Barclay Ward, now a professor at Sewanee, the University of the South in Tennessee, who was a fellow graduate student at Iowa and has remained a friend. 'She doesn't like to see people excluded. That really seems to bother her. If someone were on the edge of a group she would find a way to bring that person in. What I remember and even though it sounds

Pollyanna-ish this has been sustained over the years – what I remember is a really good person, a really really good person.'[3]

Her decision to enrol at the university was a little unplanned. She initially went to Iowa on Martin Pumphrey's coattails – although he laughs now at this suggestion. 'Mo never tagged along with anyone,' he says. They had both been uncertain about what to do next after they'd finished their degrees and had discussed it a great deal during their year in London. Their attention began increasingly to focus on the United States, partly because that was where Martin's academic career was pointing. Mo began to feel that it would suit her, too, to study in the States.

Martin Pumphrey got a place at Iowa on a course to do Black Studies, an important academic growth area in the 1970s, and he managed to secure enough funding to make it possible. He arrived in Iowa City in the summer of 1972 in order to start his study in the new academic year that autumn. Mo was a few months behind him, however, as she had problems with her visa. She joined him in Iowa before Christmas, but by then had missed the academic year. According to one of her friends at the time, Anthony Mughan, she still had visa problems when she arrived, which would best be resolved if she got herself accepted as a student. She started looking around but she had some months to decide what area to pursue. Initially she flirted with the idea of doing an MA and a doctorate in sociology, which was both a fashionable area and a naturally consequential one to her first degree in human anthropology, but eventually she settled on political science. It wasn't a specific career move, although she always had one eye on the possibility of a political career.

Another friend from those days, Susan Cowart – now Susan Loomis – distinctly recalls that Mo had arrived with no particular intention of signing on for graduate school. She remembers this because when she herself arrived in Iowa City in 1974 she was in a very similar position. She, like Mo, had come to Iowa without a particular commitment to enrol in graduate school, but in her case because she was accompanying her then husband who was taking up a post as a faculty member in the Political Science department. She met Mo – who had by then already embarked upon her course and made the considerable commitment that a PhD necessarily involves – and they became friends, and Susan in turn also decided to enrol for a doctorate in the same department. They were to have lots of fun together over the years.

'She was a very determined person and well-disciplined when she was working,' says Susan. 'But she was always up for some fun.'[4] Friday evenings members of the department would always go out for a beer together downtown. The Dead Wood bar was one favoured location and another was The Mill, an old restaurant where they would have pizza or sandwiches. Sometimes they would go dancing later. Susan separated from her husband during this period and Mo was both a supportive friend and something of a social pivot. Susan would call Mo if she had a problem – like the time she found herself alone in a house with a bat – and there were lots of parties. Mo seems to have had considerably more fun than most.

Anthony Mughan, a Liverpool-born academic who is now a professor of political science at the University of Ohio, was already working on his doctorate when Mo arrived in Iowa and takes credit for suggesting that she should pursue the political field – not that he particularly enjoyed the post-graduate work himself. By all accounts it was extraordinarily hard work and Dr Mughan still looks back on it as the worst three years of his life, with very little to relieve the pressure of work. He hated graduate school and wanted to get through it as quickly as possible.[5] Mo seems to have approached her work in a similarly expeditious fashion: the time factor also appears to have been one reason why she opted for political science. She could get her masters in one year and her doctorate in another three; she would be at the university for a minimum period – but at least one or two years less than most graduate students – and she would qualify at the same time as Martin Pumphrey who was signed up on a five-year course.

Most significant of all though was, of course, that she would acquire a qualification – and in politics, too. Martin was very aware of her desire to put her abilities to good use. One of her sterling qualities he says was wanting to do things that improved the world.

Dr Claudia Beyer – then Claudia Lewis – specifically remembers that time mattered. Once she had decided to pursue academic life for a further period, Mo Mowlam was a woman on a mission. 'I think the thing that stood out the most was the fact that she was very serious about getting that degree – and that always came first.' The two of them were in the same entering class in the same group programme of the 1973–74 year. 'I don't think she was sure what she wanted to do,' says Dr Beyer. 'She chose political science for her doctorate because you could finish it in three years and it was a natural fit for her.'[6] Finishing in four years is 'going it some' in the American system, according to Martin. It was an impressive achievement which she was able to pull off because she was sharp and she applied herself.

Mo may not be naturally academic but she impressed those with whom she worked. Barclay Ward thinks that she was a lot brighter than most of the other students, self-deprecatingly including himself. 'She was just incredibly quick. She was very straightforward in what she said and I think everyone really appreciated that – what you saw was what you got.' Barclay Ward sees her still when he teaches in the UK and doesn't find her to have changed in this respect. 'She says exactly what she thinks in her own special way, which often is very funny. She must be one of the funniest people I ever met.' In graduate school Professor Ward was older than most of his contemporary students; he was also married with small children and on leave of absence from the US State Department. Iowa had very high academic standards and he found the work imposed great pressure. 'I didn't have time to smell the roses along the way. Maybe Mo didn't feel it so much because she's a lot brighter than I am. She could do in an hour what would take me most of the morning.' The one regular bright spot in the Ward family week, though, was when Mo would arrive to babysit so that Barclay and his wife could go out together. She was a popular choice. 'If there was such a thing as a babysitters' hall of fame, our kids would have inducted her.' The other thing that he remembers particularly is Mo's energy levels. She was always in motion and he used to worry about the extent to which she pushed herself.

It was a curious time to be on an American campus. It was the tailend of the Vietnam War and the upsurge of student protest that had swept across the United States had scarcely subsided. The University of Iowa had been shut because of the trouble and Dr Beyer's recollection is that this atmosphere permeated their arrival on campus. 'It was right after the heavy stuff had happened at Iowa.' Student demonstrations were still very much a thing of the moment because American troops only began to withdraw from Vietnam in 1973 and the war did not actually end until 1975. In Mo's first week they were formally introduced to the state of play. 'The faculty had a meeting and laid it on the line that we were there to study, we were not there to demonstrate,' says Claudia Beyer. 'Then the graduate students had a meeting for us and told us that was a lot of bunk.' It made for heady stuff for some students, many of whom were intellectually uncertain of exactly what they were doing because of the instability that the Vietnam War had induced in American society. This was not the case with Mo. She knew precisely what she was about – and it was, primarily, working. Although she had been very involved in student politics before in Britain, she now had only one priority.

The word that people use about her approach is focused. She impressed everybody with her extraordinarily diligent approach to her work. She had to clock up seventy-two hours of course credits that would contribute first to her MA and then to her PhD and she just got on with it. Her dissertation supervisor was Professor Gerhard ('Jerry') Loewenberg, who remains a professor in the department in Iowa. He is a hugely respected academic, widely applauded by all his former students both for his scholarship and for just being a gentleman. He is a European specialist, having written his own dissertation in 1955 on the currently very pertinent subject of 'The Effect of Governing on the British Labour Party' – although his was an analysis of the 1945 post-war British Labour Government. He remembers Mo's arrival on the scene clearly. 'She seemed like a very live wire,' he says, with careful professorial understatement. 'She was a very energetic, very friendly person who was anxious to learn everything she could about political science, the University of Iowa and Iowa City. She was quite consistent with the sort of person she still is.'[7] He saw her again when she revisited Iowa City in the fall of 1998 to accept a Distinguished Alumni Award from the University and another from the American Political Science Association.

In the early 1970s Professor Loewenberg was involved in a major research project on legislative politics in Belgium, Switzerland and Italy and this was to lead Mo to the subject of her doctorate, entitled 'The Impact of Direct Democracy on the Influence of Voters, Members of Parliament and Interest Group Leaders in Switzerland'. It may not sound exactly gripping and was, even in academic circles, an obscure area for study, but it did equip Mo with a specific knowledge of the referendum and its application in divided communities, which was perhaps to be quite useful later in Northern Ireland. Professor Loewenberg's interest was prompted by the fact that since Switzerland is both a representative democracy and a direct democracy that permits widespread use of the referendum, it would be a worthwhile project to examine the interaction between those decisions made as a result of a referendum and those made by parliament. 'Mo found that a fascinating subject,' he says, giving a revealing indication of her seriousness. 'Although I may have prompted it, she grabbed the idea and turned it into a very good dissertation.'

She used some data that had been collected by her tutor but later went to Switzerland for some months in 1976 and 1977 to pursue the research through the University of Geneva. That, too, was a measure of her seriousness, he thinks. He did find that she was sometimes a little impatient, however. He describes himself as somewhat fussy and orderly in a traditional way. Mo in contrast was energetic, quick and in a fantastic hurry. 'I was fussy about her writing and her prose and I wanted to slow her down a little bit.' He was only partly successful. Claudia Beyer remembers, 'He expected a lot from her and she delivered for him', but she was also aware of how frustrated Mo could be by her work. She would work very hard and then find that she had been marked down because, for example, on one occasion, she had used English rather than American spellings. 'She wondered how she was ever going to survive.' Mo acknowledged the debt she owed Professor Loewenberg in her dissertation, expressing her special gratitude to him – 'who bore with my prose and my impatience in directing this study'. She has said in an interview with the Iowa *Alumni Quarterly* that she lived in awe-tinged fear of him at the time, although she also credits him for valuable lessons in 'tolerance, humanity and the decency about human nature'.

Mo had, of course, swiftly made lots of friends across the university, several in Martin's department because, according to Anthony Mughan, they were a bit more lively than political scientists whom collectively he compares to 'a gang of undertakers'. She and Martin lived initially on South Lucas Street in a small clapboard house with shingling on the sides and a garden. In the summers she demonstrated a previously unsuspected domesticity and grew tomatoes and sweetcorn and squash in the backyard. Susan Loomis, who now works in educational research in Iowa City, remembers first meeting Mo at a party given by her and Martin in the fall of 1974, thrown partly to celebrate Mo's success in growing an enormous marrow, about three feet in length. Mo exulted in the first lesson she claimed to have learned from living in Iowa: that if you left something in the ground for long enough, it wouldn't rot or die – it would just keep growing. Another party Mo gave one year was to celebrate the Kentucky Derby. She organised croquet in the garden and, because she came from Georgia, she got Susan Loomis to make mint juleps. 'Everyone imagines we sit on our verandahs sipping mint juleps – I'd never made a mint julep before in my life.'

There were not many women post-graduate students in the department. They were not made to feel particularly welcome either and Claudia Beyer says they all felt they were not taken seriously because they were women. There were no women members of the faculty and Claudia relates how one professor was on record as saying that women didn't have any business to be in this field at all. It was a time when women were starting to push the boundaries forward – 'I think most of us were feminists but just not saying a whole lot about it,' according to Claudia – and because of her established feminist views, it isn't too difficult to imagine how Mo would have responded to such an opinion. One little episode organised by the half-dozen or so women post-graduate students had Mo's fingerprints all over it. They decided to frighten the men and have a laugh at their expense: they would do nothing more threatening than arrange to have lunch together, but in order to put the wind up their male colleagues and the faculty they would announce this in advance. So they put a notice on the bulletin board declaring their intention of having lunch and to their considerable delight it had precisely the desired effect: the men were terrified that they were meeting in order to foment some sort of feminist revolution.

Dr Beyer, who is now a tax attorney in Iowa, worked with Mo and they were both concerned with research methodology in their different fields. She perceptively recognised something fundamental about Mo: 'she was a very deep person. I probably only knew her superficially. I was a country kid from South Dakota. She had been involved in politics before she came to the United States – and I always sensed she was going back to it.'

She also remarked on the difference between Mo and Martin Pumphrey: he was the dedicated scholar, very capable, very academic, interested in the intellectual pursuit for its own sake; Mo had extraordinary personal skills. 'Her character transcended so much. She was always aware of what was going on and what needed to happen to get people together and talking. She's always had that knack. That's part of what I mean when I say that there are depths there which I felt I never really plumbed. She had skills from the beginning that most of us don't have.'[8]

It is a considerable judgement – particularly after the elapse of nearly thirty years. Dr Mughan makes a similar one. He didn't think that she was heading for an academic life because she was far more interested in people. 'She was a woman of the people – bright, lively and with time for everyone.' He liked her very much; he describes her as having been 'a terrible flirt' and happily admits to fancying her. He also admired her diligence and the characteristic way in which she managed to organise her life into compartments in order to get the most out of each area. 'It's nice being around lively people with a good sense of humour. Mo scored high on those characteristics.' She was also a very independent woman: 'She didn't take shit from anybody and she'd stand up to anybody.'[9]

It was in the latter years of their time in Iowa that Mo and Martin split up. There doesn't seem to have been much acrimony and her friends don't remember anything particular that precipitated the break. Martin ascribes the cause to the fact that they were going in different directions by 1976. Student relationships tend not to endure and theirs had lasted a long time – seven years, in fact, since 1969, when she was only 20 and Martin 21. Now here they were, seven years older and on the verge of collecting their third degrees. Significantly they had also been together through an odd period of social change and revolution in the late sixties and early seventies, which greatly affected the lives of people who grew into adulthood at that time. They had a sexual freedom that was unimaginable to previous generations and it was allied to an explosion in the possibilities for individual opportunity. Martin believes that these were very important years for society in many different ways that have not yet perhaps been sufficiently assessed. 'The world was changing and we tried to make sense of it,' is how he puts it.

One particular way that they were developing separately was in his more academic leanings and her more political ones. Their friends say that he was a much quieter person than Mo. He was certainly a very private person. He returned to England when he qualified in 1977 and has remained an academic. 'Her life has taken her into the public arena and I certainly didn't envisage my life going that way.' He is not sure if either or both of them were hurt. 'It was a longish time to be together. We'd done things together, been through things together. I think it was a natural parting.' Seven years is a long time, though, in your twenties, and her mother would say years later that she believed it was because Mo and Martin had been together for so long that Mo found it difficult to settle into another long-lasting relationship. Her friend Susan certainly thinks that at the time Mo found it very difficult to adjust to the life of someone who was not one of a couple. She believes that Mo even briefly toyed with the idea of abandoning her doctorate.

Instead she went to Switzerland in pursuit of her research for her dissertation and the work must have helped her focus her attentions. Even so, she was certainly not happy there. She hated Geneva. It seemed even colder than Iowa City. 'It was a very cold place and for the first two months I was lonely, nobody invited me anywhere,' she disclosed in an uncharacteristically revealing interview shortly after she was first elected to Westminster and before she learned to restrict the kind of personal information she gave to journalists.[10] There was some fun when her friend from Coventry, Anne Bailey, came out to stay in the February of 1977. They had a lively time. There was much drinking of a local liqueur and lots of laughs and some high jinks of the kind that would have cheered Mo up a bit. By and large it was a miserable time for her, though. She had a few flings but the relationships she had were inconsequential

She returned to Iowa to complete her dissertation and then in the spring of 1977 spent a semester teaching at the University of Wisconsin in Milwaukee, where one or two other former colleagues had landed up. It was a temporary job, filling in for an absent member of staff in political science. She had a rented an apartment on the East Side of town and had graduated from the ricketty old bike she had been in the habit of riding around Iowa City to a ricketty old car. Mo was her usual sociable self in Milwaukee and, as ever, she made some new friends for life. In this case it was Professor Marvin Summers, who was then chairman of the Department of Political Science, and his wife Patricia. The Summers were about to leave that fall for a post at Warwick University and Mo volunteered her mother to help them find a house – an assignment Tina readily took on. The Summers and Tina Mowlam were of a similar age and became good friends.

Professor Summers has one abiding memory. 'I remember going with her one time to her automobile to fetch something from the trunk. She opened it and the trunk was filled, just littered, with fifty, sixty, maybe a hundred parking tickets. She just parked wherever she wanted to and she just collected innumerable tickets and she just threw them all in there. It reflected I think her rebellious attitude towards established authority at that time.'[11]

Back in Iowa, with her dissertation finished, she collected her PhD and celebrated her release with a series of parties. She had already secured herself a permanent teaching post in Florida and she left to take it up in the fall after one last party thrown in her honour by the then head of faculty, Professor Jim Murray, and his wife Patti. The Murrays, who have both since died, were a popular sociable couple, close friends with Mo and, like many others, including Jerry Loewenberg, sorry to see her go. Jerry Loewenberg admits he could never have predicted the political eminence his impatient former student would achieve, but he thinks that she was ahead of the game with the subject of her dissertation, now a very fashionable area of study in American political science. He told the audience that gathered to hear her speak when she revisited Iowa in 1998: 'I'm tempted to point to Mo Mowlam and say "There you are – you write a doctoral dissertation on the Swiss referendum at the University of Iowa in 1977 and twenty years later you help resolve the thorniest political conflict of our era".' It was something of a non sequitur, but it was meant as a handsome tribute and it was one that must have mattered to her. Her days in

Iowa, although tinged with the sadness of her break with Martin Pumphrey, had been mostly happy and fulfilling. She remembered wistfully in a later interview with the Iowa *Alumni Quarterly* how much she had relished having the time to enjoy life. In the same interview she even referred, puzzlingly, to going shopping – something she has never liked but perhaps Iowa was indicative of a normality and at least initially a domestic tranquillity with Martin that she would not find again for a very long time.

When she returned to Iowa City on the nostalgic 1998 visit she behaved in some ways like a child who had been let out of school. Her security team decided there was little risk and allowed her out on her own. Even better from her point of view, she had no press in tow. 'Isn't this fun!' she exulted at one point on the trip, clearly liberated by her escape from the official programme and the endless television interviews, formal speeches to business leaders and obligatory dinners and drinks parties which impinge upon visiting ministers. In Iowa, she and Jerry Loewenberg drove around the city visiting her former addresses, peering in the windows of her house and taking photographs with her old friends – copies of which, with a typically thoughtful touch, they were later to receive with their Christmas cards.

The Department of Political Science at Florida State University in Tallahassee was a fractious place in the late 1970s. People disagreed about everything. It was still a complicated time in the political life of the United States, particularly in the South where civil rights remained a source of trouble; Watergate was only just over; Vietnam a recent bitter memory. People who taught politics naturally had differing ideas about the way the world was going and it was difficult for any of them to agree about much. That is how Paul Piccard, a professor in the department at the time, remembers things and that is why there was such an astonishing reaction when a young English woman with bags of energy and enthusiasm and a brand-new PhD from the University of Iowa applied for the vacancy in the departmental teaching staff. 'This woman knocked us off our feet,' says Piccard, now Professor Emeritus. 'Everybody wanted her for the post. If she'd turned us down we'd have been like a bunch of teenage boys rejected by the beauty queen.'[12]

When she came for the interview every motel in town was booked for some reason and Mo stayed with Paul Piccard and his wife Betty, a social work professor. Although the Piccards were older – the eldest of their five children was only a year younger than Mo (and at one stage he briefly took a bit of a shine to her) – they formed an immediate friendship. At the time Paul was just over 50 and was wistfully bewailing the fact that he was getting too old to do what he wanted to do: take the whole summer off, go and stay in the Swiss Alps and learn French. 'Mo said: "That's ridiculous! You can still do that."' They were charmed by her up-and-at-it attitude to life. They were also particularly impressed by the impressive degree of last-minute panache she displayed when she arrived at their house and disclosed that she was still working on the presentation she was required to make to the department for her interview. In fact, of course, this was because she was preparing with her usual carefulness.

She was offered the job, accepted it and swiftly became a popular member of the faculty and the university. Paul Piccard was president of the steering committee of the faculty senate and knew a great many people on the campus. 'After she'd been on campus for one school year she knew more people, more faculty members and more parts of the university than I did,' he says. She was less popular with the higher administration on the campus and, subsequently, with 'town' opinion. Tallahassee is a small place; although it is the state capital, it has a population of only 100,000. There is a strong town-gown divide there and local opinion was not best impressed when, for example, Mo had the idea of organising a university trip to Cuba, to the World Youth Festival, *Havana Libre*. 'That was absolutely forbidden,' says Betty Piccard. 'People from the United States were not allowed to go there – but there were some people on the campus who were interested in going. It was quite a big deal.' The visit went ahead despite the myriad problems of visas and travelling through a third country to reach Cuba. Oddly enough, it was to lead Mo to a meeting that would later have great significance for her political future. When they eventually made it to the event that had inspired the trip, Mo met a young student leader from Britain who had spent months in Cuba helping organise the international rally. He was Charles Clarke, later to become the Minister of State at the Home Office and one of the most able and most swiftly promoted new MPs in the 1997 intake. When they met at this curious political crossroad twenty years earlier in 1977, he was the President of the National Union of Students in Britain, but only six years later he would be running the Labour Party leadership election campaign on behalf of Neil Kinnock and Mo Mowlam, the young academic from Florida State, would be one of the first people to come knocking on his door to ask if she could help.

This episode relates much about Mo Mowlam. First, her readiness to challenge authority and to seek to do something that is difficult but not impossible. It wasn't the done thing for people in the United States to visit Cuba at that time, yet she proved that, with a degree of determination, it could be organised. And it was an attractive idea for radicals: this was 1977 and Fidel Castro was at the time still a considerable hero to anyone on the left. But more important even than challenging the accepted norm, the visit demonstrates at a personal level not only her can-do approach but also her appreciation of the attractive possibilities of such a visit. She would have known that there would be other interesting and politically motivated visitors in Havana and she might have guessed that she might make contacts that could be useful. She learned early on in her political career the advantages of making contacts – and making as many of them as possible.

There was a chilling incident shortly after she arrived at Florida State University. She had found herself somewhere to stay within easy walking distance of the campus. The university is within the city limits, not far from downtown Tallahassee and close to an area of inner-city deprivation; on one edge of the campus is a Black neighbourhood of poor housing called Frenchtown. With typical disregard for her personal circumstances and with her naturally casual self-confidence, Mo rented a couple of rooms in a decrepit small house – 'better thought of as a shack', as one of her American colleagues put it – only a couple of hundred metres away from Frenchtown, on the other side of a busy thoroughfare. The day was not long coming when she was sitting in her front room and heard someone breaking down the back door. Fortunately, she recognised that this was no time for either confrontation or attempted heroics. 'She hi-tailed it out the front door and ran 200 metres to this busy street where she got to the phone,' recalls Paul Piccard. She rang the police and then the Piccards, who came to pick her up from where she was nervously waiting at a small grocery store.

The Piccards took her home to stay with them for a couple of days because the incident proved somewhat unnerving. When the police arrived at her apartment they found that nothing had been stolen and Paul Piccard remembers a cop commenting: 'I guess we know what he was after.' Everybody, particularly Mo of course, felt very uncomfortable at the possibility that the intruder might have been a stalker intent upon personal assault, but she repeatedly said to Paul and Betty Piccard during this brief stay: 'I have to go back sometime.' Despite her friends' misgivings she insisted on returning to the seedy apartment. It was not to be for very long. A matter of weeks later a man later identified as the psychopathic serial killer Theodore 'Ted' Bundy broke into a sorority house on the other side of the campus and murdered two women students. After the murders had been discovered, the police showed up at Mo's house in the middle of that night to check that she was all right because of their concern about her vulnerable location and their suspicions about the identity of her earlier intruder. In the aftermath she recognised that she could not sensibly remain living there.

Bundy, a handsome young law school drop-out with a nasty taste for pornography, was later to be captured after the murder of a 12-year-old schoolgirl and spent ten years on Death Row before being executed in 1989, aged 42, in Florida State Prison. He had confessed to 23 murders, a number of them in various parts of the county, and was linked to at least another 13. What is chilling here is that his crimes had all followed a similar pattern – he stalked his attractive women victims, sometimes to their homes. He was one of the psychotics on whom the character of Hannibal Lecter, unforgettably portrayed by Anthony Hopkins in *The Silence of the Lambs*, was based. 'I always asked myself if that man at Mo's back door was Bundy,' Paul Piccard says. She was sure that it was.

Mo rented a house in a much nicer part of town with another colleague, Candace West, from the sociology department. Professor West, as she is now, is a distinguished and much-published academic, now working at the University of California in Santa Cruz and specialising in the sociology of gender and conversation analysis – and specifically the different sorts of conversations between men and women. Living with Mo must have given her a considerable amount of research material. She was a very different sort of person from Mo, according to Russell Dalton, another member of the faculty. He became an assistant professor at Tallahassee at the same time as Mo and regards the friendship he forged with her during those years as one of the highlights of his time in Florida. 'Marjorie was one of the most unforgettable characters and she was one of the things that made Tallahassee enjoyable,' he says with great affection. Mo was an extrovert, she was people-oriented and very personable, he says, and he assumes that the friendship between her and Candy – as she was known – must have resulted from the attraction of opposites because Candy was very much more reserved and inward-looking. 'Mo was positive, Candy was negative and she was always complaining about something,' he says. 'It was more of a pleasure to go over to see Marjorie than to know that Candace was home.'[13]

Mo and Candy gave some good parties. Members of faculty in a place like Tallahassee naturally spend a great deal of time in each other's company. There was no urban centre and although the majority of the students at the university are from all over the US, the culture of the area was Southern and provincial and, according to Professor

Dalton, going to live there was a considerable culture shock. 'It was a small town with a limited number of restaurants and a limited number of things to do socially.' The university was therefore something of a cultural oasis. Assistant professors didn't have much money and struggled to pay their bills – both he and Mo fell into this category – so going to restaurants was not high on their list of priorities, anyway, and they tended to go out to dinner at each other's houses. The Piccards, in particular, were very kind and protective towards the young teachers, often asking them round to play cards at their house. Professor Dalton thinks that for someone like Mo, who had grown up in Europe, it must have been a very curious environment – even though she had already experienced small-town America in the Midwest.

Tallahassee is on the western side of the top of the Florida peninsula and just an hour's drive from the Gulf of Mexico, which made for great weather. So Mo and Candy and their boyfriends would head off for the beach when they could get away. Mo met a man named Dan Sammons in Florida and they started a relationship which became increasingly serious. Sometimes they would go for day trips, sometimes for the weekend, occasionally renting a place on St George's Island, a little further west on the Gulf. The sand on the beach of the Gulf is like icing sugar and it is easy to find a spot on the beach where you can't see anybody else for 100 yards in either direction. On other occasions they went hiking or canoeing; or they would indulge in the wonderfully indolent practice of 'tubing'. A group of friends would each get inside a large tyre tube, equipped with a can of beer, and then float leisurely down stream. They went swimming, too, in the sink holes around the town or in the 'Dog Lake' – so called because it was a place where people took their dogs to exercise them or swim.

Mo's friend Anne Bailey, who went to stay with her for a holiday in July 1978, remarked how well she fitted into American society and with her academic circle of friends. 'She got on great with them. She was well liked. She had that kind of confidence wherever she went: she would arrive and immediately get herself organised, get talking to people – she had a confidence in getting herself established. Wherever she went – she was in there, nothing bothered her.' Mo made Anne very welcome in her own way – 'she's never been domesticated. She lived in total chaos' – and Anne saw how hard her friend was working. 'She was extremely industrious. Nothing would get in the way of what she had to do work-wise. She did everything she could to make sure I had a good time – but she expected you to get on with things and be independent.'

Professor Dalton, who now teaches political science at the University of California in Irvine, had an overlapping area of professional interest with Mo because they were both specialists in European politics. They were both in their first jobs as assistant professors and at the start of their careers. He retains very good memories of those times: a feeling that the world was young, an excitement about all the possibilities that lay ahead. The department was pre-eminent in political science in Florida, one of the top four or five institutions in the South and ranked highly nation-ally as well. The work was productive and stimulating and it was an active department with lots of intellectual momentum. 'Those early years were professionally enjoyable, creative and stimulating.'

The two of them collaborated on their work during this time and wrote papers together. One was on the attitudes of Communist Party supporters and was presented at the Southern Political Science Association Meetings in Atlanta in 1978.[14] He recalls that she also published an article based on one of the chapters in her PhD disserta-tion and another on British Government and Opposition and he remembers them working together on a paper about European foreign policy. Betty Piccard believes that Mo had a problem with the American academic 'publish or perish' syndrome, whereby an academic is required to publish work regularly as a matter of course and specifi-cally in order to secure tenure within a faculty. The requirement is that an academic must publish one or two articles a year and that this must reach a total of between seven and ten papers over a period of five to seven years. 'She had a hard time with that,' says Betty Piccard. 'She felt that if you published something it ought to be worthwhile. She felt she was not likely to get tenure – although we'd have broken our backs to get it for her, if she'd stayed.' Russell Dalton does not entirely agree: 'If she had decided that she did want to have an academic life she would have been able to follow that trajectory.' He is certain she would have had no difficulty publishing the necessary work and securing tenure, but he is quite sure that, although she was clearly good at what she did, she was not committed to teaching and had already made up her mind in favour of a political career. 'She was also a wonderful teacher. You can imagine how engaging she was with young graduates. She would always challenge them, but in a very informal style – and the British accent helped.' She reportedly ran an unconventional classroom, but she was popular and successful.

Another member of the political science department, Burt Atkins, remembered an outgoing, chatty, enthusiastic woman – 'she was a great teacher, the students loved her'[15] – with a considerable interest in British Labour politics. He was surprised that she stayed as long as she did at FSU, because it was a small town and a long way away from her political concerns. A few years later he visited her in Newcastle-upon-Tyne to give a guest lecture to her students and was gratified to find that she was as engaged in Labour politics as she was by then.

It was recognised that Mo was on the left in politics and she was quite active while at FSU, but she was still, of course, a visitor to the US. She managed to avoid any contention by separating her personal beliefs from her teaching and while she enjoyed argument and debate, according to Professor Dalton, she was not seen as an ideologue. She prodded the department a bit, for example to be more conscious about women's issues, and Betty Piccard also remembers Mo's irritation at the inequalities of her life and times. She got annoyed because members of her department – who were, of course, mostly men – would always enquire about her love life while they would ask male colleagues about the progress of their research. As she was doing some serious research, just as they were, she found this particularly galling.

One of the original attractions of the job at Tallahassee for Mo was that FSU has a study programme in London. Every year half a dozen members of the faculty are sent there for a term, accompanying about a hundred students. It was an obvious opportunity for her to have occasional assignments in the UK and when she joined FSU it had a particular appeal as her father was not well. At the time she mentioned to several friends that she was concerned about him, although with typical reserve she revealed nothing of his alcoholism. It was no surprise to anyone therefore when she had fulfilled the qualification of being a member of faculty for a year and she applied for the London programme. Her mother desperately wanted her nearer home and, according to Mo, used to apply for jobs on her daughter's behalf.

While she was in London she made some contacts at the University of Newcastle-upon-Tyne and was offered a post as a lecturer back in the north-east of England. There were two very strong factors drawing her back to Britain: her family and her political future. But there was also a strong draw keeping her in Florida and that was Dan Sammons. She had been very close to him for much of the time that she was in Florida but appears to have been undecided about what to do next. Dan worked in a school for children from dysfunctional families, teaching kids with very serious problems. He seems to have been very popular and widely liked by Mo's friends. Anne Bailey met him when she went to stay on holiday and was charmed by him. 'He was the most lovely person you could wish to meet,' Anne said.[16] 'He was attractive. He was gentle and he worked with kids in a way that was quite inspirational.' And she remembered: 'Mo came back to England in two minds about what to do next: whether to stay here or whether to go back and start a new life with Dan.' Everyone who knew her agreed that at the time Mo was not someone who was about to settle down in any suburbia anywhere, but Dan had made a difference to her. She decided to take up the post in Newcastle, starting in April 1979, but was clearly wondering whether she had made the right decision. Then on June 3 tragedy struck.

Dan had gone swimming in one of the lakes near town with a friend. The two men had a can of beer on the beach and Dan went for a swim while his friend sunbathed. Dan was a strong swimmer and known as such, so his friend wasn't looking when Dan got into trouble with what was assumed later to have been cramp. It pulled him under the water. By the time his friend noticed and got out to him and brought him back to the beach it was too late. Naturally Dan's parents were distraught and so it fell to Mo to go out to Florida and sort out his affairs. She had to deal with his house and his financial affairs and, presumably, with her emotions. It was a terrible time.

CHAPTER 6

'She had her eyes on her political future'

Newcastle-upon-Tyne 1979–1983

The word was that they were looking for a man to fill the vacant post of Lecturer in Politics at the University of Newcastle-upon-Tyne in the spring of 1979. Professor Hugh Berrington, Professor of Political Principles, had been head of the department for nearly fifteen years and he disclosed later that he did not want to appoint a woman to his staff when Dr Marjorie Mowlam, BA, MA, PhD, applied for the post. 'He said: "I had to have her for the vacancy. She was head and shoulders above the rest",' Tina Mowlam recounted with great pride.[1] From her own point of view, she was also very glad that her second daughter, who had been living abroad for so long, was coming back to live in Britain.

As soon as Mo turned up for the interview, there was never much doubt that the job was hers if she wanted it. Professor Tim Gray, Professor of Political Thought, who followed Professor Berrington as head of department from 1994–99, met her for the first time when she arrived for that interview. 'She took the place by storm. She was quite flamboyant and dynamic but also extremely shrewd and sharp and answered questions impeccably. There was no question in my mind that she was far ahead of any of the competitors.'[2] He described what he called the magnetic aura that surrounded Mo, and the transparency, frankness and honesty that she conveyed which seemed so unusual. He was impressed and Professor Gray has the mien of a man who is not easily impressed. When she got to know him a little better, Mo, with her usual casual irreverence, called him 'Dad' – even though at the time she was 29 and he only 36. She called Professor Berrington 'Grandad'.

The Politics department is to be found beside the old A1 in a nine-teenth-century two-storey terrace of houses to which an additional modern storey has been added. Mo Mowlam taught British politics here and by all accounts she was a good teacher. She spoke rapidly and without notes when she was lecturing, while to her colleagues she gave the impression of needing to prepare relatively little in order to give an effective and popular course. She was much liked in the depart-ment and, according to Professor Gray, the students loved her throwaway remarks and casual sallies which pricked the pomposity that others sometimes brought to teaching. She had a wide range of knowledge, which meant that she was also used to teach on other courses – something she resented slightly but which came about because she didn't have what is known as an academic identity of her own. Eventually she would have developed her own particular area, but although she stayed nearly five years that wasn't very long in academic terms.

Her somewhat arcane PhD on the Swiss use of the referendum put her in the field of comparative politics. She was, in the words of Tim Gray, 'an empirical behavioural academic' interested in voting behav-iour, why people did things – particularly in mass party politics. In view of the interest she displayed in the need for fundamental re-thinking and reform within the Labour Party during this time in Newcastle, it seems highly probable that her opinion on what ought to happen to the party was much informed by her academic work. She didn't explore these revisionist ideas on paper, however. 'She didn't write a lot,' Tim Gray said. 'She wasn't a dyed-in-the-wool academic. I think she had her eyes on her political future a lot earlier than we recognised.'

He was right there. She was in fact already devoting a great deal of time to this political end. She has two academic publications to her name, both of which she produced during this period as a result of her intense interest in the fashionable political topic of nuclear disarmament. Neither could be said to have involved much writing: one was a contribution to a book of essays on the subject;[3] the other a collection of lectures which she jointly edited with one of her departmental colleagues, Professor Michael Clarke,[4] who had a strong commitment to CND.[5] They worked together very closely but he was always aware that her real interest was in becoming an active politician. 'She had a promising academic career in front of her if she wanted,' he said, but as soon as he got to know her he realised she was primarily interested in political power.[6] She actually liked the very processes of politics, he thought. 'She enjoyed local Labour Party politics even though they were wearing – and very emotionally wearing. She liked to throw herself into the gossip and the backbiting, even though she was quite vulnerable in some ways. The Tyneside Labour Party structure – well, it wasn't pretty.'

The politics of Newcastle-upon-Tyne were actually pretty ugly. They were certainly not very woman-friendly in the late 1970s and early 1980s. There had been no women MPs in the north-east of England since the death of Ellen Wilkinson as the Labour MP for Jarrow in 1947. There were lots of other women members of the local Labour Party when Mo joined it in 1979, but, other than a vague sort of commitment to the principles of the party, they were not encouraged to have political ambition. The women members of the Labour Party on Tyneside were expected to do the dreary dogsbody jobs that keep political parties in business, but, by and large, not to express their opinions on political matters in public. They were most certainly not expected to have any ambition of their own, such as might secure them a seat in an election or even propel them into Parliament. The idea was as unthinkable as allowing a woman into some of the pubs in Newcastle city centre. So the arrival of someone like Mo Mowlam in the Labour Party on Tyneside at this time was altogether something of a mixed blessing: she was ready and willing to work all the hours given for the greater good of the party and for the benefit of the poor benighted residents of the inner city, but she also wanted to play a part in political affairs herself. This was never going to make her popular and it didn't.

Her first point of contact with the Labour Party after her years abroad was in the old Newcastle-upon-Tyne Central constituency, a rock-solid safe Labour seat held by Harry Cowans.[7] She joined the West City ward. She was living off the Westgate Road at 1 Summerhill Terrace, a large, turn-of-the-last-century terraced house in a little pocket of relative respectability within a desperately run-down area. She would regularly have come out of her front door and seen glue-sniffing children in the park across the way. It wasn't where the other Newcastle University lecturers lived, but that would have made it even more attractive to Mo. The academic crowd lived in Jesmond and had dinner parties in each other's homes. That wasn't what Mo was after. She quickly made friends in rock bands and lesbian groups and law centres and housing action groups across a huge swathe of the Tyneside left. She had come back to Britain because she wanted to get involved in British politics and it wasn't her style to try to do that by living in an academic enclave. Besides, she was, as usual, compartmentalising her life, and as she intended to become an activist within the Labour Party, she needed to put some distance between her political life and her professional colleagues at the university. Not that there would have been any problem at the university with her being politically active – although, as it turned out, she did manage to offend in this regard – it was, rather, that she wanted to keep the different aspects of her life separate. It didn't stop odd and interesting people turning up outside her office at the university and following her around. 'She took a certain amount of pleasure in knowing that she functioned in lots of different groups,' said Michael Clarke. She also needed a life outside the university, as he put it, 'to keep her sanity'.

This chimed precisely with the recollection of Laurie Taylor, sociologist, broadcaster and journalist, who had a relationship with Mo that lasted for a couple of what he remembers as fun-filled years. He was very aware of something that they did not realise at the university – how distant she felt from the academic life she was leading. The two had met when Laurie Taylor, who was working at York University, was invited to Newcastle University to give a lecture – 'God knows what it was on' – after which there was a dinner. He had to continue singing for his supper in the presence of a rather stiff and formal group of other academics. And Mo. They liked each other immediately. 'I suddenly found myself in the company of someone who regarded academic life as a bit of a joke. Although she was a lecturer in politics, you never felt that she was – she never talked about the lectures she was giving very much. She was much more amused by the foibles of the members of the staff and how to have a good time. I always thought she regarded her presence there as something of an absurdity. She was much more anarchic than I was – I was hoping to become a professor – and it was wonderful to meet someone who regarded the whole academic thing as funny.'[8]

He holds an immensely affectionate recollection of her. She was, in his view, 'a tomboy', a personality who was equally appealing to men and to women. 'She'd always go where the fun was,' he recalls. They would go to the pub in the evening and he would turn round and suddenly she wouldn't be there any more – and then there she was again, behind the bar now, life and soul of the party, having a great time with the barman. 'She was totally against deep sententious conversations – she just loved good times. I've no idea what her lectures were like. I don't think we ever had an academic conversation in our lives – to her it was a slightly funny job to be doing and I don't think she ever thought she was going to be doing it for the rest of her life. She was seeking to be a Labour candidate. I was vaguely trying to support her and help things come off.'

But, as with Chris Pye, he didn't remember them ever talking about politics. He saw her political ambition as being a way out of an academic life she didn't particularly enjoy and while he would ring her up to find out the outcome of some meeting that he knew was important to her, he was emphatic that they didn't actually have political conversations as such. This has to be another example of Mo's ability to put her life into different compartments. It would be quite wrong to deduce that she didn't have political conversations at all. On the contrary, she had plenty of them, almost all the time, but she had them at work with her students or with those who peopled her 'political' life; Laurie was her boyfriend, her relaxation, her fun. She was inevitably involved in politics all day at the college yet she did also enjoy theoretical discussions: Martin Spence, a friend she made through her political activities, remembered having 'hammer and tong arguments' with her on a regular basis. She was someone with whom he enjoyed settling down for a challenging conversation in which she would often raise issues he hadn't previously considered, things which he would then realise needed to be addressed. In his view she was a stimulating conversationalist on the subject.

And of course she talked politics within the local Labour Party, which didn't make her acceptability to the party old guard any easier. Andy McSmith, the political journalist, described the former constituency of Newcastle Central where she was a member at that time as 'a rotten Labour borough'.[9] It was slap in the middle of the city; there was a small electorate, male unemployment of 55 per cent, miserable housing and a percentage Labour vote that was nudging 70 per cent. It had been taken for granted for years and so had the voters who loyally contributed to it. The Labour Party was given a bit of a fright when Andrew Ellis, a famed Liberal Party by-election strategist in the 1970s who had previously contested this parliamentary seat three times, decided to apply his party's theories about pavement politics to these precise pavements in the middle of Newcastle – and won a seat for himself on the council. It brought the party up sharp, but not to the point at which anyone was prepared to do much about it. And the last thing the tightly knit group of politically motivated men who ran the area was prepared to do was to let an incomer like Mo Mowlam get a toe-hold.

But she was indefatigable. She worked relentlessly. Sid Butcher was a long-distance lorry driver who had been a long-serving member of Tyne and Wear County Council and was secretary of the Labour Party's West City ward. He found her to be energetic, hard-working and reliable. 'If I went to her house with a load of leaflets and said, "OK. You've got a week", I'd knew they'd be out and the job would be done.'[10] He and his wife Alma befriended Mo and liked her style. Her ability to walk into strangers' houses and make herself at home was an asset in political campaigning and they admired her commitment to the party. She was also prepared to work anywhere to help the party and didn't restrict herself to turning out on her own political patch. Jonathan Upton, an official of the National Union of Public Employees (NUPE) at the time and an active party member, was very impressed by how much effort she put into political campaigning. 'She did have this tremendous capacity to motivate and enthuse people. She had a particular empathy with working-class people, the people who lived in some of the more moribund wards and areas of the constituency. They all loved her and adored her.'[11] He particularly remarked on her ability to convey her sincerity to people, as well as being practical about helping those who needed something done.

One reason Mo has always been so popular as a politician is because of this diaphanous quality she possesses. People can see that she means what she says and that she is telling the truth. But the work she was putting in on the ground was not entirely altruistic; she was also looking at the bigger picture. She knew what she was doing, and one thing she didn't want to do, for example, was to go on the council. 'I broached her once or twice to go on the Labour Party panel[12],' said Sid

Butcher. 'She just said at the present time she was too busy.' This must be one of the very few recorded instances of Mo refusing to take on something: some ambitious politicians regard a local council seat as a route to Parliament and a help in selection as a candidate, but she felt that she could make the grade without such a step. It was probably a wise decision: she would undoubtedly have been a highly responsible councillor and would have had to commit more time to it than she would have gained in political credibility. She did much better for herself by her work within the party and other political organisations in the city.

One of her main commitments was nuclear disarmament. It seems a little unlikely now for someone with her political stance, but it was an all-embracing, hot political issue in the first years of the Thatcher Government. It dominated the left-wing political agenda and the publicity accorded to the Greenham women's peace camp, which was set up at Greenham Common in 1981 in an attempt to stop the British base being used for American Cruise missiles, ensured that it remained highly topical. It was a political cause with which Mo identified at a number of levels. She was active both in the peace movement as a member of CND and in the related organisation opposing the use of civil nuclear power. It was a cause that was of great importance to her during this time and it had an impact on her life both politically and professionally because it took up so much time. It also meant that she made many new political contacts who were swept up into her endlessly expanding network.

Lots of these new contacts had started when she walked through the door of the left-wing bookshop, Days of Hope, in the city centre. This was a focal point of much of the left-wing contingent in Newcastle in the 1980s. The name was inspired by the television series made by Ken Loach and written by Jim Allen. It is sometimes said now that the bookshop was actually known as 'Haze of Dope' but in truth this seems to be a recent witticism mocking the youthful idealism that was the motivating force of the bookshop. There was certainly lots of idealism around, some of it no doubt wreathed in the smoke from the cannabis joints of those who promulgated their ideas to anybody who would listen, but Jonathan Upton, now elevated to Head of Corporate Development and of the General Secretary's office in Tony Blair's model 'new' Labour Party, insisted that the image of the place has been changed in the telling of it. 'Those were the days of the puritanical Left,' he said.

There were many able young politicians in Newcastle, some more puritanical than others and many of them far more left-wing than Mo. But Mo never compromised her politics in order to enhance her chances of selection for a parliamentary seat. She has always remained loyal to her beliefs. Oddly enough, two outspoken Lefties who were prominent on the political Left in Newcastle at the time, Stephen Byers, who was a member of North Tyneside council, and Alan Milburn, who worked in the bookshop and was treasurer of the trades union CND group, would both end up sitting in the same Cabinet with Mo twenty years later. There was a difference here, though: by then, of course, the two men were reformed characters who had renounced the wild days of their youth, whereas all Mo Mowlam's friends from Newcastle would agree that when she became a Cabinet minister her politics were almost exactly the same as they had always been. Martin Spence, who was one of the two young men who ran Days of Hope and who saw a great deal of Mo during her years on Tyneside, is one of many who doesn't think her politics have changed at all – 'I saw her as right-wing in an inclusive, libertarian sort of way.'[13]

The other young man who ran the bookshop was Andy McSmith,[14] a journalist who was active in the Labour Party and later went to work as a press officer at the party's national headquarters. Martin Spence was what might be called a practising anarchist. He was very involved in Newcastle politics, particularly in CND, and later moved into Mo's house for a while as her lodger. They both remember her first appearance in Days of Hope very clearly. She wandered in and struck up a conversation with Andy. She asked whether they had shifts of volunteers to help run the place and, if so, whether she could volunteer in exchange for a discount on the books she bought. This practical and businesslike suggestion completely threw the two young idealists. 'We couldn't possibly have allowed it because we had people who were unemployed coming in and doing shifts and they weren't getting deals on books,' said McSmith. His colleague and friend recalled their mutual indignation: 'She said: "What's in it for me? Will I be able to buy books at a discount?" And this wasn't the deal! You did it out of commitment to the cause! At that point it was a bit out of order – in fact we had a discussion about how out of order this was and how lacking in commitment it was: "Is there a comeback? Is there something in it for me?"'[13] But Spence was reflective: 'It's consistent with Mo: "Socialist bookshop? Great idea! But if I'm going to give up some of my time, maybe there's a deal where I will benefit from this as well?"'

Despite this shock to their puritanical socialist souls, their initial reservations were quickly dispelled and it wasn't long before Mo was installed as a regular in the bookshop, doing shifts, buying books (at full price) for the courses in the political department at the university and doing an immense amount of good business for them. As ever, she was an attraction. Everybody liked her. She was friendly and funny. She was knowledgeable about politics. She sat at the till, affably chatting to customers, helping them, encouraging them – the only problem was her rather alarming propensity unthinkingly to give things away when she felt like it. But the two men greatly appreciated her help and friendship as well as the marketing advantages of her presence.

And there were always lots of laughs when Mo was around. Andy McSmith told her once that his partner, Sue Dearie, who worked in the reference section of the city library, had been complaining about the daft and trivial questions she got from the public. This immediately started Mo scheming. She planned to ring Sue and ask her how many sections there were to a caterpillar. At her first attempt Sue immediately recognised her voice. Mo pretended she was ringing for another reason, rang off and then grabbed some innocent customer in the bookshop.

This poor sap was obliged to ring the reference library and seek information about caterpillar sections. Sue sighed and said she would need to look this up and ring him back. When he gave Sue the number on the telephone, she instantly recognised it. 'Has Mo Mowlam put you up to this?' she demanded.

What is extraordinary is that Mo found the time for the bookshop, let alone the pranks. She was working extremely hard within the Labour Party and also at the university. 'People didn't realise she wrecked herself with work,' Michael Clarke said. Everybody speaks of her attractiveness and the word vivacity is used time and again. Yet Clarke also remembered that she often looked washed-out and exhausted, something that didn't really surprise him because of the amount that she put in to every aspect of her demanding lifestyle. She was very committed, in particular, to the students. The university was at the time rather traditional, and she presented the antithesis of the way in which university lecturers were expected to behave; the inevitable consequence was, said Clarke, that half the students fell in love with her.

However, those students who were not swept up in her aura had considerable reservations. Michael Clarke said it was hard to put a finger on the reason. 'A lot of people who reacted against her were quite suspicious. One or two after they graduated said things like: "I always kept out of Mo's way because she was so aggressive, she bullied people in seminars, she was a control freak." They felt she was very manipulative.' He described a known academic problem which arises when a charismatic lecturer entrances their students and then uses the subsequent power gained as a means to manipulate them. 'I don't think Mo did that. She worked so hard and took such a deep interest in those people. She would spend the whole evening sometimes talking to people and she would go round to their homes and sort them out. She entered into not just their work, but their development. Most of the students thought she was great and she had some very very devoted followers.'

116

The students invited her to all their parties and she was a particular hit at the annual Christmas revues when the staff poked fun at the students and vice versa. With no preparation, she would entrance the company with her comic skills. She was often asked to front things on behalf of the department and the other staff were similarly appreciative that there was somebody who was prepared to take on such things. With the benefit of hindsight, Tim Gray said: 'She was a natural politician basically. She could speak with a certain amount of credibility on almost anything at any time. She had very good projection, she was extrovert and always animated.' She also had personal courage.

All of these things were to prove useful in the course of her activities as a member of CND. Single-handedly on one occasion, she defused a potentially ugly political situation. It came about after the dramatic rise in interest in nuclear disarmament. Days of Hope was attempting to turn this, in a small degree, to pecuniary advantage. As a way of stimulating trade at the bookshop, the boys organised political meetings in the evenings at which they would set up a stall to sell books. In May 1980 they had one such meeting and Ken Coates[16] spoke powerfully about CND and what he described as its imminent resurgence. The meeting was a success and it was decided to hire a theatre that autumn and invite the revered left-wing writer E.P. Thompson to address the issue. This too was a terrific success – the theatre, hired with bookshop funds, was crammed to overflowing – and again it was agreed that it would be an excellent idea to repeat the exercise, only this time with more space in order to accommodate the evident numbers of people on Tyneside who would be interested to hear such powerful and influential speakers.

Meanwhile in another and more well-ordered part of the forest, Professor Laurence Martin, the Vice-chancellor of the University of Newcastle-upon-Tyne, was preparing for the great honour of delivering the Reith Lectures. Sir Laurence, as he later became, had been known throughout his distinguished career as a strategic thinker of a somewhat traditional kind who believed in preserving the nuclear balance.[17]

The fact that he had been invited to become the Reith Lecturer in 1981 necessarily stirred up members of the university CND who held a meeting to consider an appropriate way to respond. Mo and Michael Clarke were on the panel of that meeting at which Carol Clewlow, later a well-known novelist, suggested they set up an alternative set of lectures. Mo and Clarke both thought this was a great idea and Mo set about organising the Alternative Reith Lectures. There were to be six lectures that would take place in the same weeks as the Reith Lectures and while the Vice-chancellor's 'Establishment' case would be published weekly in *The Listener*, the CND alternative views were to appear weekly in *New Society*. Among the lecturers chosen were Jonathan Dimbleby, Mary Kaldor and E.P. Thompson, who were to deliver their addresses under the title 'Perspectives of Disarmament'. The university's Nuclear Disarmament Group sponsored the exercise and Mo Mowlam and Michael Clarke then found a publisher prepared to produce a book which the two lecturers would jointly edit. All proceeds to CND. It was intended to demonstrate that there was 'a second voice distinct from that of the government and media establishment.'

None of this went down at all well within the orthodox circles of the university. A considerable amount of flak was directed at the two rebels. The Vice-chancellor was affronted by what he regarded as a slight which was also 'really rather rude'.[18] Although he was said to have behaved with great dignity in the circumstances, he nevertheless wrote a frosty letter to the head of the Politics department, Professor Berrington, suggesting that the two lecturers should either refrain from engaging in such evidently insolent practices – or choose somewhere other than Newcastle to pursue their interests. They seem to have been lucky and to have got off lightly as the situation was regarded with some seriousness. It was an incident that everyone then involved at the university recalled very clearly nearly twenty years later.

But the event that said much about Mo's personality was on the night of the lecture by E.P. Thompson, who was fast becoming a left-wing folk hero. Mo had been responsible for the organisation of the lectures and she had performed in a spectacular fashion. She had got the word around and she had booked an auditorium within the university. But then disaster struck!

Andy McSmith recalled: 'There was a catastrophe. The hall filled and hordes and hordes more people just kept turning up.' Michael Clarke remembered that there were two overspill theatres filled with people too. The university authorities decided that, for obvious safety reasons, they had to stop any more people coming in and the doors were closed. Still people were turning up. It was a dark, winter evening and people anxious to see and hear the great guru E.P. Thompson had come from all over Tyneside only to find themselves outside on the street. There were hundreds outside and they were very angry. It was a potentially nasty situation.

'Someone was going to have to go out and address them and apologise and tell them all to go away,' said McSmith. It wasn't going to be an easy job. He admitted, frankly, that he didn't like the idea of doing it himself. Mo wasn't disconcerted, however. 'Dear old Mo! She went out and she said to them: "Sorry. The auditorium is full. You can't come in." I'd never heard the expression "street credibility" before: people were shouting at her about why she hadn't booked a bigger theatre in the city and she told them: "E.P. Thompson already had street credibility. We felt he needed intellectual credibility – that's why we brought him to the university."' McSmith thought she was magnificent and very brave.

Michael Clarke much admired her ability to put their message across. 'I became a disarmer in 1976, having lectured on the damn stuff. Mo came to it in a much more political and instinctive way – that's why there was a kind of a partnership. The reason we got on well was because I was the practical, boring one who had all the details but she had all the flair to take it out to people. She was a 29-year-old, young, unattached, female lecturer, so when there were TV cameras around they homed in on her.' She also displayed a natural sense of how to appeal to her audience. Martin Spence remembered one incident when a television camera crew turned up at a CND demonstration. Other members of the group were always rather precious about how to handle publicity, but Mo snatched up a passing child, held the infant in her arms and did an interview straight to camera about why CND was campaigning for the future of this child and all the other children of the world. 'While the rest of us were flapping around, she was brilliant,' he said. 'She was always prepared to do what the occasion demanded – but I don't think she would ever let her passion cloud her very pragmatic judgement.'

Pragmatism is a word Mo has always used to describe herself. Michael Clarke agreed that their general approach to the subject was more an emotional one than intellectual. Mo was clearly profoundly committed to the cause at the time, but it does seem to have been politically pragmatic: it was the issue that then most motivated the Left and no self-respecting socialist, particularly not a member of the Labour Party who was serious about seeking a seat in the House of Commons, could afford to ignore the question. She could have opposed disarmament, but that would have been highly idiosyncratic: she was a right-winger in what was then a very left-leaning Labour Party – but she wasn't *that* right wing.

Mo's old colleague Tim Gray perceptively summed this up: 'I never had the idea that Mo had fundamental political principles that organised her life. I tend to think that she was a politician who would see the sense of moving on when the political climate changed. She wouldn't stand and resist the waves when the waves were swamping you. She's not a Canute. She didn't have any very fixed political landmarks – she wouldn't die for a principle if the principle was obviously otiose in the light of circumstances. There was a flexibility and a pragmatism there and it never surprised me that she got on well with Kinnock, Smith and Blair successively, because she struck me as a team player and she would see the sense of adjusting in the light of political winds and sensibly keeping on message.'[19]

Whatever fuelled her endorsement of CND, she certainly put a great deal of effort into it. She worked with Martin Spence both in the peace movement and the anti-nuclear power movement and she would usually be involved with at least one meeting a week. There were as many as a dozen different CND groups on Tyneside and they were all for ever individually occupied with organising various events, planning future strategy or just designing posters. Mo often chaired meetings and was good at it. She was mistress of ceremonies at an inaugural demonstration in Eldon Square in 1980 and was credited with having pulled the whole thing together. Spence gave a telling example of another event at a national conference in Sheffield. 'There was some guy making a long and rambling speech. He'd lost his way and the audience was restless. Mo was in the chair and she came up behind him and started tickling him. He collapsed in giggles, his pomposity was undermined but she had recharged the whole meeting.' There were a great many demos, both locally and in London and sometimes at other places like Torness in Scotland. They brought some famous faces to Newcastle – the actress Julie Christie on one occasion – and at other times the Tyneside contingent would travel to distant destinations by coach. This all required organisation, at which Mo was extremely good.

It should have helped with her personal projection in the Labour Party but it most certainly didn't. The constituency party to which Mo originally belonged was predominantly right-wing but there were also a fair number of hard left-wingers. It was dominated by a Tyne and Wear county councillor of the old school, a former Lord Mayor named Arthur Stabler who had been an officer of the party since the end of the Second World War. Mo did not conform to his view of how a woman ought to behave and he couldn't abide her. 'It was traditional for women to sit at the back at ward meetings, they didn't speak and they made the tea,' said McSmith. Another figure of the local party establishment was an elderly woman, Iris Steadman, a former full-time Labour organiser, and she apparently endorsed this view. She was certainly anti-feminist, she referred to all the younger members of the party as 'the young socialists' – assuming, quite wrongly, that they were all left-wing Bennites[20] – and she used to tell them: 'I've seen you come and I'll see you go.'

Despite this antipathy, in early 1981 Mo succeeded in getting nominated as the Newcastle Central delegate to the special Labour Party conference held in London that January. It was a mark of some honour for whomsoever was chosen and it was going to be an important political event. It was this rules revision conference and its endorsement of a complicated electoral college system for the election of the party leader that provoked the formation of the SDP by the Gang of Four.[21] The nature of the debate all seems as obscure now as perhaps it should have done to the left-wing activists at the time, but the contribution of the young delegate from Newcastle Central was to speak against a move that left the choice of party leader with Labour MPs. 'The impotence of backbench MPs is well known to many of us, so to suggest that the MPs will have to control in some way the leader who is put forward is a myth that we ought to stamp on right now,' she said.[22]

The real significance of her role as delegate, though, was what it meant for her later in that same year when she found that she was deliberately blocked from fulfilling the same function at the annual conference in Brighton. This was the occasion that saw the culmination of the deputy leadership contest in which Tony Benn had stood against Denis Healey and was only narrowly beaten – partly as a result of the abstentions of some members of the 'soft' Left led by the then Shadow Education spokesman Neil Kinnock, who had publicly and controversially abstained rather than support Benn. When Newcastle Central came to choose its delegate, Arthur Stabler swung the vote against Mo in favour of a known supporter of the Militant tendency, John Noble. This meant that a very right-wing constituency was sending a Militant left-winger to one of the most crucial party conferences of the generation no doubt to block Mo Mowlam going instead. 'Stabler preferred someone who was male with a Geordie accent,' said McSmith, who witnessed all this. 'It really hacked her off that they had done that simply because she was a woman.'

It was a warning and it was personal. Mo was caught in the middle between the right-wing old guard and the hard Left and it was not a happy position to occupy. Happily, her experience was not unique. Joyce Quin[23] and Hilary Armstrong[24] were two other politically ambitious young women who were also both moderates in the Labour Party and hoping to find Westminster parliamentary seats in the north-east. They could at least all have a mutual moan from time to time. 'We used to gossip to each other about these bloody awful men and the so-called left-wing idealists,' Hilary Armstrong said.[25] She and Joyce Quin were both selected for safe seats in 1985 and, in the event, all three of them entered the Commons together in 1987.

Even though Mo's Labour Party branch was so right-wing, the constituency party decided to back Tony Benn in the deputy leadership election and gave the delegate a mandate to this effect. But although the vote itself was not at issue, it still provoked further trouble in the party afterwards. Harry Cowans, who as the Member of Parliament had a separate vote in his own right, had not voted for Benn. He attended a post-conference post mortem with his local members, where Mo challenged him, on the grounds of democratic accountability, about the fact that he had departed from the constituency decision. Cowans wrongly interpreted this as a Bennite-inspired attack upon him. Mo was not a Bennite, but someone who was independently minded, prepared to defend her own stance and was surprised when others didn't. Two years later, in 1983, when she succeeded once again in being elected conference delegate, she returned to her local party and defended her very eclectic votes for the Labour National Executive. She had not voted for any slate but had supported among others Tony Benn on the left, Jack Ashley on the right and Peter Shore whose stance was strongly anti-European. She had also voted in favour of the expulsion of some members of Militant. 'I remember her coming to the ward meeting and disarming everybody. She had voted for everybody – it was very cleverly done and the old Right were very pleased about her voting to expel Ted Grant and co.[26],' said Andy McSmith.

She had two setbacks in terms of selection as a parliamentary candidate for a seat in Newcastle. One was at the end of 1985, after she had left the city and gone to live in Barnsley. But the first, which was in some ways probably more disappointing, was before the 1983 election when the boundary changes altered the constituency map of the city. She put up to fight the new Newcastle Central seat, which had now become a Tory marginal but which Labour could certainly hope to win in a good year. She was optimistic about winning the selection because, despite the old guard, she had chaired the West City branch of the old constituency, and also because of the effort she had thrown into helping the Labour Party on Tyneside make sense of the boundary changes. A new seat called Tyne Bridge, combining the most run-down areas of Newcastle with the most run-down areas of Gateshead, had been created which was clearly going to be a safe Labour seat and it was the one which Harry Cowans effectively inherited. But there was a problem about motivating the people on the ground in the local parties, specifically because of the rather illogical linking of two places, Newcastle and Gateshead, divided by the River Tyne with distinctive and inimical identities – at least to the people who lived within them.

Someone had to pull the new constituency party together and deal with all the political and organisational problems that had been thrown up as a consequence of the boundary revision. As usual, Mo was right in there. She chaired the shadow constituency party before the changes came into effect at the 1983 general election – and, indeed, remained in the chair afterwards. She shook up the party workers, gave everybody a job to do, mediated in the rivalries between the two disparate groups within the new constituency and provided a powerful motivating force where none had existed.

And to what effect? Well, there was certainly to be little reward for all this effort when she went for selection for the redrawn Central seat. She lost it by one vote to a city councillor named Nigel Todd, an official of the Co-op who was considerably further to the left than she was. This despite the fact that by several accounts she was the more charismatic candidate; many thought she *ought to* have won the selection, if for no other reason than simply because she performed better. 'She didn't swallow the Bennite line,' said Jonathan Upton. 'If she'd wanted to get Newcastle Central she should have gone to the left of Nigel Todd – a Marxist intellectual type.'[27] She wasn't prepared to do that even though, arguably, given her personality and campaigning skills, she might even have won the seat for Labour when the election arrived and could then have adjusted her politics later. In the event Nigel Todd lost to the Conservative candidate, Piers Merchant, but the Tory majority was only just over 2,000.

What was plain to many and now to Mo herself was that she had made a great many enemies. It is a curious function of politics, perhaps because it is such a personally competitive business, that success by any one individual is resented by others. There is an old joke at Westminster which says that every time you make an enemy in the House of Commons, you can console yourself with the fact that you have simultaneously made 658 friends. There is jealousy and rivalry and animosity wherever you turn in politics and that is as true in local politics as anywhere. It perhaps particularly affects women. There was certainly a tide against Mo Mowlam at this selection conference. One example is provided by what happened in Jesmond. She and Todd had both addressed a hustings meeting in the Jesmond ward of the constituency in the run-up to the selection and that ward – in what was in effect a primary – had chosen to back Mo. Yet at the selection meeting, a delegate, who was personally hostile to Mo, voted instead for Todd – although all those present had been reminded that under party rules mandating was not allowed and that delegates should vote as they wished. That alone, unfair as it seems, was enough to prevent her winning.

Andy McSmith was astonished by the display of enmity and vitriol that Mo had stirred up by putting herself up for this public position. There were those, and he was among them, who thought she might even throw in the towel on politics at this point. He had wondered about this possibility before, when she was prevented from being the conference delegate in the autumn of 1981 and was clearly very hurt by what occurred and showed as much: he remembered her being very brusque and uncharacteristically dismissive on the telephone when he rang about something just after that meeting. But she had rung him back forty-eight hours later to apologise, having swallowed her disappointment. On this occasion, she managed to do the same. She was to show that she was more serious about her commitment to a political career than most could have imagined – in spite of all that was to be thrown at her.

By this time she knew that there was one specific reason that could have swung the selection conference against her. That was the extraordinary rumour about her that had recently started to circulate. Everybody heard it. Andy McSmith heard it first on the telephone, from a 'well-connected' person whom he refused to identify. 'This person said: "Avoid all contact with her. We think she's a spy, working for British intelligence." I thought: "This can't be true!"'

The more widespread version of the rumour was that she was working for the Central Intelligence Agency. The total of the evidence against her was that she had worked for Tony Benn and that she had then studied and worked in the United States. But this appeared to be quite enough to set the rumour mills grinding through the Newcastle political networks. People didn't really believe it was true. There was certainly no supporting information of any activity on her part that could have been interpreted as suspicious. But politics being the bitchy business it is, none of this prevented people from passing on the information with alacrity. As the former Labour Prime Minister James Callaghan had said in another context a few years beforehand: 'A lie can be halfway round the world before the truth has got its boots on.'

Jonathan Upton, who was to be Nigel Todd's agent for the 1983 election and who didn't know Mo Mowlam personally until this time, said: 'The [rumour about the] CIA was seriously being suggested – and being posited as a very strong reason why she didn't get the selection for '83.'

These days Jonathan Upton, now elevated to his distinguished position at 'new' Labour headquarters in Millbank, speaks frankly of 'how awful' the politics were at that time, citing this as a specific example.

Martin Spence, who was at this time lodging with Mo, had no hesitation about asking her directly about it and was quite convinced by her response that the story was sheer fantasy. That didn't stop it damaging her politically. She was angry and hurt about it and, according to her friend Hilary Armstrong, blamed powerful factions within the party. 'It was linked to her going for the selection,' said Hilary Armstrong, who at the time was a lecturer at Sunderland Polytechnic. 'She always used to think that the far left had fuelled the rumours. I don't know whether this was paranoia getting in. She had worked for Tony Benn and then gone to the United States, of course.'

Michael Clarke said that she was very angry about the smear. She regarded it as a whispering campaign against her and it upset her a great deal. 'The reason it sticks in my memory is because she was so angry and annoyed and depressed,' said Clarke. 'She would say: "Where's this come from?" and "What's the problem?"'

When asked about this nearly twenty years later, Tony Benn said he had no recollection of even having heard the suggestion that Mo Mowlam was any sort of spy.[28] He produced a list of all the specific references to his contacts with her that he holds on his data base[29] and there is no record in his remarkable daily diaries of him having heard such a story. He did observe, however, in this context that such rumours may have originated because Alvin Toffler, whom he knew was an acquaintance of Mo Mowlam, was known to lecture on defence and security issues.

It was a strange episode. It seems probable that it was exactly what it looked like: a deliberate smear, possibly conceived by her political critics in a specific attempt to damage her reputation and lessen her chances of any selection for a parliamentary seat on Tyneside. 'We were both done over by the hard left,' observes Hilary Armstrong,[30] speaking of their mutual experience during those years.

In retrospect, it is easy to see how, in such a febrile political climate, doubts about Mo's political authenticity might have been floated. It is important to remember the amount of antipathy – and naked hatred – that there was then within the Labour Party. It was virtual civil war and members of the hard left were quite happy to use whatever weapons they could to do down an opponent. In this poisonous political atmosphere the smallest snippet of innuendo could easily be embroidered overnight into a full-size quilt of guilt. Mo Mowlam was not prepared to compromise herself and to choose what would have been a far easier political course by presenting herself, as so many did, as holding more left-wing views than she in fact held.

It was not the only time that she would be a victim of this particularly vicious kind of whispering campaign. The very same rumour was to surface again a few years later when she was living and working in Barnsley during the miners' strike, and although she had already been obliged to ride out this experience of personal vilification, it was not something that she did easily. She is a woman who presents herself sometimes as invulnerable, because she appears so strong and tough and resilient. Neil Kinnock once spoke of her 'Tungsten toughness'.[31] The reality is that she is very vulnerable. The tough outer shell is just that: a shell that she developed as a child to protect herself against her circumstances and to enable her to function despite what was happening around her. It was a means, literally, of survival. On both occasions that this particular story surfaced she survived. She minded like mad, but she managed to beat it, making it through to the other side with her sanity and self-respect intact. However, the next time the same sort of thing happened, more than ten years later, at the time of her departure from the Northern Ireland office, it would not be so easy.

Martin Spence saw all this from the viewpoint of a close friend. He remembered on one occasion her being quite depressed and then to his utter astonishment being told by a mutual friend that she was upset with him because, according to Spence, 'we had been on different sides of an argument, which had quite hurt her – which gob-smacked me because my perception of her was as someone who wasn't like that.' He realised then that she was more sensitive and more vulnerable than he had imagined.

Most of the time, the atmosphere in Mo's house in Summerhill Terrace, even when they were arguing about the relative virtues of anarchy and a participatory democracy, was a cheerful one. Martin was a member of a housing co-operative, five doors down the terrace, and he had moved in with Mo while some serious structural work was under way on his own premises. As part of the arrangement he decorated the room he was living in and helped around the house, which was sizeable. There were always people around: Mo quite regularly had others taking rooms for a short period, probably to help with the bills although she also had a propensity for taking in lame ducks. It was certainly an expensive house to heat: he remembered her screeching every time she opened the gas bill. But it was a well-appointed establishment, it wasn't scruffy; she was past the period of student squalor.

Her boyfriend at the time, Laurie Taylor, also remembers a pleasant, communal, affable atmosphere. 'You'd come down for breakfast and there'd be six people there – three of whom you didn't know. She eclipsed people around her, so you didn't notice them.' Nobody remembers anybody ever cooking; according to Taylor people 'rooted round in the fridge' and coffee was made. That was about it. And despite whatever problems Mo had elsewhere, these were happy times at Number 1. Martin admitted to being mildly reluctant to leave and return to the less genial surroundings of his co-op when the time came.

Mo and Laurie did not meet only in Newcastle, of course. She was often in London and he vividly remembered introducing her to his colleagues from the radio programme *Stop the Week* on which he appeared at that time. The regulars, amongst whom Taylor was numbered, were an eclectic bunch of journalists – Robert Robinson, Ann Leslie, Milton Shulman – bound together primarily by wit and egotism and a healthy cynicism. Mo would meet him at The George in Great Portland Street, to which those involved with the programme would repair from Broadcasting House.

'They were a fairly cynical crowd – and she was – well, a lecturer at Newcastle. It was very difficult for anyone to get in on the act – even on the programme we used to play "Hunt the Guest" – and the idea of *anyone* being able to insert themselves into this company was . . . well, there we were standing at the bar of The George drinking large whiskies and she said to Milton: "Why do you keep hiding your right hand?" He said: "A little patch of eczema", and he produced his hand and she said: "Oh! That must be so so painful!" And then she said: "Don't worry about it. It doesn't *look* too bad." She always had that extraordinary capacity to home in on anybody's anxiety or anyone's troubles and be exceedingly and genuinely concerned. It was terribly disconcerting but effective: everybody would stand around and pay attention to her. I have seen her do that on so many occasions – when people feel they're being disregarded, she just brings them in. And afterwards they think: "She's marvellous!" "Mo noticed me!".'

Friends who witnessed the relationship were surprised by the effect that it had on Laurie. 'He was completely dotty about her', according to one of them, who had become accustomed to meeting a succession of girlfriends of quite a different kind. Those who had preceded Mo had all tried to split him off from his friends, and when they failed, hung about gazing adoringly at him. Mo wasn't like that. She was feisty and feminist and very much her own person. 'When he said it was a fun relationship, he meant it – but she was the only one who took him at his word. Other girls would moon around but she didn't. She was extremely cheerful about the fact that she could do just exactly what she liked. She was certainly not going to do what his usual women did and if he didn't like it – well tough.' His friends found this quite amusing, particularly as they all liked Mo – so much so that Laurie began to panic and kept saying: 'She can be quite cold, you know . . .'

But 'fun' was what the relationship was meant to be all about. They had several holidays together. They went to Turkey once for six weeks or so, and on another occasion, in 1981, they went to North Africa. They stayed there with Mo's friend from Coventry, Chris Dammers, who was a development worker in Cairo at that time. When Mo wrote to Dammers in Cairo to propose herself as a guest, she described Laurie in her letter: 'The companion: rather old, but good fun.' (Taylor was about 44 at the time, twelve years older than Mo.) When they arrived they were both clearly on form and their visit was good fun all round. Chris remembers that she was still the same person as the teenager who had glittered in Coventry only 'she had become even more self-confident and funny and entertaining'. While in Egypt, the couple went to Alexandria and got into trouble with the morality police for walking down the street with their arms around each other.[32]

Laurie himself described their affair as 'funny, vigorous, lots of laughs – I can't remember anything about it which wasn't great fun.' It does sound as if it might have had the potential for developing further, but Mo seems to have resisted that. She played it for laughs and shrugged off commitment. Although she didn't talk about it, she must still have been recovering from the death of Dan Sammons, her boyfriend in Florida, which had affected her profoundly. She had also been touched deeply by the deaths of her father in March 1980, aged just sixty-four, and her grandfather later that year.

Mo talked little of any of this. Many of those who thought they were her friends were probably scarcely even aware that these things were going on in other – closed – parts of her life. Sometimes she would open a small door on her emotions. She talked to Michael Clarke about Dan, for example. 'She told me about him. The reason was that a parcel of stuff that he had sent to her turned up.' It emerged that before he died Dan had sent Mo a parcel containing a memento of a holiday they had taken together in Peru in the autumn of 1978. It had been lost in the post for eight months. Presumably, she didn't even know that it was en route and its unexpected arrival must have been unbearably poignant. She told Clarke about the hopes that she had had about her future with Dan: 'We were thinking we would sort something out.' Her friend from Coventry Anne Bailey also thought that the relationship was a very profound one: 'I don't know what would have happened because at that time she was definitely not the marrying kind.'[33] Later she would tell Martin Drew, another Coventry friend, that Dan was 'the love of her life'.[34] Michael Clarke said: 'She spoke very warmly about the States. I think she found the adjustment quite difficult to start with. She was very American and she was going on about Tallahassee. I said: "Why've you come back?" She kind of looked at me and said: "I wanted to come home." I later added to that the thought that she was having a lot of trouble.' He meant at home in Coventry.

She was not often so revelatory. She pushed away from getting too close to anyone. Laurie Taylor once tried to tell her how much she meant to him; having realised this in the course of an evening in London, while Mo was in Newcastle, he raced out to Heathrow in order to fly immediately to Tyneside and convey the news. When he got to the airport he found he had missed the last plane, but still he wasn't diverted from his mission. He spent the night at the airport, took the first flight of the morning and was knocking on the door of 1 Summerhill Terrace at 7.15 a.m. in order to tell her how he felt. He didn't describe precisely what happened but he said: 'Nothing in life ever disturbed her. The important thing at that moment was that she didn't have any shampoo.'

It was Laurie who brought their relationship to a close. He said: 'The only reason that it ended was because of some silly ascetic idea that you can't go on having fun. That was my fault rather than hers.' He was aware, though, that there was something in Mo that backed away from commitment. She didn't want to talk to him about how she felt, any more than she would talk to him about academic life or about politics. But they have remained friends. She obviously appreciated Laurie's capacity for having fun but wasn't prepared to move beyond that. Her favourite record at that time was Rikki Lee Jones's 'Chuckee's In Love'. 'You couldn't get out of bed in the morning without that being on,'

Laurie remembered, more than a little wistfully. And then he added: 'But being in love meant you couldn't have much fun.'

They broke up a few months before the 1983 election campaign got under way and so Mo had plenty of other things in her political life to distract her. According to one of her friends: 'At that time she didn't really feel she was going to meet somebody who gave her everything.' She had a network of women friends to whom she could turn for succour and she put a huge amount of effort into maintaining those friendships and keeping them in good order. She would spend long periods on the phone and she was systematic about it, which fitted in with the way in which she ran her life – with as many segments as a caterpillar. Martin Spence commented: 'She had bits of her life that I didn't know anything about. She had friends working in TV for example – and I used to think: "Where does she meet these people?" "Where does she find the time to go to places to meet them?"' She did start a new relationship in the few months that she remained in Newcastle, with Jonathan Upton, whose marriage had just broken up. It was not a very serious relationship, though, and seemed to observers to be unimportant to them both.

When the election was announced Mo worked energetically for Nigel Todd in the seat she had herself hoped to contest. 'She was absolutely a total good egg about it,' one of the party activists said. And while she apparently did believe it possible for Labour to win the seat of Newcastle Central,[35] she knew very well that the party would not win the election and Michael Foot was not going to be forming the next government. What is of great interest is that she is on record describing how important it was for the Labour Party to do something to redress what she saw as this coming electoral humiliation. She was filmed three days before that election, on Monday, 6 June, saying precisely that. It is the earliest footage of Mo Mowlam, the moderniser. It is even arguably the first film of any of those who would form Tony Blair's 'new' Labour Government detailing what needed to be done.

Bob Davies, who runs a film company in Newcastle, was making a documentary for Channel 4 called 'Who'll Keep The Red Flag Flying Here?', and in pursuit of material for the programme he filmed two hours of discussion about the party among a small group of Labour Party members in the Blakelaw branch. Mo was one of the five people present; she was campaigning there in the course of the election because her own patch was a solid Labour area. This segment of film was never screened, however, because the Labour Party branch concerned decided that it was too revealing and too critical. In the film, Mo, wearing jeans and a tartan shirt and smoking incessantly, leads much of the conversation, speaking eloquently and often. She is wearing no make-up and she looks tired, no doubt as a result of the effort she had been putting in to the election, but she is animated and interested and often rocks with laughter.

She describes the party as in 'an untenable position' with regard to the election manifesto. 'I think it's a very good manifesto and one I support,' she says of the document – famously described by Gerald Kaufman as 'the longest suicide note in history'. However, she adds: 'We haven't got the electorate to the point of supporting that manifesto. We are in a ridiculous position.' She describes herself as a strong unilateralist, but points out that the electorate is unconvinced on this subject and she speaks about the 'inconsistencies' in the way Labour's national campaign is being run. 'I don't think the press is very fair to us. But I'm coming to the position where I'm not sure I'm going to put it all at the press's door because I think that we have failed as a party to a certain extent to put the unilateral position across.' It is quite a perceptive analysis, especially in the immediate run-up to election day when the heat of the campaign can easily cloud political objectivity.

She goes on: 'You've got to work with people. If we stop listening to people – which is what we have done in the party – we won't get their votes.' She has a dig at some of her local enemies by suggesting that councillors take people for granted – particularly in the north-east where Labour takes its supporters for granted, she adds – and goes on to say that the party has stopped thinking and talking to people and trying to include them. 'I'm not saying "Sell out on policies". I'm saying we've got to get back to listening to what is important to people.' It's little wonder that there is a credibility gap, she continues, holding her hands two feet apart to illustrate the point. 'It's not a very popular thing to say: on the Left, we've pushed a number of things through [she was referring to the constitutional changes], we've partly split the party and we haven't taken the electorate with us . . . Until we do it on both levels, we're going to have problems.' Then providing a classic proto-type for Tony Blair's future policies, she speaks of the importance of the 'lower middle-class group', a group she describes as having been lost to the Labour Party. She insists that this must be changed through forging a very different coalition in future. 'That is going to be very problem-atic but it is something we've got to start thinking about.' It is a remarkable testament and it isn't hard now to see how much Tony Blair would have approved of someone who was thinking like this.

But it wasn't Tony Blair then of course who was her hope for the future. It was Neil Kinnock. She had met him already, at a rally in Newcastle. Charles Clarke was now working for Kinnock as a research assistant. After the Newcastle rally, Mo and Hilary Armstrong, whose father, the MP Ernest Armstrong, had, it turned out, gone to the same school as Charles's mother, drove Kinnock across the Pennines to Carlisle. It was a useful opportunity to make contact and talk and Mo was never one to pass up the chance of such a thing.

After Labour's catastrophic result in the election, she built on that contact. Margaret Thatcher had a landslide. The Conservatives had an overall majority of 144 and a majority over Labour of 188. Within twenty-four hours of the result of the election, even before Michael Foot had announced his resignation as Labour Party leader, Mo Mowlam had been instrumental in contacting Neil Kinnock's office. She did so by organising for a telegram to be sent from the Newcastle Central campaign team. Jonathan Upton, the election agent for the constituency, recalled: 'She suggested it. Immediately after we lost the election. It went to Neil Kinnock and it said something like: "Down but not out in Newcastle Central. Please come and talk to us to rebuild for the future.'"

Once Neil Kinnock's candidature was secure for the leadership, Mo contacted Charles Clarke, who was running the Kinnock campaign, to ask if she could do anything to help. In the summer of 1983 her academic post gave her a long summer holiday, and Clarke brought her into the Kinnock office during the run-up to the election at the party conference in September. She acted as treasurer and impressed everybody – as ever – with her fantastic energy.

Mo also showed that she was strongly motivated about the parlous situation of the Labour Party. She believed it was the time for changing the party, and according to one source, that was what prompted her to volunteer. 'It wasn't even for love of Neil. There was no materialism or ambition about it. It was entirely about what was good for the party.'[36] Perhaps it crossed her mind that it wouldn't do her career any harm either, as it was to prove.

Later that year she surprised everybody by deciding that her own future was elsewhere and applied for a job at Northern College in Barnsley. Professor Tim Gray was particularly surprised because of the nature of the post. He rated her professional skills in the following order: 1) teaching; 2) research; and 3) administration, and she was going for the third. 'We couldn't understand it at the time,' he said. There were plenty of others who did, though. She wanted to find a way to add to her qualifications as a politician and, besides, she had been in Newcastle for over four years. There were several leaving parties, to say goodbye both to her colleagues at the Department of Politics and her fellow Labour Party members. She hired an Indian restaurant for her Labour Party farewell. There was usually a complete divide in the city between the middle-class intellectual Left and the indigenous Labour Party, despite her ability to make enemies as well as friends, it was some tribute to her that both sides turned out on this occasion.

She still liked the city and would have liked a seat there. Indeed eighteen months after she had left for Barnsley, when Harry Cowans died unexpectedly, aged 52, she thought, with some justification, that she might be in with a chance in Tyne Bridge, the constituency she had nursed into existence and which she had chaired. She rang her old friend Sid Butcher. 'She said: "I want to know if you're standing for Tyne Bridge because if you are, I'm wasting my time coming up."'[37] Butcher told her he'd been 29 years on the roads as a lorry driver and he'd seen quite enough of London, thank you. Mo got her campaign under way. She came to stay with the Butchers for two weeks and Sid secured her the backing of his union, the Transport and General Workers' Union. He coached her for the selection conference: she would have to speak for ten minutes and answer questions for another ten. He was on the constituency executive and he had an early political feeling – which he didn't share with Mo beforehand – that she wasn't going to win, however well she performed. He sensed 'there was something going on'.

The 'something' was that she was up against David Clelland, the leader of Gateshead District Council, who had strong union backing from his own Engineering Union and from the General Municipal and Boilermakers' Union. Earlier that same year he had been beaten by both Joyce Quin and then by Hilary Armstrong at their respective selection conferences in Gateshead and Durham; this time he would get the better of the third of this group of women. He won by 46 to 35 on the fourth ballot. There was a shortlist of five and Mo made it to the last three before dropping out in the third round. Shortly afterwards three TGWU members dropped in at the Butchers'. They were bus drivers, members of A34 branch, and they had called by to see Mo who was out. Alma Butcher recalled: 'They'd come to say they'd never been to a meeting like it and they were very sorry she didn't get it. They'd never thought a woman could hold a meeting like that – a couple of lads had got up to go and she'd said to them: "Where are you going? I haven't finished yet!" and they came back like little lambs and sat down. They were so impressed that a woman could do that. They were really chuffed with her.'

CHAPTER 7

'A bit of a bloody nuisance'

Barnsley 1984–1987

The name Northern College, Barnsley, has a gritty-sounding ring to it, appropriate for an adult education establishment with strong community, trade union and left-wing links. The reality therefore comes as something of a surprise. The college is to be found at Wentworth Castle, a magnificent seventeenth-century country house, Palladian on one front, baroque on another, a gem of English architecture with a remarkable staircase, a fabulous overmantel in the entrance hall and arguably one of the most beautifully situated student libraries in Britain. In 1948 the last member of the Wentworth family to live in the house, a bachelor named Captain Bruce Vernon-Wentworth, was obliged by a combination of death-watch beetle, dry rot, the after-effects of military occupation during the war and practical finances to sell. The house, outbuildings and 60 acres of garden and parklands, including an impressive range of garden monuments, an eighteenth-century pillared barn and no fewer than three obelisks, were bought by the Barnsley Education Committee – a snip at £26,000, particularly in view of the fact that it cost £14,000 in 1708. The house at

Stainborough in the rolling countryside just outside Barnsley became a teacher training college until, in 1978, it opened as a residential college for local people who had not previously had the opportunity of such access to education. It was the pioneering vision of the distinguished socialist economist, Michael Barratt Brown, the founding principal, and in January 1984 Mo Mowlam took up the post of college administrator. She has always said that Northern College isn't so much somewhere to give people a second chance, as somewhere for people who didn't have a chance in the first place.[1]

To a number of people at the time it seemed an odd job for her to take. She had told her mother that she had got fed up at Newcastle University 'teaching politics to kids who were never going to use it',[2] and she was interested in the post at Northern College because she felt she would be able to help people who had never had a decent chance. But there was another much more pragmatic reason for taking up the post. 'She had political ambitions,' says her friend Hilary Armstrong. 'We neither of us hid our political ambitions. She decided that her profile simply wasn't right: she was seen as an intellectual and not seen as having the trade union roots and stuff that she needed. She needed to demonstrate that she could manage. Academic life can't give you the contact with the real world that a lot of them – constituency parties – are looking for.'[3]

In the view of Jonathan Upton her intentions were absolutely unambiguous. She wanted to be a Labour MP and she systematically plotted the way to do it. 'It was no good being a wanky academic in the Labour Party in the early eighties. If you wanted to be selected, you'd got to get the trade unions behind you. So what does she do? She goes to an organisation which has got something to do with the trade unions, even though she was hugely over-qualified for the job.'[4]

Coincidentally, it was a friend of Hilary's who employed Mo in her new job at Northern College. Professor Bob Fryer has long been active at the interface between politics and education and as an adviser to the Labour Party. He is now the Director of Policy and External Relations at the University for Industry and the Assistant Vice-chancellor at New College, Southampton, but in September 1983 he took over from Professor Barratt Brown as Director of Northern College. He wanted to appoint a senior administrative officer to raise the profile of the place, get some more money for funding development and generally shake things up a bit. He was friendly with Hilary and her now husband, Paul Corrigan (they married in 1993), with whom he had taught at Warwick University, while Mo knew Paul from her undergraduate days at Durham. The four met for a drink in the autumn of 1983, shortly after Mo applied for the post, to discuss what was involved. Subsequently she turned up for the formal interview at Northern College and in typical fashion bowled over the governors and other members of the panel with her energy and her ideas. The chairman of the governors at the time was Councillor William 'Bill' Owen, later the Lord Mayor of Sheffield, and he felt immediately that she was exactly the right person for the job.[5] She had personality and flair and she exuded both. According to Jonathan Upton: 'She must have absolutely knocked the socks off them.'

She has always had a terrific presence. At the time she was an athletic and attractive woman of 34. 'When Mo goes into a room she always creates an impression,' Bob Fryer said. 'She has a directness about her. She immediately engages with people in a very up-front manner. It's a very open approach; in that sense there's no side to her.' This manner is not always as casual as it may seem, however; it would be quite wrong to think that she is unaware of the impact she may be making or that the way she behaves is unconsidered. 'Don't underestimate all of that. It is a consummate performance,' one former boyfriend observed, not unkindly.[6]

Mo knows that while she is not a great public speaker on platforms she can put herself over extremely well in more intimate circumstances such as job interviews and, as she was to prove in due course, selection conferences. She relates to people. She communicates her own personality. She is very quick, very intelligent and intellectually very sharp.

Her mother once said that she was 'bloody-minded and determined' rather than clever, but that rather underplays the reality for she is extremely bright, although, as Bob Fryer puts it, 'she wears her intellect lightly.' When she first meets people, she has an extraordinary ability to reach out to them and charm them. Her remarkable ability to remember people's names – and use them – is an attractive skill that makes others feel good and yet at the same time reflects extremely well on her. She can be introduced to someone in the morning, meet dozens more people in the course of the day and still remember that first individual's name to say goodbye. This is very flattering, particularly when the person involved may not be someone of political importance but perhaps a driver or a doorman. She remembers people who other politicians sometimes don't even notice are there.

There are endless examples of this: 'Where are Jack and Lorna?' the visiting Secretary of State demanded at the end of a day's ministerial tour in Yorkshire in 1998, naming two police officers she had met five hours beforehand and hadn't seen since. They were naturally charmed and they had every right to be. It is a reflection of a genuine concern for the tea ladies of life, but it is also a skill she uses for effect. In the middle of making a speech to the House of Commons Press Gallery Luncheon Club once, she interrupted herself to make a passing comment to the head waiter, who was moving discreetly around the tables. 'It's all right, Joe . . .' she began. This was very impressive to the audience of journalists and politicians, as indeed it was meant to be. Although MPs eat infrequently in the press gallery restaurant, she was demonstrating that she knew Joe's name when half the regular clientele had probably never taken the trouble to find it out. But Joe, as he admitted later, was greatly embarrassed; the last thing an efficient head waiter would want is to be singled out in such a fashion. On this occasion, however, it was his bad luck that he was not the person she was seeking to impress.

This gift is something her mother believed was inherited from her father Frank, who had the same well-developed skill. Mo herself has ascribed it variously to her Saturday job as a telephonist when she was a teenager and as a spin-off from being a teacher. It seems probable that it was also something she learned during her years in the United States, since most Americans regard it as a routine matter of courtesy to commit to memory the names of people to whom they are introduced. However she came by it, she has refined the skill to an art.

But Mo Mowlam doesn't rely on social competence when she is after a job, or when she is employed doing one. She prepares her ground. She works exceedingly hard to this end, talking to people beforehand, finding out the lie of the land and the information that will be useful and could be impressive. She also thinks and plans ahead. At about the time she went for this interview one of her friends in Newcastle came upon her reading a copy of George Orwell's *1984* – it wasn't clear whether or not it was for the first time. He innocently asked what had prompted her to read it. 'Because,' she replied, 'next year is 1984 and everybody is going to be talking about the book *1984* – but in fact everybody will be talking about it and nobody will have read it. So I'm reading it now because it's going to be a very good thing to know about next year.'[7]

She mounted a military-style campaign to get the job in Barnsley, according to Jonathan Upton, who, because of his work with NUPE, was one of those whose help she sought because he knew which side was 'Up' with the trades unions. She put in an extraordinary amount of effort, ringing people and seeking advice. He gave her a list of 'ten things you need to know about trades unions'. Paul Corrigan helped put her through her paces. Even after the interview at Northern College when she stayed overnight on the premises before returning to Newcastle, she was still guarded and initially careful not to be too casual or, literally or figuratively, to let her hair down. Bob Fryer had asked two of the second-year students, Jim McKenna and Aileen Larsen, to look after the interviewee, take her to the college bar and entertain her. 'Mo's appearance was quite out of character,' Jim McKenna says now, having become a close friend and knowing what passes for normal in terms of her appearance and behaviour. 'She was the schoolmarm: hair in a bunch, floral dress, tight lips, very reserved, listening more than talking – quite a different image. I thought: "This woman is very reserved, she's a bit of a prude" but as the evening wore on we realised we liked each other.'[8]

The approach she had adopted proved, of course, to be outstandingly successful. When she was offered the job, she took it on with enthusiasm and commitment. But she had seriously underestimated the difficulties of working in an adult residential college and of being an incomer in the close-knit traditional male-dominated mining community of South Yorkshire. 'If people aren't brought up here we tend to be a bit xenophobic. Coming from Coventry, you're like from another planet,' said Jean Marshall, who was to become a close friend of Mo's and who was born, brought up and still lives in Silkstone Common, a village just a couple of miles away from Wentworth Castle.[9]

Mo's years at Barnsley were to prove among the most difficult periods of her life to date, for personal and political reasons as well as professional ones. Her personal life was unsatisfactory and endlessly complicated or, in the phrase that she herself always used in interviews in her attempt to head off further enquiries, 'spectacularly untidy'. She did have a number of relationships with different men at this time, none of them particularly serious. One was with a married man who lived in London. At about this time she was beginning to play more of a role on the national stage and as someone who had helped organise his campaign she naturally went to the Labour Party conference in Brighton in 1983 to see Neil Kinnock's election as leader. She met this particular man that year in the place where many political alliances of one sort or another have been forged over the years – the bar of the Grand Hotel. He was very taken with her, they met again at the party conference in Blackpool the following year and then, eventually, found themselves as people do at party conferences, waiting for a taxi together late one evening. 'Where are we going?' she asked. He was diffident. 'I don't know,' he said. 'Right. We'll go to my hotel,' she said. She told him later that if he had taken the initiative, they would have gone their separate ways. 'She was asserting her right to choose. She only likes blokes who are "new men",' he explained.[10] It is a telling anecdote.

As well as casual flings, she had a series of affairs with several married men. Mo was a risk-taker and it was part of what made her sexually attractive. She was also an independent woman who had grown into womanhood in the sexually liberated sixties and to whom sex was as natural as eating or drinking. She became accidentally pregnant and either miscarried or had an abortion. This was not something that she confided to many although it was a situation of which at least two of her friends were aware. It was obviously a time of great private unhappiness. Her political life was scarcely less complicated, partly as a result of being an outsider who became active in a very institutionalised local Labour Party, but also because she was in Barnsley during the devastating and politically difficult miners' strike of 1984–85. And professionally she found herself doing the wrong job: she did it well, but she was wasted in it and it was an enormous emotional drain on her. Still, she didn't see any of this ahead of her when she moved south from Newcastle. It was the end of one era of her life and the beginning of another. She spent New Year's Eve 1983 with Jonathan Upton and it was the end of their brief affair, if not of their friendship. They said goodbye and she drove off to this new life, the new job and many new friends.

She found one of the first through the local Labour Party which she had contacted to find temporary lodgings. She was put in touch with Jean Marshall – known at that time by her married name of Blackburn – who was then in the process of getting divorced. She was an active member of the party and Mo moved in briefly with her and her son while looking around for somewhere permanent to live. She settled initially on a unit in a large house called Keresforth Hall, at Ward Green, but it didn't really suit her. 'The other people were retired school mistress types and she was a bit noisy and came in at funny times of the day and night,' said Jean. Living with Mo, who has always been wildly untidy, can be difficult, as Jean found out. 'She had this terrible habit: when she left the house not only did she not lock the door, she didn't even remember to shut the door. Things like that didn't matter to her – she'd be far too busy planning things.' There are myriad stories about Mo's untidiness, of which one of the most reveal- ing was when she was contacted by some apologetic police officers who regretfully informed her that she had been burgled; when she got to the scene of the alleged crime she was able to reassure the police that in fact the scene of devastation in her home was not the result of any- thing untoward. She had merely forgotten to shut the door when she left home and as for the state of the house, 'I left it like that,' she told the police.[10] Her mother Tina would come to visit her from time to time wherever Mo was living, 'to muck her out' as her friend Jean put it.

After staying in a couple of other places in the area Mo bought her- self a small house in Silkstone Common, a nineteenth-century village on a high ridge of land, a few winding miles from both Wentworth Castle and Barnsley. There is no coal industry now, of course, but there is still a railway station on the line which used to transport the coal from the valleys. There is a shop, a garage and two pubs at the central crossroads. The big pit in the area used to be at Dodworth and there were a number of little day holes around. It is also an agricultural area with a string of little villages dotted here and there and nowadays some pleasant modern estates that have grown up alongside the grimy stone cottages of the last century. Mo bought a two-bedroomed ter- raced Victorian worker's cottage on the end of the village which, when she left the region, she was eventually to sell to Jean, who lives there still.

At the time it had one room downstairs with a breakfast bar divid- ing the kitchen and the sitting room and, of course, a coal fire. As with all Mo's houses, it was cold but the new owner was actually quite good at making fires, through long practice. One of her ex-boyfriends remembers someone failing to get the fire going when they were all sitting around and freezing. 'He's a - - - - miner! And he can't make a - - - - fire!' said Mo, qualifying both miner and fire with an unnecessary adjective.[13] Among her friends were Michael[13] and Yvonne Clapham; he was an Industrial Relations Officer with the miners' union, who sometimes taught on NUM courses at the college and Yvonne had been a student on the first intake. Their son, Jonathan, did some gardening for Mo and their daughter, Paula, helped her decorate the house in Silkstone Common.

The house always had a good feeling, according to Jean; they had some happy times. She remembers them drying their hair together of an evening, laughing and having a natter, or watching *Question Time* together. 'She'd spend half the time ringing up the programme – she'd be on the blower registering her complaint about some bias.' Later Jean was greatly to enjoy watching *her* on *Question Time* and remembering how it used to be.

As usual Mo quickly made lots of friends. There was a number of houses in the area where she could just turn up and muck in as part of the family. She would look by and see Mick Clapham's elderly mother or turn up at the Claphams to borrow their children. She has always been the sort of person who doesn't make arrangements but turns up unexpectedly and takes part in whatever is going on. That included mealtimes. Jean said: 'She'd start eating your dinner if she was hungry, without meaning to be rude – although it is rude, really, when she eats it off your plate.' Peter and Doris Clarney, close friends she made at Northern College, remembered exactly the same. 'She'll walk in,' said Peter, 'and it doesn't matter what's on the table – she'll have a pick of it.'[14] This is actually something she has done all her life. 'She's always been a picker,' her mother, Tina, said. 'If you had the Christmas turkey and hid it, she'd still find it and pick bits off it.'[15] The Clarneys often had meals with Mo in her years in Barnsley, sometimes at her house. When she did remember to lock the door, they knew where the key was hidden and Doris would usually take over the cooking in such an instance. 'Mo was the worst bloody cook in the world,' Peter said, while Doris spoke affectionately of Mo's ability to cook roast potatoes 'like bell metal'.

Her friendship was particularly important to Jean Marshall. 'I knew Mo on a different level to other people. She was quite a revelation to me. She lifted me up – it's easy to get a bit low when you're going through a divorce – and I think her independence was quite an inspiration. We both detested being called "Miss" or "Mrs" and she would say: "You have to study hard and get a doctorate and then when they try and do that, you say, 'Well, actually . . . it's Dr'".' Jean admired Mo's ability to walk into a room full of strangers and get to know people just by being herself; she found her to be an education in that respect, all this of course at a time and in an area where women's independence was still not really encouraged.

It was an approach that got Mo into trouble and made her plenty of enemies, but to Jean she was, as people often say about her, a breath of fresh air. There could easily have been political differences between them. Jean had worked for the NUM for some time, had been Arthur Scargill's secretary for ten years until he took over the national presidency in 1983 and she was specifically *not* a supporter of Neil Kinnock, with whose leadership of the Labour Party Mo was at this point inextricably linked. Moreover shortly after Mo's arrival in Barnsley, the miners' strike over pit closures began, heralding an exceedingly difficult time for relations between the Labour leadership and the NUM. After she left the NUM, Jean worked for the Labour Member of the European Parliament for the area, Norman West, someone who, according to a number of those around at the time, didn't like Mo. Amazingly, the friendship between Mo and Jean transcended their politics.

Like many people, Jean found that Mo was the sort of person who had time for everybody; she was sympathetic and endlessly helpful with other's problems. Jean thinks she actually took on too much in that respect and sometimes she would do more than would normally be considered reasonable to try to help others. There was a heavy fall of snow one winter and all the villages were cut off, no traffic could move down the steep narrow lanes of the surrounding countryside. Mo walked to Northern College and then into Dodworth – a distance of something like six miles, in very difficult circumstances – in order to take the canteen workers their wages due that day. She knew that the women depended on the money.

Someone prepared to perform kindnesses or show initiative like that was unusual, but it was noticeable that while being a good friend to others, Mo didn't often share her own problems with those close to her. Some of her friends were quite unaware that she was often profoundly unhappy during her years in South Yorkshire. She compensated by trying to help others and by working. 'She was working so hard to make up for the fact that she hadn't got anyone to go home to,' said one long-standing friend.[16] 'She could be up and down in terms of being happy but she really missed the lack of a real relationship. She didn't talk about it a lot, but you always felt there was something missing in her life – and that she felt there was something missing. She never let it get her down but if she had a drink she'd get a bit fed up. Then she'd just get on and work – and she does have this incredible ability to drive herself.'

Her lack of a permanent emotional commitment at home helped her fulfil her role at the college. In the relatively brief time that she was there – just under three years – she hurled her formidable energy at the task of raising money and pulling in fresh support and she did it very successfully. Bob Fryer said that the impact was enormous. 'Lots of people knew about Mo Mowlam and the college.' And that was important for Mo personally as well as professionally. She was very conscientious about her job and she was very conscious of the importance of getting her name known within the Labour Party. She wanted to find a parliamentary seat and she was desperately anxious not to do the wrong thing.

But she wanted to do the right thing as well and she faced a major dilemma, inadvertently set by Neil Kinnock, who had by now been

In the garden at Aunty Jean's in Oxford.
From L: cousins Bridget and Michael, Jimmy, Marjorie and Jean, 1952.

The family at the Hughes' house in Oxford.
From L: Frank, Jimmy, Tina, Jean and
Marjorie, 1952.

Bridget (left) Jean (right) and Marjorie with
Jimmy playing behind at Oxford, 1952.

Marjorie, Jimmy and Jean in the garden of Richmond Drive in 1952.

In the garden at Richmond Drive, Cassiobury Park, Watford in 1953.
From R: Jean, Marjorie, Jimmy and friends.

On holiday in the Lake District, 1953. Marjorie (left) Jean and Jimmy.

On the beach at Bognor. Marjorie (centre) with Jean and Jimmy, 1955.

Marjorie and Jean at Bognor.

Tina with Marjorie (centre) and two friends in the front garden of
17 Shaftesbury Avenue, Southall, about 1957.

Jimmy (left) and Marjorie as Little Bo Peep, Southall.

Marjorie (on the right) sitting next to Jimmy with two friends at Southall.

A family picnic in Bushey Park with the Morris Minor. Tina, Frank and Jim with Marjorie in the foreground, 1958.

Picking apples with Jimmy in the back garden of the house in Shaftesbury Avenue.

At Guide camp (Marjorie second from right).

Jean, Marjorie and Jimmy in Southall about 1959.

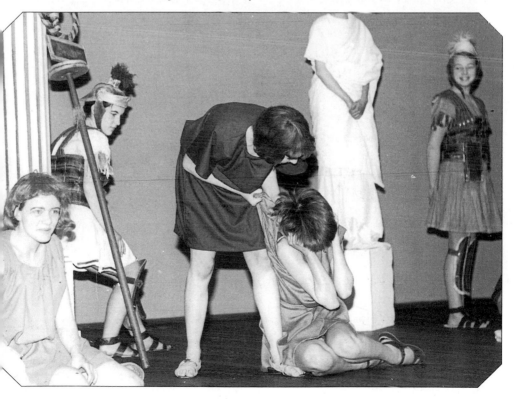

Marjorie Mowlam, the star in 'Androcles and the Lion' at Coundon Court, Coventry.

63 Styvechale Avenue, Earlsdon, Coventry.

Marjorie, growing up.

Mo with Tina at the White House, about 1967.

Mo with Martin Pumphrey.

During her first year at Durham University.

Martin Pumphrey and Mo.

With Martin Pumphrey during their years in Iowa.

Mo in June 1974 when studying at Iowa in the United States.

Mo at a conference in Venice during her years at Newcastle University in the early 1980s.

On holiday in China with Tina, March 1985.

Tina's 70th birthday. Marjorie, Jim and Jean with their mother.

A handshake in history. David Trimble and Marjorie Mowlam are introduced at a British Irish Association conference in Cambridge, 1989.

Acknowledging the applause, Blackpool, 1998. How long would the smiles last?

Marjorie Mowlam sculpture by Shenda Amery for Durham University.

© Steve Bell, 1999

© Gerald Scarfe, 1999

elected leader of the Labour Party. Mo had, of course, helped to organise his campaign, and he so admired her political skills and her personable style that he thought she might be a suitable person to take on the horrendous task of clearing out the membership and cleaning up the mess made by the Militant tendency within the Labour Party in Liverpool. She was approached by Charles Clarke, now the head of Kinnock's office, and specifically asked to do this. She agonised over the offer. Untypically, she seems to have taken advice from a wide range of her friends. 'She couldn't decide whether she could turn it down and still be in their good books,' said one. On the other hand, if she agreed to this task, she would lose serious political credibility with the traditional Left in other constituencies and she already had enough problems in this regard. Another of her friends remembered that she was worried that she wouldn't get a seat at all; such a role would have had a profound effect on her relationship within her own regional Labour Party. 'I said: "Let Kinnock do his own dirty work." If it goes wrong it's Mo Mowlam's fault,' Peter Clarney advised her.[17] In the event she managed to turn down the invitation without causing offence. Peter Kilfoyle, the man who did do the dirty job the party wanted done on Merseyside – and who later became an MP and a close personal friend of Mo Mowlam's – would say afterwards that she had a lucky escape. In any event, she redressed the political balance in Kinnock's office in her favour during the miners' strike. She was seen in the leader's office as invaluable, as she tried to correct what she saw as the misrepresentation of the party view to the striking miners, while simultaneously relaying the miners' thoughts and the prevailing atmosphere in South Yorkshire to the leader's team.

The miners' strike was the most important political issue of Mo's years in Barnsley and it coloured much of her time there. As soon as she arrived in the area she became active in the local Labour Party, which in South Yorkshire was heavily dominated by the NUM. She adopted the same approach to the Labour Party as she did to her job at Northern College, which was to look at how things were operating, consider how they might be improved and then set about telling people how to get on with it. What's the issue? What are the problems? What have we got to do? She threw herself into this activity with characteristic verve which was admirable but, inevitably, she rubbed people up the wrong way. She shook up the college administration, the trades union bureaucracies, the local Labour Party machinery and she upset people.

'I think they were quite taken aback,' said Bob Fryer. 'Here was a comer-in, arriving in their Labour Party, telling them what to do. It wasn't long before people were thinking this energetic, dynamic person was a bit of a bloody nuisance. It was a minority of people, but nevertheless . . .'

She was always very direct. She used to visit trade union conferences to raise the profile of the college and Bob Fryer, who was often there as well, remembers how at least one trade union general secretary was more than slightly taken aback by her uninhibited, in-your-face style. She marched up to Ken Cameron of the Fire Brigades Union at a conference in Bridlington, introduced herself, told him he should be supporting Northern College and giving resources to provide educational opportunities for working people. But such an approach didn't always work; she could offend people by being over-familiar.

'People often use that to criticise her but actually the main reason people don't like her is because she goes to the heart of difficult issues and confronts people with problems they're not facing,' according to Bob Fryer. She would sometimes leave a meeting while it was still under way in order to get on with something that had just been decided, because, being a do-er, she wanted to do it there and then. But it didn't always work, because, according to Fryer, 'She can be more careless than you might want about how many eggshells get broken.' It wasn't clumsiness, but commitment, getting on with the job in hand to the exclusion of all else. 'I'm terribly fond of Mo and I'd defend her to the death, but I do understand why she irritates people: by being upfront, by familiarity – but what most irritates them is that she challenges them.'

He added: 'The up-front directness can get dangerous. She is not the most traditionally diplomatic of persons. She is not mellifluous. She can be very sharp and focused and some people take a dislike to it. That was what happened in South Yorkshire with some staff and students and part of the Labour Party. Mo divides people into close friends and people who find her irritating and difficult.'

She was popular with most of the students, though. There were about 150 residents, aged mostly between 25 to 45, and another 2,000 or so going through the college on part-time courses during any one year. She became close to a number of them, promoted some whose careers she would foster and encourage, and made a whole raft of friendships. Many of the students who attend Northern College have children who also live in at the college and Mo became very involved with helping people with their child care, babysitting and all the other things that inevitably cropped up. Some of the children, Jean Marshall recalled, were fairly clued-up city kids who found themselves transplanted into a highly unusual environment in the middle of the countryside, far from anywhere. Jean's son would come home from the local school, which the children from Northern College also attended, with appalling stories of the goings-on. It didn't appal Mo, but it did make more for her to do. She relished it: during the vacations when other members of the staff might take a holiday, she got involved in running play schemes for deprived children.

Mature students are necessarily more committed, more demanding and, with many coming from trade union backgrounds, they were impatient to do things with their own lives and in politics. They wanted results. They went to Mo because she was seen as someone who could deliver. She was often to be found in the college bar, talking to people, helping them with their problems and sometimes perhaps she became too involved. 'Adult residential colleges are very demanding places to work,' said Bob Fryer. 'The students are engaged, energetic, opinionated; going through crises in their own lives – divorce or unemployment. Add that to the effervescence of learning and living cheek by jowl with others in the same circumstances – and it means that when turbulence breaks out, it can get very turbulent. There are always issues to be resolved and Mo was the one who would pick up all the difficulties and conflicts and turmoil because she was that kind of woman. She felt it was her responsibility and she was close to the students.'

John McMahon, a student at the time who returned to work for the college as a member of staff on Mo's team, remembered an exuberant person who was full of life and could talk about any subject whatsoever. He had come from Glasgow where he had been active in the Union of Shopworkers Distributive and Allied Workers (USDAW) and his years at the college were a very formative time. 'It was a changing point in anybody's life who went there as a student,' he said. There are many other former students who are happy to testify to Mo's popularity. There were more women than men among the students and for them Mo was a particular focus. Doris Clarney cannot speak warmly enough of what Mo meant to them all: 'If you had a problem she was always there for you. She always had time – she made time. Every woman on the course went seeking her for one reason or another. She was always there – honestly, you couldn't describe the help she gave. She always had a listening ear. She was brilliant. She was one of the loveliest people.'[18]

'Most people fell in love with Mo,' said Jim McKenna, who was a student at Northern College when Mo first joined. He gave up driving buses to study and is now Chairman of the Governors at Northern College and a Leeds City councillor. 'What a wonderful attractive woman she was.'[19] At the time he was with Aileen Larsen, also a former bus driver, and they married in December 1984, although they have since separated. They all became very good friends. Mo was at their wedding and along with a number of the other guests stayed the night after the party. He recalled that she wasn't particularly brilliant with the washing-up the next day, preferring to stay in bed and eat the children's Roses chocolates until the dishes were all safely seen to.

But washing-up seems to be the only thing that she dodged. The college was going through a difficult time then. It had few friends in any of the educational establishments; there was a hostile Tory Government in office; there was a great deal in the newspapers about the 'Socialist republic of South Yorkshire', while Northern College was projected as an exercise in what was derogatively termed 'revolution on the rates'. McKenna recalled Mo being active and enthusiastic about creating interest in what was really happening at the college, bringing in finance and embarking upon ambitious projects like turning the old stables into additional student accommodation. It worked: he is justifiably proud that in the spring of 2000 Northern College was named among the top twenty colleges in the country and awarded 'Beacon' status, an achievement which obviously owes much to those who worked there in the first ten years as well as subsequently.

But there were many strains on her life. Peter Clarney, now a community development worker, was a former miner. He remembered the difficult days of the miners' strike. 'People either loved Mo or hated her,' he said. Many of the students at the college came from mining families, and some went on the picket lines, others gave up their meal entitlements. Mo was very supportive of the students, although her own politics were identified with the Labour leadership which was in conflict with the NUM and its President Arthur Scargill in particular.[20] She helped organise play schemes and collected toys for miners' children, and her organising skills were put to considerable use in a 'Police Watch' established by some people at the college to assess objectively what was happening on the increasingly violent picket lines. One of her relationships at this time was with her old friend from Coventry Martin Drew. His marriage had broken up and he would come to Barnsley at weekends to spend time with Mo. They seem to have spent most of their time raising money for the miners' families and Martin was extraordinarily impressed by what she was doing.

She talked, of course, a great deal about politics. 'I was not aware of her commitment before because I wasn't exposed to it. There I was exposed to just the force of her . . .' – he grappled for the word – '. . . goodness. I've never seen anybody do so much work for people. Every weekend we would be raising money – she was always raising money.' He compared what she did with others who were involved in politics but didn't actually do anything. 'This wasn't agit-prop stuff. It was hands on.' She had what he described as a missionary zeal to help the miners' wives.[21]

The relationship lasted for a year or so but 'drifted', according to Martin. She told her old friend Anne, who had gone out with Martin for six years in their late teens and early twenties, that one reason it didn't work was because Martin was drinking very heavily at the time and wanted to stay up all night talking. 'She found it very difficult to cope,' Anne said. 'Getting up in the morning was a problem when you're drinking all night. She couldn't keep up with the pace when she had a lot of hard work to do.' She was working very assiduously, as ever, and she knew where her priorities lay.

And, in political terms, where her sympathies lay, too. She went with another boyfriend to a pantomime in Manchester during the miners' strike. The actor John Nettles was the big name draw and on the first night he came on stage and declared: 'I'm the Sheriff of Nottingham.' Mo jumped up in her seat and shouted, 'Scab bastard!' It got a good laugh although it took Nettles somewhat by surprise.

She did try to keep clear of the NUM politics of the strike[22] but she had already unsettled the surface of the local political pond. There are three constituencies covering the Barnsley area and Mo joined the Barnsley West and Penistone party and promptly set about trying to change things. There were not many young women involved – Jean Marshall recalled that they were the only two in their ward. It was very difficult. There were a lot of differences among the party members. Mo managed to get herself elected Social Secretary and later – bearing in mind that she has never presented herself as an upfront feminist – she was made Women's Officer. This was a post with strong overtones of tea-making. Mo wanted to get on to the Party Executive, but found herself constantly thwarted. 'People round here don't like you to get on,' Jean Marshall explained. 'It's above your station – and a woman as well to boot! This has always been a male-dominated working village.'

But Mo was not put off. She got a hold of the branch organisation and set about turning it around. The party had never troubled much with what went on in the two wards in Penistone, a scattering of villages with some new estates housing Tory-voting managers, professionals and commuters, surrounded by land-owning farmers. But Mo completely changed this approach. At a council election, a student at the college called David Hunter, a friend of Mo's, stood as the Labour candidate. Mo's systematic efficiency was a wonder to behold according to several involved. She was a phenomenal organiser: the students were turned out to canvass and distribute leaflets and check the registers and campaign. She introduced them to the Reading system[23]. David Hunter was duly elected. 'She was very capable and she had some really radical ideas about campaigning,' Jean Marshall said. 'I must say that we still follow the kind of advice that came from Mo about campaigning, about really getting out there.'

But it didn't help her get on the Executive. Everything had to be done by the rule book in Barnsley and people like Arthur Scargill and Norman West, who was both the South Yorkshire MEP and the chairman of the constituency party, had taken against her, almost certainly because she was a free spirit and, as such, a threat. Michael Clapham remembered Mo presenting her report as the Social Secretary to the constituency General Management Committee meeting. 'She stood up to say what she'd organised – and it turned out it hadn't gone through the Executive. She was given a real bollocking because of that, because it hadn't been approved and she was taken aback. She thought she'd done something that was really good for the party. Norman West didn't like her: he had a view on how women should do things in the party – and he didn't like women in the party anyway.'[24]

It was after the miners' strike that the CIA rumour started to circulate again. Bob Fryer explained: 'Here's Mo: she's making waves in the local party, she's making waves in the college. She's arguing and criticising and pushing.' The strike was over, but the NUM was very damaged by it. Many people felt that it was, at least, mildly diversionary for the NUM that there should be a focus for gossip. The suggestion was that there was an infiltrator in the party. Mo's political background with CND and Tony Benn, and her time in the US were maliciously used against her. It was that simple.

'It was an absurd, completely groundless rumour,' Bob Fryer said. 'The allegation was: "You can't trust this woman. She's not what she seems". It hurt her deeply. It's a kind of smear and how do you repudiate such a smear? What do you do about it?' Everybody heard the rumour and everybody knew it was a nonsense.

'There was never any evidence for any of the stuff that was going on, but there was a fair amount of shit flying around her,' said Hilary Armstrong indignantly. 'She couldn't just be a good straightforward left-wing woman – they'd got to find something to have a go at her about. How do you persuade people that something like that's not true? The feeling is: if you're linked to it, there must be something in it. The trouble was that by now there was no compromise: you were either with Arthur – or seen as against. She did a hell of a lot of work to try to hold things together, to find a way forward that had political credibility but Arthur would manipulate and use people in ways that were very very difficult.'

It was probably this that made up her mind to leave Barnsley. For one thing, she knew, as she said to Mick Clapham when Roy Mason[22] announced that he would not stand at the next election for his seat in Barnsley Central, that a woman was unlikely to get selected for Parliament in this area. Her close friends weren't surprised when she decided to leave Northern College. 'She had a miserable time there,' one of them recounts. 'It was a battle for someone with metropolitan tastes and interests to survive in that environment.' She had always made it plain that she was seeking a political career and although she hadn't got a seat for the general election anticipated in the summer of

1987, she told Bob Fryer: 'I've done what I came here for. I think it's time for me to move on.'[26] She wasn't the sort of person who would back away from difficulties, yet she left feeling dissatisfied and unhappy – not because she was sorry to be going, she most certainly wasn't, but because she knew that she was leaving because she had had enough. She was worn down by the constant back-biting in the party, by difficult and demanding students, by college staff who resented changes in their work practices. It wasn't that she had failed – she knew she hadn't and Bob Fryer is emphatic that she had achieved precisely what she had been hired to do – but she felt as if she was giving up.

Despite her mood, she had got a great deal from the experience of those three years. She learned much about the Labour movement, the unions, how to deal with very difficult men, and, in particular, she had come face to face with how working-class people lived and what their values were. Living among the 'heroes' of her political life had been salutary.

She gave in her notice at the college and set about looking for another job. She went to see her old friend the journalist Andy McSmith, who was by then working in the press office of the Labour Party headquarters in Walworth Road, and discussed whether she should apply for a job in the party Research Department. He was not very encouraging, thinking that it wouldn't suit her. Another possibility she explored was a post as political adviser to George Mudie, now the MP for Leeds East but who had been the leader of Leeds City Council throughout the 1980s. The idea of employing political assistants in large local authorities had only recently been introduced and she was keen on the Leeds job. However, to her considerable frustration, a formal offer never materialised. A similar position came up at Doncaster and she went for an interview there. She was offered the job and might well have accepted, but for a strange incident that arose after the final interview process. A correspondence connected with her appointment had been found to be already opened when it reached the councillor to whom it was addressed. Mo was oblivious to this incident but when she went for a meeting with senior politicians on the council about the proposed job, she found herself being cross-examined. She didn't like the innuendoes and told them, in typically earthy terms, exactly where they could put their job. It was a lucky escape. She had inadvertently stubbed a toe against 'Donnygate', what was later to be revealed as scandalous and illegal goings-on within the council.

The date of the 1987 election was announced on Monday, 11 May. A June date had been expected for some time and was irresistible to the Conservatives after their sweeping successes in the local elections on 7 May. Mrs Thatcher held a special Cabinet meeting at Chequers on Sunday, 10 May to agree the timetable, and polling day was set for Thursday, 11 June. Mo had been having a somewhat dejected holiday the week before the election was called, staying with Hilary Armstrong. It didn't make it any better for Mo that several of her friends, including Hilary, who had been selected two years previously to fight Durham North-west, had been selected to fight winnable seats, whereas she had not, despite her diligent application to her political career and her miserable recent experience to that end in Barnsley. She will often claim in interviews that she is never depressed, but it is not true and this was one such occasion. She was very down at that time – about her personal circumstances, her lack of a job and the imminence of an election in which she had no meaningful role. 'She was very frustrated. She was just really pig-sick,' said Hilary Armstrong. Yet even so, in typical fashion, she tried to be useful: she offered to be Hilary's driver, minder and gofor when the time came. It would at least give her something to do and stop her moping. In the meantime, she went back to Barnsley to finish tying up loose ends and she had then planned to go away for the weekend.

There are differing versions of how the news broke about the decision made by James Tinn, the long-serving Labour MP for Redcar, a solid Labour seat, that he would not contest the election. One very attractive apocryphal version has it that Tinn turned up to his adoption meeting in the constituency and said: 'I don't think I'll bother.' Hilary

Armstrong heard it first from her father, an MP since 1964, who was a former whip, currently one of the deputy Speakers and a man who was always plugged in to everything that moved at Westminster. 'My dad rang and said Jim Tinn had just told him he was going – "so you'd better tell Mo." I rang her and said: "Don't go away!"'[24] The chairman of the Redcar Constituency Labour Party, Dr Richard Lewis, who had been at the forefront of trying to keep the peace in this troubled local organisation, heard it from the man himself. 'Literally on the morning of the day the election was called, I tried to contact Jim because he was still our MP. When I phoned him I said: "We've got our differences, but you are our candidate" and he dropped the bombshell.'[28]

What actually happened is that a week or so before the election was called James Tinn had been to see Neil Kinnock to inform him of his plans. He was 'prepared not to run' for Redcar, although, surprisingly, he did not have an agenda, such as a request for elevation to the House of Lords, as is often the case in such circumstances. He explained the reasons for the timing of his decision, which centred on the recent selection of a man called Paul Harford as the Labour candidate for the next-door constituency to Redcar. Tinn had been particularly anxious that Harford should not be selected to replace him. Kinnock was grateful for this warning of an impending vacancy and all its implications but he asked Tinn to delay an announcement of his intentions for a short while.

Tinn, who died in 1999, had been MP for the area since 1964. He was first elected for the constituency known as Cleveland, a seat he held until 1974 and then, after a major boundary revision, he represented the seat known for a period as Teesside, Redcar. In the years before the 1987 election, he had fallen out with members of the constituency party for various reasons: he ascribed it to infiltration by left-wingers, but in fact he had been inadvertently caught up in the backwash of a classic story of old-style local authority mismanagement. A man named Arthur Seed, at one time the leader of Langbaurgh Council, dominated local affairs and exerted an inappropriate degree of political control over everything that happened in the area. Tinn had accepted this. Seed, who has also since died, provoked a considerable amount of local controversy because of his political practices and a number of left-wing party members, in association with a group of teachers and other professionals, formed a loose leftish alliance among party members who didn't like the way the party was run. At this precise time Neil Kinnock was trying to deal with the Militant problem and what Richard Lewis described as the Bennite civil war within the Labour Party. It all got rolled up together in Redcar, where Jim Tinn had declared that his party was trying to throw him out and had demanded an inquiry by Labour's National Executive. This had met early in 1987 in what was privately viewed by some members of staff at Labour headquarters as an unnecessary effort to try to protect Jim Tinn.

Whatever, it was a waste of time. The party now found itself with an election already under way and no candidate to defend what ought to be a safe seat. Jim Tinn's 1983 majority had been only 3,104, but the results of the 1983 election had been appalling for the Labour Party everywhere and the party's percentage of the vote still guaranteed the seat. The question was whether a candidate should now be imposed upon the party, a practice that would be pursued increasingly at by-elections under Kinnock's leadership in order to avoid unsuitable candidates. After the loss of the Labour-held seat of Greenwich to the Social Democratic Party in a by-election in February 1987, which was widely blamed on the unfortunate Labour candidate, Neil Kinnock had been privately reconciled to the eventual defeat of the Labour Party in the general election. In fact his acknowledgement of this forthcoming failure preceded even the result in Greenwich: when he first learned of the selection of Deirdre Wood as Labour's candidate for that by-election he was at first incredibly angry and then depressed because he correctly foresaw that it meant the loss of Greenwich and he could see the wider implications of that on national politics.[29] It was at this point that he determined that in future the party leadership would have the final say on the identity of candidates in crucially important seats.

It has been held that the Redcar seat was fixed up for Mo Mowlam, a known friend and active supporter of Kinnock's. That is not the case, although it did coincide with Kinnock's recognition of this selection problem and his determination to change things. Unknown to Mo, circumstances had moved to assist her, but she still had to show what she was made of. Someone behind the scenes in the Kinnock office said: 'We didn't actually promote Mo. We said we would have a shortlist of competent people and make sure there was a generally competent list. We worked to make sure she was on the shortlist. The only criterion we had at that time was to have a good list for the local party to choose from so we would try to exclude idiots. Mo completely won it herself.'[30]

In fact things had been moving fast without the knowledge of most of those who would be affected. The reason Kinnock asked Tinn to delay his public announcement was because the announcement of an election was known to be imminent and, under existing party rules, it was only after that had happened that Labour's Executive would have the freedom to impose a shortlist on Redcar. When the day came, Richard Lewis rang Kinnock's office as soon as he had spoken to Tinn. He spoke to Richard Clements who worked there and who said that they had 'just heard about it'. A short while later the party General Secretary, Larry Whitty[31], and the National Organiser, Joyce Gould,[32] announced that there would be an imposed shortlist of potential candidates for Redcar. Lewis, a lecturer at Teesside Polytechnic and a blameless member of the party for over twenty years, got a telephone call informing him of this and additionally that as the objective was to have a local candidate, the party's regional office would like him to allow his name to go forward. Richard Lewis, who had never had personal political ambitions, was stunned. He took this call at 11 p.m. and had to give his answer the following morning. Little wonder that, poor man, he didn't sleep that night. And in the morning he said yes.

'I had no idea who else would be on the shortlist and I took a rather fatalistic view at that point. The key thing was that although I was

161

Chairman of the constituency party, it was a party that had been riven for a little while by problems: simply being chairman would not guarantee my selection. There was a very, very strong Seed-ite element, a solid block of ten to fifteen members closely associated with Arthur, and a very strong left-wing group. There were one or two actual Militants who resented the fact that a shortlist was being imposed at all and saw my name as a betrayal of the constituency party. It was not until the afternoon of the day after that I learned what the shortlist was. I must confess I didn't know anything about Mo. I'd not heard of her, although others had.'[33]

The other names on the list were Arthur Taylor, then the Labour group leader on Langbaurgh Council who had been Jim Tinn's agent for many years, and the Co-operative Party's education officer, Paul Tinnion, a councillor from Gateshead. In fact Kinnock's office had already got what one member of the team described as 'a pretty good idea' of the shortlist of three men within a very short time of Tinn's announcement. The name of Mo Mowlam was said by some to have been added at the insistence of Joyce Gould because no women were included. But this was not accurate. Joyce Gould thought very highly of Mo, who had performed well when seeking selection in Newcastle, but it was actually Kinnock himself who suggested her. Kinnock's office also made a couple of calls on Mo's behalf – completely without her knowledge – to Tom Burlison[34], the GMB[35] official in the north-east, and to Joe Mills, the regional secretary of the TGWU. The object was not to stitch up the seat for her but to ensure that she got a fair chance; Kinnock's primary objective was to get someone good elected.

Significantly missing from the list was the name of the one person who would have been most likely to succeed Jim Tinn until his selection for the neighbouring Tory marginal seat of Langbaurgh – Paul Harford. He was a prominent and very able local politician who was in the forefront of the opposition to Arthur Seed and who was very much liked and admired – by everyone except Tinn, that is. His exclusion did not escape the notice of others. Richard Lewis explained: 'The theory was that Jim Tinn waited until Paul Harford could not be selected for Redcar. When he knew that was then certain, he announced his resignation.' This was precisely the case, as Tinn had confirmed privately to Kinnock when he first went to announce his intended retirement.

Given Harford's exclusion, it looked to many local party members in Redcar as if the selection of the still rather startled Dr Lewis was a foregone conclusion. Despite his own feelings – or hopes – he looked like the favourite. Paul Tinnion didn't have much chance: he was being pushed by the Transport Workers' Union and had the support of the national party, but that didn't help him as he looked to the locals like someone who was being imposed upon them. Arthur Taylor was strongly associated with the legacy of Jim Tinn; and as for Mo Mowlam – nobody really knew who she was.

Mo had been predictably busy in the short time since Tinn's announcement, pulling out every stop she could to put her name around within the Redcar party. She made a number of contacts with local union officials and through Tony Finn, a well-known official in the GMB, she found a place to stay. She was put up by John Pallister, a former steelworker, and his wife Dot, who are active party members living in Eston, one of the purpose-built communities constructed to service the giant industrial complex on Teesside. In an attempt to meet more members in advance of the selection conference, Mo held a couple of meetings in the Eston Hotel, a pub in the centre of Eston with a large meeting room more frequently used for weddings than anything political. It is opposite the Town Hall, which services the borough, architect one John Poulson[36]. Hilary Armstrong used her influence and made some more union contacts for her: the moment she had put down the telephone after breaking the news of the vacant candidacy to Mo, she got on to the ASTMS[37], her own union, and in the hope that he could help her friend contacted a Redcar official called Ian Jeffrey, who is still an active member of the party there. It all helped.

The selection meeting was held less than a week after Tinn's announcement, on the morning of Sunday, 24 May at the Community

Centre in South Bank, a distinctly grim area practically in the shadow of the giant British Steel works, which stretches bleakly along a distance of about four miles on the southern bank of the River Tees from South Bank to South Gare. It was, according to several people present, a tense occasion. There were about fifty members of the CLP there and, as expected, Arthur Taylor and Paul Tinnion were knocked out in the first round. 'It was always going to be between Mo and Richard Lewis,' said Brian Roberts, a well-known local councillor who was on a promise to act as agent for Lewis. 'And after we'd seen Mo perform it was going to be Mo. She performed very well. She was really going for it. You could see she was appealing to all sections of the party.'

Richard Lewis was charmingly philosophical about the outcome. The other candidates were outside the room where the meeting was held while each addressed the party in turn. 'I knew that Mo had been very very successful. She was much more polished and a more effective operator than I ever was.' She took the left-wing vote – indeed for some time the left-wingers in the party erroneously believed they had a strong left-wing candidate – she picked up the votes of the disgruntled Seed-ites and she won over others just by being an attractive personality. One unexpected vote she picked up was that of Brian Roberts. Before the vote Roberts had a chat with Richard Lewis's wife, Ruth, the vice-chairwoman of the party, and discovered that she was not at all enthusiastic about her husband going to Westminster. 'I didn't vote for you because your lass doesn't want you to be an MP,' Roberts told the much-relieved Lewis later. As he remembers it, Mo won the selection on the second round by one vote and, in the way of apocryphal stories of this nature, he likes to think that it was his vote that decided the outcome. The more prosaic reality is that Mo beat Richard Lewis by 28 votes to 21. But one would have been enough. She was on her way.

CHAPTER 8

'I have as much right to be here as they have'

Westminster 1987–1991

'Hello! I'm the MP for Redcar!' It was June 1987 and Harriet Harman was in the Members' Lobby shortly after the general election when a smiling blonde stranger in a flowery Laura Ashley dress suddenly introduced herself. For Harriet Harman it was a revelation. She had been in the Commons as the Member for Peckham in south London since winning a by-election there in 1982 and she had been, frankly, a little lonely, in a way that people who know the House of Commons will understand. After her own victory, she had hoped that friends of hers, other ambitious younger women, like Patricia Hewitt and Kate Hoey, who had been selected for winnable seats might join her as a result of the general election the following year. But after the disaster of the 1983 election for the Labour Party it wasn't to be. And the appearance of this new woman MP was surprising to Harriet Harman in other ways. In January of 1987 she had given birth to her third child and the run-up to the election had therefore been understandably more than usually busy and distracting. She was vaguely aware that Jim Tinn had stood down as the Labour candidate for

Redcar at the last minute – but little else. Now here was a woman of a similar age to herself, who had been elected for an industrial seat in the Labour heartlands of the north and yet who, untypically, was actually being *nice* to her and not chippy about Members with southern seats. The impression was considerable. 'I distinctly remember meeting her – although if you asked me I couldn't remember anyone else I met in the whole of 1987,' says Harriet Harman. 'She made an immediate impact because she was so different – and very glamorous.'

And, of course, she had such winning ways. Shortly after their first encounter Harriet Harman was at a party meeting with other MPs in the Commons with her baby daughter, Amy, on her hip. She was managing, according to the usual practices of accomplished motherhood, to play her role in the meeting while dandling the child, when suddenly Mo appeared unexpectedly at her side and whisked the baby away. It was a blessed relief. A few minutes later Harriet heard loud slurping noises behind her and looked around to see the engaging picture of Mo sucking Amy's 'probably very dirty' fingers while the baby giggled in sheer delight. It was a charming, practical gesture and completely typical of Mo. She has always been someone who just rolls up her sleeves and gets on with it. Sometimes even literally. When she was the 'minder' for the Labour MP Peter Kilfoyle at the Liverpool Walton by-election in 1991 she arrived at his house one morning to collect him for campaign duties at the height of the daily domestic chaos that besets any household with five children. She walked in the door, assessed the scene and imme-diately went over to the kitchen sink and, without asking or being asked, started doing the washing-up. She doesn't make a fuss, just gets stuck in.

And that was the approach she adopted towards her political career as soon as she arrived at Westminster. She established herself very early on as someone who was going places in the Labour Party. It was widely recognised, of course, that as a former member of Neil Kinnock's election campaign team, she was closely associated with the leader, but that didn't prevent the predictable sorts of jealousy surfacing. There was a reference to her 'wearing out the carpet to the leader's door'[1] in an early biographical piece about her, which clearly reflected the extent to which she was on the inside track. 'She was someone who was seen as having access to the leader,' said a friend and fellow Labour MP,[2] speaking without resentment, and adding, 'She was always at the end of the Shadow Cabinet corridor.'

During the time Mo worked on the Kinnock election campaign she got on very well with others in his office. Now here she was four years later, a new MP, with a great advantage over others elected for the first time. Far from having to concentrate on finding her way around at Westminster, both geographically and politically, she not only knew the ground but also the most direct route to the leader's office. She knew the staff there personally and had made a considerable number of friends and contacts among people who mattered. Better even than that she and Neil Kinnock were, to use a word they would both employ, 'mates'. Kinnock had already decided to promote her at the first opportunity for two reasons. One was her skill as someone who was inclusive, who brought people into debates, decisions, whatever was going on; the second was his belief that because she was 'a smart lady', she would be able to pick up any brief and master it.[3]

She made an early impact with the press. The 1987 election produced a record number of women MPs although that still added up to only forty-one. It was inevitable that a clever, vivacious, academic blonde was going to make an impression. She was a natural candidate for the profile writers and one of the first new Members to feature in a series of interviews written by Colin Brown in the *Independent*. The article started in a fairly flamboyant fashion:

'I've got a new bra on and it's killing me,' the Member for Redcar said as she settled down on the Commons terrace to talk about her life since becoming a Labour MP 11 months ago.[4]

It was perhaps not the wisest comment to make to a journalist but it was quintessential Mo. It is the sort of thing that she says – not necessarily to shock, but because it's the way she is. It probably wouldn't have occurred to her *not* to mention that her bra was uncomfortable.

She did a similar thing a few years later when being interviewed for the *Observer*. While trying to find a handkerchief in her handbag to bind the wounds of a cameraman who had gashed himself on his camera, she pulled out a pair of knickers.[5] Now any modern woman may have a pair of knickers in her handbag for any number of reasons, but it is a curious Shadow minister, as she was by then, who would disclose as much in the course of an interview. It is beguiling. But more than that, undoubtedly it is meant to beguile. In the same interview with Colin Brown, she acknowledged that she does not feel any sense of awe at being entitled to walk into the chamber of the House of Commons as a Member of Parliament. She told him: 'I think: "Bugger it. I have as much right to be here as they have". The Commons is more than just individuals, but it is made up of individuals and you just don't let it get to you.'[6]

Being so forthright is a peculiar trait. Her friend Bob Fryer believes her open readiness to deal with the truth, however difficult, is of immense value: 'Some politicians argue that it is not a good idea to be upfront. I think it is that which enamours her to people. It is not that she remembers people's names; I think people like her because of her direct style, her cool willingness to say the world is like it is.' Although she is merely being herself, and certainly not usually intending to cause offence, that is often the effect she has. She startles people by how candid she is and often her language and her actions can be offensive. 'She doesn't recognise the distance between other people's bodies and her own,' says one colleague.

At one level her style gives her a tremendous advantage. It is the essence of the touchy-feely Mo that was so lauded when she first became a nationally known figure – but was subsequently also disparaged by her critics. Nevertheless, it is how she relates to people. It is this approach that enables her to walk into working men's clubs in her constituency – where the very appearance of a woman would in ordinary circumstances cause consternation – pick up someone's pint and have the effrontery to take a swig out of it. Such behaviour may seem at the least impolite in conventional circumstances; on Teesside it would be regarded as an outrage, nothing short of sacrilege. Yet Mo is forgiven since from her, because of the humanity and warmth she exudes, it is a piece of cheek that is usually not only welcomed but gives the recipient a glow of pride, causing them to feel special.

Yet at another level she can be grossly inappropriate. The same routine of casually drinking someone else's drink doesn't always go down so well. One account that serves to illustrate the point involves Maria Vaz, wife of the Labour MP Keith Vaz, who was standing drinking a cup of tea at a social event. She was holding her drink by the saucer when Mo waltzed up beside her, seized the cup from the saucer and helped herself to a slurp of the contents before putting back what remained and then drifting off. Even someone who is not excessively fastidious might find this a little surprising at the least. Yet Mo seems unaware of the dangerous social territory on which she sometimes treads.

The Mayor of London, Ken Livingstone, once said about her relationship with Ulster Unionists that 'she touches them in ways that nobody except their wives has ever touched them before.'[7] She is sometimes excessively intimate in an inappropriate way, failing to recognise other people's space. 'She stands too close when talking to you and uses your Christian name excessively,' the journalist Lynn Barber wrote perceptively in an interview with Mo at a time when her star was in the ascendant.[8] She put this down to 'New Labour style', but it is actually Mo's own style. 'It is one of the things you have to come to terms with about Mo,' says a colleague. Some people are delighted by the intimacy she extends, overwhelmed by her normality and how down-to-earth she is. Others simply feel uncomfortable. One of those in this latter group, although she would not have known this at the time, was another relatively new young Labour MP called Tony Blair.

And she can be vulgar. Even her mother acknowledged as much. On one occasion when there was a suggestion that the Northern Ireland Secretary had said something very rude indeed to the Rev. Ian Paisley, Tina Mowlam said, 'I am sure she did say it. She *is* vulgar.'[9] It is not only her 'industrial' language that offends. While being fiercely protective of her personal privacy in some respects, she wholly disregards it in others. For example, she swiftly became known among her fellow women MPs as someone who regularly fails to shut the door when she is in the lavatory in the Lady Members' Room, and who seems neither embarrassed nor even remotely aware of the potential for embarrassing others. In a similar vein, when she became a minister a few years later, she made it plain that she thought nothing of continuing to conduct political business in the 'Ladies' if the person to whom she happened to be talking when she wanted to go to the loo was also a woman. She happily boasted that she did a lot of talking to other women in the loo. Some people were amused by this; others were bemused. On occasion it caused consternation among civil servants, particularly junior ones. However, her women press officers, like Sheree Dodd, loyally claimed to find it a useful way of being able to catch up with what the minister was thinking.

Mo's indiscretions are not limited to her female colleagues. There are numerous accounts after she became Northern Ireland Secretary of her asking her male protection officers to nip off and buy her some tampons, something which naturally provoked some comment – responsibility for sanitary protection not having previously been included in their duties. Her friends laugh this off. 'At least you would know it was that time of the month again,' one of her ministerial friends – a man – said. 'At least you would understand why she was crabby – and anyway the police loved her.' This was certainly the case and indeed she did involve them in her life at every level, including choosing her clothes.

In an earlier incident, not long after she arrived in the Commons, she went for a drink in Annie's Bar. This is the watering hole where MPs and lobby correspondents can meet on equal terms, which is to say anyone can buy the drinks. It is no longer widely frequented, but at the time it was a congenial place where a number of influential journalists would congregate and politicians of some significance – and none – would often look in for a drink at the cocktail hour. Some women went there and were welcome, but it was still a place with a masculine, club-like aura. On this occasion Mo came in to the small room that housed the bar and declared loudly that she needed a drink and she needed to sit down and she needed these things *now* 'because I've got the curse'. As far as she was concerned, it was a perfectly straightforward statement and she seemed unaware of the slight frisson it caused. But almost certainly if she had noticed, she wouldn't have cared anyway. She admitted when she had been in the House of Commons for just over a year that she thought some of her colleagues 'think I am a bit gross'[10] but she said bluntly that they would just have to get used to her. 'My mother worries that when televising comes I won't sit like a lady and I'll pick my nose, but we all have our weaknesses and we have to learn how to live with them.' She actually meant that other people would have to learn to live with hers.

Some of her colleagues are convinced, however, that she actually sets out to shock or take people by surprise as part of a deliberately considered strategy. There is some evidence for this. For example, in an interview for the *Mail on Sunday* in early 1998, the writer and photographer waited to see the Northern Ireland Secretary for quite some time in an anteroom. She suddenly burst in to the room wearing no shoes, no wig and no jacket, and on seeing them exclaimed in apparent surprise in a fruity four-letter way. The reporter, Louette Harding, wrote that the freelance photographer who was with her later disclosed privately that he had photographed Mo Mowlam before for another publication in another location, and that, curiously, exactly the same thing had happened on that occasion. He had waited, she had burst in, appeared aghast, done a double-take and then cursed in surprise.[11]

She makes a speciality of borrowing make-up and hairbrushes from women interviewers, too. On another occasion she asked to try on the guitar-string bracelets belonging to the writer Ginny Dougary – and ended up keeping them and wearing them both as a trophy and as a joke she enjoyed. There are numerous somewhat coy instances of her behaving like this in interviews. It makes the journalist feel special and it makes her appear accessible, friendly and normal. The journalist cannot resist writing about the little personal foibles she displays. But the apparent carelessness about her appearance is assumed in part because she does actually mind how she looks and she pays more attention than she sometimes lets on. On a series of visits in Doncaster in May 1998 her two-car entourage was suddenly brought to an abrupt halt just before arriving at a school. There was an atmosphere of heightened security at that time and the police in the support car were naturally nervous when they were radioed to pull in to the side of the road immediately. It turned out to be because the Secretary of State was applying her lipstick.

The surprise tactics she employs helped present her at Westminster and later to the wider world as someone who was different, a woman who was prepared to challenge the norm. It would prove a great assistance to her politically, particularly in Northern Ireland, and she enjoyed discomforting some people. But others were more likely to be puzzled. John Prescott, for instance, couldn't understand why she would take the trouble to tell him, as she did, about sending policemen to buy her sanitary requirements. His reaction was: why is she telling me this? Others had a more extreme reaction than puzzlement. She profoundly offended some older 'traditional' working-class Labour MPs of the old school who disliked her language and were not susceptible to her charm. They didn't expect women to behave or talk as she did and they didn't like it one bit. They said so in unrepeatable terms.

It may have been that sometimes she just went too far in trying to be one of the lads. Or it may all have been an elaborate structure of personal defence. When she first arrived, she quickly realised that the combination of her looks and the shortage of other young, unmarried women MPs in a masculine environment rendered her as prey of some kind. 'The laddishness was about not being coy and kittenish,' said another woman MP. 'It was saying: "I may have long thin legs and blonde hair but I'm not a baby doll".' Put more succinctly she was aware that she could be regarded as what is sometimes known as 'crumpet quarry' and, according to this colleague: 'Her way of not being crumpet quarry was to be not eligible for crumpet status.'

She made it plain, perhaps to a wider audience than she may originally have intended, that she did not intend to get involved in casual sexual relationships with 'the boys' at Westminster. 'I'm not going to,' she told one surprised journalist when he took her to lunch at L'Amico, an Italian restaurant at Westminster which has a division bell and can sometimes rather resemble a Commons' dining room. 'If you do that, well, you just get a reputation for doing that.' The trouble was that being Mo she added another verb to her explanation of what she wasn't going to do and she used this verb three times and forcefully. She apparently didn't notice that everyone in the vicinity in the restaurant had stopped eating and was listening with interest and amusement. 'You could have heard a souffle collapse,' the journalist said. What puzzled the journalist was the way in which she quite unexpectedly raised the topic of sex as if she wanted to talk about it, when he had simply been planning to sound her out on the political issues of the day.[12]

It could perhaps be another example of her laddish defence against being crumpet quarry. It is the sort of thing that a man might possibly say to another and Mo had already established that this approach could be politically useful in the Parliamentary Labour Party. She was genuinely popular with most other MPs and she was good fun. Even so her friend Neil Kinnock was certainly wrong when he suggested that she was never a target of criticism for being what he called 'a hell of a lass'. He described her arriving in his office: 'She'd come in and kick off her shoes and sit on the sofa with her toes tucked under her and sip a drink and smoke a ciggy and we'd get down to the case. And you'd know that nobody was going to be critical of Mo because nobody ever mistook her candour for being a lack of seriousness.'[13] She was in fact often criticised for being a hell of a lass, but the last point, at least, is true: nobody ever doubted that she was very serious indeed about her career.

As far as her formal parliamentary work was concerned, the first few months at Westminster were taken up with the normal routine for new Members. She had the early excitement in July of being appointed to the Fifth Standing Committee on Statutory Instruments, and she was initially appointed to the Social Services Select Committee in November and then almost immediately dropped by the Whips in favour of Frank Field. Subsequently she was appointed to the Public Accounts Committee, which was probably a more congenial position for her as it is the parliamentary watchdog on public spending and can get into the news a bit. On other issues she displayed an early pragmatic populism: she supported the establishment of a women's refuge in her region, called for an inquiry in the wake of the 'Spycatcher'[14] affair to prevent the security services using the Government's social security data base in Newcastle, and used the publicity potential of the Ten Minute Rule Bill[15] to propose concessionary television licences for pensioners.

She made her maiden speech early in the Parliament,[16] on unemployment in her constituency. Being Mo she prepared for it very thoroughly and she contacted her friend Bob Fryer to check it out with him. It reads well, but one of her former boyfriends who was present remembers an almost empty House and a somewhat strained delivery. Mo has never been particularly good at making speeches and, as this man commented, 'she actually hasn't got that much better'. He doesn't find it altogether surprising, however, that she hasn't made more of an effort to improve her speech-making skills in the present electronic age, because in a way this weakness doesn't really matter. Her communication skills are so good in other ways – in personal contact and on television – that this is almost more important. 'It's part of why people like her,' he said. 'That kind of artlessness travels quite well.'

She made the speech during the progress of a Bill on the borrowing powers of British Shipbuilders and paid the customary graceful compliment to her predecessor, if in somewhat limited fashion. It is noticeable that while what she had to say about Jim Tinn ('a quiet man . . . well respected . . . wish him well') takes up under five lines in Hansard, her tribute to the pioneering achievements of Ellen Wilkinson, the last woman Member for a Teesside constituency, takes fourteen lines. 'Ellen' – as Mo called her with typical familiarity – had made her maiden speech as the MP for Middlesbrough East over sixty years before when she was the only woman on the Opposition benches. 'She was a practical woman who liked to get things done,' said Mo, expressing her desire to emulate her. She went on to attack the Tory Government in quite forceful terms for a maiden speech, something which is traditionally supposed not to be controversial. She even provoked a Tory MP, Michael Fallon, to protest sufficiently strongly for it to be noted in Hansard. She lambasted the Government's legislative programme as a collection of 'obscene fantasies' and used the subject of the debate to focus on the 22.5 per cent unemployment on Teesside. Fallon, who spoke next, complimented her on the passion and urgency of her speech and made what seems to have been a kind remark about her eloquence.

In some ways she found her first months in the House of Commons easier than life in her constituency. She made a great many friends among the new generation of MPs, others like her who were interested in reforming the party in the hope of reversing the electoral tide that had flowed for so long against Labour. 'We are not changing our beliefs or our principles, we're just looking at different ways of implementing them,' she said in an interview in October 1988,[17] explaining the need for reform. 'That's necessary because time has moved on, we have not been in power since the late seventies and we need to rethink.'

Her political stance was the same as it has always been: what her friend Bob Fryer describes as slightly to the right of centre, reformist, unquestionably egalitarian. This disappointed those who had misread the years that she spent at Northern College as a statement of a more left-wing commitment. John Prescott, who had met her at Barnsley a few times, was heard to complain that she 'joined the "Beautiful People"' as soon as she got to Westminster but this seems rather unfair. She supported the 'dream ticket' of Neil Kinnock and Roy Hattersley in the 1988 leadership election and, according to his friends, Prescott found this difficult to understand. He asked Bob Fryer: 'Why isn't she supporting me?' Prescott had been to Northern College, met Mo there and was taken aback when she arrived at Westminster and was not in his camp. Fryer reported: 'I remember saying to him: "You mustn't make assumptions about her simply because she's come from Northern College, she's active and she's supportive of women's issues. It isn't personal against you. It's Mo's politics. It's where she's always been. She's not being opportunist. This is quite consistent."' Despite Fryer's efforts, Prescott was not convinced.

Neil Kinnock had no hesitation in describing her as a Socialist. 'She has got a very well-developed sense of justice and the conviction that the privilege of the strong is to help those who aren't,' he said. 'That's as good a definition of Mo's engine as anything. In a democratic society she thinks that all activity should be made consistent with the needs of that society – that's where the word socialist comes from in the first place. It sounds awfully grandiose – and that's not how she thinks about it – but anyone with a sense of justice wants to try to ensure that as far as possible people should get a fair shake.'[18]

The reality is that she has a chameleon quality as Michael Barratt Brown, the founder of Northern College, said of her. He was still teaching at the college when she was the administrator and hugely admired her social skills and her professional competence. 'Really she is a chameleon,' he said. 'She's so attractive and lovely and warm and friendly – and the trouble is that she is that to everybody. I don't mean it in an unkind sense. She does take the colour of the people she's with – it's part of her charm.' He added: 'I don't mean she was unprincipled, just that she was too nice to *everybody*.'[19]

Those who knew her best were always aware that her own politics were difficult to define. 'There's something slightly rootless about her,' said one former boyfriend. 'She had lots of strong views about things but there wasn't an underlying passion – unideological would be more the word.' But he was wrong if he thought that she didn't understand this about herself. She often described herself as rootless in interviews and she saw it as a positive political advantage. She knew that she was a chameleon as well.

'You see, when you're like me, lower middle class, you're rootless, floating between levels without the strong identity a working-class or a middle-class person might have,' she said in an unusually revealing interview in 1996.[20] 'That forces you to become adaptable. So I'm annoying in the sense that I'm difficult to place and that I can switch my accent to confuse whomever I'm with. But I like being a chameleon. It's probably to do with me wanting to be liked, wanting life to be as smooth and enjoyable as possible.'

'The first year was tough because people [the inhabitants of Redcar] didn't really know who they'd got,' she said of herself in the interview she gave to *House* magazine.[21] 'I had to prove myself by working in the constituency.' She wasn't overawed by the Commons and the work didn't bother her, although she thought the hours were loony. She had thrown herself into things. She played for the House of Commons football and hockey teams and was the first woman member of both; even so she admitted that she had put on a stone and a half in weight in just over a year. 'I like the House of Commons and I like to get involved in things,' she said and then, interestingly, she acknowledged that she recognised she did sometimes attract criticism: 'People say that you're ambitious and media-seeking; I just feel that I'm not going to let the place inhibit me from enjoying myself.'[22]

She was doing that, enjoying herself, having a good time – yet she knew that having been elected to the House of Commons was not enough on its own, not for her. There were many MPs who would boast that they came to Westminster, proud of the responsibility of representing their constituency but not planning to make any kind of political splash. Her predecessor, James Tinn, after all, in a largely blameless parliamentary career spanning nearly a quarter of a century, had progressed to no greater heights than the post of Assistant Government Whip for the three years before 1979. Mo was not in this category. She was very aware of the possibilities of what might happen to her next, still looking to the future, still driven by ambition. One good friend of hers had no doubt that this drive was a result of the difficulties in her family when she was a child: 'It means you only survive by taking hold of things yourself, by throwing out what you don't want and don't like and being very focused on what you can succeed in.'[23] According to this friend, it affected her personal relationships, although she didn't apparently see it. 'Something I always felt was difficult about Mo was that her ambitions would frequently get in the way of normal friendship.' It had always been her huge strength that she was so driven by her desire to succeed, but it was also a real problem. It meant that Mo was always looking at what was going on around her, looking at her friends and those who were likely to be in competition with her to see what they were doing in political terms, who they were with, who they were supporting for what and whether this was the same person as she was supporting. Her motivation was simple, her friend said, 'It was pure political rivalry.'

The same friend admitted an enormous sense of personal relief when Neil Kinnock appointed Mo Mowlam as a Shadow spokeswoman. It happened on 14 April 1988, just ten months after she was first elected. Hers was not the first appointment of the reshuffle, but after watching others from the same parliamentary intake of 1987 get a post – 'she was hyper-conscious of it' – at last she too was summoned. As a result, from then on her parliamentary life was going to be lived far more in the public eye. She was on the Front Bench; she was on her way. And the first job she was given, her very first responsibility – although this particular post only lasted for just over a year – was as an assistant spokeswoman for Northern Ireland. It was the subject that would come to dominate her life.

She had not had much previous involvement with the Irish question, except inasmuch as it would affect anyone growing up in Britain through the early years of the Troubles. It had not been an issue during her school years. There was some IRA activity in Coventry, which had led to at least one bomb scare at her old school, Coundon Court, but that was after she had left. It is something of which she must have been aware when she was working for Tony Benn at his home in Holland Park during 1972, because there was a heightened need for security in London at that time, but then she left Britain for six years so it was still not an issue that had touched her life personally.

She got this particular post for two reasons: Kinnock was anxious to promote her, and Kevin McNamara, the party's Shadow spokesman on Northern Ireland, whom she would later replace, wanted an additional member on his team to accommodate the amount of legislation currently going through the Commons with implications for Northern Ireland. He was aware that no party had ever had a woman speaking from the Front Bench on Northern Ireland and believed that this was something that should be remedied. He put it to Kinnock. 'I said: "Could I have a woman and could I have Mowlam?" because she struck me as being able.'[24] And thus, in a way, was her political fate settled. She only stayed in the job for eighteen months but it was time put to good use. She made lots of contacts, some friends and a good impression on the community of political opinion that had continued to try to seek some way forward throughout the previous twenty years. It would serve her well later.

179

But before she reached the Northern Ireland post that would catapult her into public prominence – which came with her appointment as Shadow spokeswoman for Northern Ireland in 1994 and then as Secretary of State in 1997 – she had a few important political lessons coming her way first. She could not possibly have imagined how this could be so at the time, but the course of her political life would be set to a very large extent by what was to happen in her second job in Opposition, at the end of November 1989, when Neil Kinnock sent her to join Gordon Brown's team. She was given the job of spokeswoman on the City and Corporate Affairs in the Trade and Industry team.

It was in itself a significant appointment, perhaps more so than she may have realised, because there were two routes to promotion under Kinnock's leadership of the Labour Party. The first was through the post of Shadow Chief Secretary to the Treasury and the second was the Shadow City job, the number two position at the DTI. Kinnock used to pick people he thought had talent and put them in one or other of those key political positions as a leg-up to help them secure election to the Shadow Cabinet. There is a striking list of those who came into this category and it includes Tony Blair, Gordon Brown, Robin Cook, Jack Straw, Mo Mowlam and Bryan Gould.

There was a further aspect to this appointment, too, and that was how, very early on in her parliamentary career, Mo Mowlam had managed to put a distance between herself and the 'traditional' women's portfolios. This was deliberate. It was once suggested – although she has herself specifically denied it – that she had told Neil Kinnock that she was happy to take any Front Bench responsibility 'except Women'.[25] When she was asked about this in 1998,[26] she denied making the comment, but at this point she had already held the post of spokeswoman for the Citizens' Charter and Women between 1992–93, so it would have been extremely difficult to admit she had ever said such a thing, even in jest. At this time, in the late 1980s, there was an unacknowledged degree of rivalry among the members of the emergent generation of young women politicians, and while Harriet Harman, for example, had specifically and intentionally defined herself as a feminist, as a politician who was also a woman, Mo did not do so. She was much more one of the lads.

Mo regarded her appointment to the City with great seriousness and applied herself with immense dedication. There were Opposition Front Benchers at this time who did not take their role wholly seriously: this was Opposition, they would say privately to each other, they would probably not be in the same department, anyway, if and when Labour ever won office again, so what was the point of working incredibly hard to such little purpose? Wouldn't it be better just to consolidate one's political position at Westminster? This was not Mo's view at all.

She was a surprise choice to the City and to some extent at Westminster as well. 'Some people thought it was an unlikely choice, but I thought she had just the qualities of getting on top of the brief and communicating in direct terms,' Neil Kinnock said. 'She became a point of reference.'[27] He regarded her in those early years of her career in the Commons as a 'roll-up-your-sleeves politician' who could have done any job. 'She's one of those people to whom you could say: "Do this job" and she would deliver. She's a good political operator – getting round the crowd, getting round the tearoom – Mo is good at politics.'

She worked, as ever, extraordinarily hard. Night after night she could be seen walking down the Library Corridor in the Commons with a huge pile of books in her arms. She had no particular expertise in City affairs and she had some catching up to do, but she was going to get on top of this portfolio and she was going to prove that she could make it a success.

First she had to negotiate her way through some predictably sexist media comments. 'The blonde taking stock of the market' was the headline on one early newspaper report of her appointment.[28] The journalist, Lesley White, opened her account:

'There are those who would say that Marjorie Mowlam's best asset in the City will be her legs. This is the attitude that

Labour's new spokeswoman for City matters will be facing. The City will not like a sharp-minded left-of-centre blonde whose only old school tie is from a Coventry comprehensive . . .'

Mo was typically robust in this interview. She did not intend to be intimidated by the City, she said, she had not been appointed to prove that a woman could do the job – 'Come on, that's Seventies stuff' – and the institutions of the City would just have to get used to her. 'They're not going to like it but they will just have to put up with it.' It was typical Mo style: gutsy and no nonsense.

Next she had to put the time in on the ground, or more specifically in the penthouse City's boardrooms over lunch – 'eating for Labour', as she called it, an initiative that took a toll on her previously lathe-like slimness. But the approach worked, in the City at least, which wasn't surprising both because of how much effort she put in and because of the extent of her charm. She was in the job for two and a half years and by the spring of 1992 they were calling her 'Ms Nice Guy' in the *Financial Times*.[29] She had become 'a familiar and courted figure in the Square Mile' wrote Ian Hargreaves – 'I can go to Brooks's in St James Street and I know the guy that waits on table,' she boasted – and despite her somewhat alarming antecedents, from the City's point of view, as a progressive Lefty she had impressed people with her command of her brief. Hargreaves gave her the opportunity to expound upon it, asking her to set out exactly what a new Labour Government would do in City affairs. She did so fluently and coherently. She was impressive. She could talk about regulation, corporate governance and mergers, compare the Conservative British Government's approach to the future of banking with that of the German administration, analyse the pragmatic view of what could be achieved against the romantic aspirations of a socialist party that had been out of office for more than a decade, and do her best to redefine Neil Kinnock's Labour Party against its immediate predecessors. What she wanted was 'a degree of market forces with a degree of social responsibility'.

A Labour political analyst and businessman who watched all this said: 'She was a great hit in the City. A woman in the boardroom was something but she made a real effort to understand the issues and what their problems were and to speak back to them in their language. She cleared the decks of old Labour bags and baggage and she paved the way for a new relationship between Labour and business. She was in the advance as a Labour moderniser.'

Her problems with the job were not, it turned out, with the chaps in the City at all. They were, rather, with the chaps much closer to home in the Trade and Industry team; more specifically, with Gordon Brown. He, like Kevin McNamara before him, had sought the appointment of at least one woman among his juniors on the Front Bench because he could see the political usefulness of such a move. Mo and her friend from the north-east Joyce Quin were appointed at the same time. In Mo's case it was not a success, internally at least.

One thing over which they had problems was the financing of her side of the Trade and Industry brief. Such money as was made available under the programme for financing Opposition research and office work went into the team's central pool. Gordon Brown's approach was that he ran the team, he hired the staff – 'all those bright young men', as one critic of this operation put it – and he instructed that if any of his junior spokesmen or spokeswomen wanted to use the services of this team as research staff they were welcome to do so. But there was no direct cash available from the fund of so-called 'Short' money[30] which was extremely irksome to Mo Mowlam. Brown took this approach because he apparently needed to keep control of everything within his remit. It upset Mo Mowlam. It was part of a bigger problem.

'When they worked together it was obvious that he was never ever going to acknowledge anything that she did,' said a friend of Mo's. 'She worked very hard. She was good at what she did. But Gordon saw her as a threat – him and Robin Cook and all – and they wouldn't take her seriously when she was doing wonders in the City on that brief. If there was anything good happening, he would take it. I don't think he ever acknowledged her ability. Culturally they were very different as well.'[31]

'Gordon is impossible to work with,' said one of her ministerial colleagues who understood only too well. 'He doesn't involve people. She wouldn't let something go if he didn't agree with it.'

Another commented: 'There was a laddishness about. It was sometimes quite difficult for women to get recognised within that system.' A third said: 'Never forget that Mo was very into Gordon Brown, then she worked in one of his teams – and as a result she couldn't stand Gordon Brown.'

It apparently irritated her that even though she felt perfectly capable of giving her views on whatever policy issues were being discussed at team meetings, her contribution would be disregarded. According to one of her political women friends to whom she grumbled at the time, her sensible analyses on any given matter would be completely ignored – 'and then three hours later one of the lads would come to the same conclusion.' The bottom line was that 'the lads' sorted things. It made for a very bad atmosphere at team meetings.

'Gordon hated her,' said one close observer. 'When she came into the House she was seen as a rising star and seen as someone on that scene with Blair and Brown and Mandelson but she went to Gordon Brown's team and they fell out quite badly during that period. I think Tony liked her and respected her – but, of course, Gordon hated her.' This man was not surprised: 'If there was anyone whom you would predict that Gordon Brown wouldn't get on with, it's Mo: she's earthy and tactile and talks about sex a lot. Gordon was uneasy with her because he's so buttoned-up sexually.'

One story that was mischievously related by those associated with Gordon Brown was that he blamed Mo Mowlam for gossiping about him when rumours about his private life circulated. The suggestion was that she was getting her own back because the two of them found it so difficult to relate to each other on a personal level, and because she didn't understand why he was not susceptible, as so many were, to her charm and personality.

But the root of the problem between them, apart from the reality that they are such different characters, was almost certainly a matter of pragmatic politics and untrammelled ambition. Gordon Brown had a very close interest in the future. So did Mo, of course, but her personal ambitions were as nothing in comparison to his. At this stage it was being suggested by Brown's friends that he was the man most likely to succeed Neil Kinnock in the event of what is known in politics as the 'bus' scenario, and this was something that increasingly irritated others, including close allies of John Smith, obviously another potential candidate. Mo Mowlam was identified[32] as one of those who did not approve of the idea of Brown as the 'Crown Prince', largely because it must already have been evident to her that her career would not prosper in a Labour Party led by him. By late 1991, because of the rumours flying around, Brown was obliged to make it clear that he would not challenge John Smith for the leadership if Kinnock lost the forthcoming election and resigned.

Yet this was by no means the end of his leadership ambitions. He was still optimistic for the long term; he was a lot younger than Smith and he represented another generation. This meant looking after his popular support within the Parliamentary Labour Party. It was here that the role of Nick Brown, MP for Newcastle-upon-Tyne East, was crucial.[33]

Nick Brown was very close to both Tony Blair and Gordon Brown and he was their self-appointed agent in cultivating their supporters. 'Nick Brown would never have been Chief Whip except for Gordon Brown,' said one minister. 'Nick Brown would never have got anything *after* being Chief Whip but for Gordon.'[34]

Nick Brown became Chief Whip when Labour won the 1997 election, having always been a wheeler-dealer, a political fixer. It is a role which is regarded in many circles as an honourable calling in politics; given the nature of the business, it is an inevitable one. A former trade union official based in Newcastle, where he had also been a member of the city council, he had established himself in a position of some authority with other Labour MPs in the north-east of England and he was a power broker. One member of the Opposition Front Bench at the time estimated that he could deliver up to fifty votes within the Parliamentary Labour Party in the annual Shadow Cabinet elections.[35] This was very important to Tony Blair, who had a seat in the north-east himself but no historic connections there and who was a middle-class lawyer, living in Islington. Gordon Brown on the other hand had his own political base in Scotland, which he had carefully tended himself, but he also badly needed additional support from Labour MPs sitting for English seats. Most of the votes in the Parliamentary Labour Party were in the north and the north-east.

According to one Labour MP who was aware of what was going on at the time, Nick Brown did not like Mo Mowlam and he did not want her to get close to Gordon Brown because that would enhance her political position. Politics is an uncomfortable and unpredictable business and Mo's arrival in the House of Commons in 1987 had not been greeted with universal delight on all sides. She was never popular among 'the barons', the people who handle the power, the votes, the way deals get done. She was too strong an individual, too wilful, too independent and therefore much too dangerous. People were also jealous of her because she was pretty and personable and popular. This MP said: 'Nick Brown couldn't bear Mo being close to Gordon. He couldn't bear a woman being close to Gordon.'

It was clear from this point onwards that she had some serious enemies within the party establishment. Remarkably, she did not complain. As she didn't have 'the barons' on her side, she didn't have powerful support to defend herself either.

Gordon Brown decided shortly after Mo's arrival on the Trade and Industry team that he did not need her as an ally. A friend of his said that he was helped to this view by Nick Brown, who was then the Front Bench spokesman on Legal Affairs. 'Nick Brown didn't like having her on his territory with Gordon. He was the one who was going to organise things. He engineered a "me-or-Mo" choice for Gordon and really there was no choice: Nick offered plenty of votes in the Shadow Cabinet elections and Mo didn't offer any.'[36] What happened then, gradually, was that she was frozen out of the Brown team deliberations. 'Gordon doesn't have rows with people. He's the great communicator – but if you're not in the team, you're out of it,' said one Shadow minister of the time. Another more bluntly said: 'He agrees with you and then stabs you in the back.'

She had an additional problem: she didn't have an individual political agenda as did some of her contemporaries. Tony Blair had a mission to revivify the Labour Party through the involvement of the middle class of middle England; Gordon Brown had a political and economic programme; Harriet Harman had a feminist agenda; Peter Mandelson always had something on the go. Mo Mowlam was able, energetic, enthusiastic and as ambitious as the rest of them but to what end? 'She was slightly hands-off,' said a friend of Gordon Brown's 'and I think the trouble was that Gordon couldn't really see what she was *for*. He couldn't see what she could contribute. He couldn't see what she actually did.' The friend meant what she did in terms of being politically useful, rather than in her job as City spokesperson.

None of this sounds particularly serious in terms of an individual politician's future career – she didn't get on with Gordon Brown, so what? Yet it was to be of desperate importance to Mo, even if she could not herself see quite what an effect it was going to have on her future. There were also other crucial relationships. There was John Smith, who would be of immediate relevance. There was Peter Mandelson, with whom she fell out in the early 1990s. And there was Tony Blair. Happily she didn't fall out with him at this point; they were friends, but he did not go out of his way to defend her when she ran into difficulties with Gordon Brown. 'Tony was not going to champion her because he didn't see the need,' said the same friend of Brown's. 'From his point of view, what was she doing that made her an essential part of the modernising team?'

There was no doubt that she was wholly behind it. She was very supportive. She said all the right things and believed them – she had, after all, been saying them publicly and privately for ten years. In a Fabian pamphlet in early 1992 she wrote: 'Until the Labour Party can mentally make the leap that says aspiring to be middle class is positive, the public will always have trouble believing that we want to help anyone less fortunate. People want more money, a decent house, a good car – and so do all of us in the Labour Party.'[37] There couldn't have been a more definitive statement of support for the Blair 'Project' as it later became known. But it was still not enough. 'She had a position but she didn't have a base in the party, like Robin Cook or Harriet Harman, nor did she have the support of the leadership – after Kinnock's departure,' according to a source close to her.

What happened in consequence of this political stand-off was that Mo Mowlam would effectively be cast out from a central role in domestic politics, not just temporarily but for the long term. All manner of things were about to change in the Labour Party and in many ways Mo Mowlam would be identified with much of what was to come. She was crucial to the developments within the Labour Party in the run-up to the 1997 general election and she was phenomenally important afterwards as Secretary of State for Northern Ireland. But because of the earlier fall-out with Gordon Brown there was never any chance that she would be given an economic portfolio at the heart of policy-making while he remained a key figure in the party.

It was the beginning of what was to be an extraordinary political exile. And it was made more extraordinary by two factors: the first was that for some time she appeared to have no comprehension of how far she had been sidelined; the second was the extent to which her political critics within the party underestimated the power of her personality and what it would mean when she later achieved public prominence and a popularity which exceeded that of any other member of the 'new' Labour Government.

CHAPTER 9

'I'll be back to see you after'

Redcar 1987–1995

There is a film sequence of Marjorie Mowlam campaigning in her first general election in Redcar in the early summer of 1987. She is wearing a scarlet suit and a white blouse and she is striding down a path, vibrant with energy and enthusiasm, walking so fast that her hair is flying behind her as she goes. She is slim and fit and she looks simply stunning. 'We just ran her up and down the borough,' said her first election agent, Brian Roberts, 'just to show her face.' There wasn't any doubt that she was going to win, but maximum exposure of her smiling face must have been a considerable help.

She hit the ground walking briskly as soon as she won the selection. She had little choice. She was selected on Sunday, 24 May and started her campaign the next day at the Bank Holiday meeting at Redcar races. Her mother came to stay in Redcar to manage her domestic arrangements, as she often would in the course of Mo's political career. The nomination papers were handed in at Langbaurgh Town Hall on Thursday, 28 May and Neil Kinnock, with typical panache, sent the new candidate a red rose bush to congratulate her on her selection, which she planted on the Glorious First of June. Mo Mowlam was exactly the sort of woman that Kinnock wanted on the Labour benches in the Commons.

Brian Roberts, meanwhile, had embarked on the organisational nightmare of trying to raise the money to run the campaign and getting the necessary posters and literature printed. He used the format of the posters designed for Frank Cook in nearby Stockton North, simply changing the name and the picture, and wrote begging letters to unions and other Labour-supporting outfits to try to finance a campaign that he had to run having started with next to nothing in the bank. He discovered, to his relief, that Mo was already quite well known within the party up and down the country even though no one in Redcar seemed to have heard of her until five minutes ago. And she was popular. That helped tremendously.[1]

Then it was off with the candidate to the clubs and the pubs and the markets and the old people's homes and in and out of the housing estates. She went down very well. She was sparkling. She looked good, she felt good and she told them she was going to do them good. 'I make you one promise,' she said to a group of elderly, bemused-looking potential voters on this BBC North-east footage,[2] 'where I've gone looking for votes, I'll be back to see you after.' She meant it and she indeed came back.

Everybody was delighted with her, including the troublesome left wing within the local constituency. Sincerity is what matters in politics. It is something that can easily be detected by the least political observer, by the unemployed steelworker, by the disaffected teenager, by the mother with no money and a family to feed, by all those who feel disenfranchised by a political system that seems to pass them by. There are many people like that in the Teesside constituency of Redcar.

The seaside town that gives the constituency its name was a 'poore fishing toune' in early days. There has been a market and a fair there since the thirteenth century and in the mid-nineteenth century the extension of the railway – the famous Stockton and Darlington

Railway – brought tourists and industry to Redcar. It boasts the world's oldest lifeboat, the *Zetland*, built two hundred years ago. As a town, it still photographs well with the fishing boats pulled up on the beach – as long as the industrial backdrop of Hartlepool on the North Bank of the Tees is kept out of the shot. It is 'an area of contrasts', as the official publicity for the local authority describes it without irony. Inland to the south stretch the Eston Hills, part of the Cleveland range, where the iron ore that gave the area its lifeblood in the nineteenth century was found. The first blast furnace was built on Teesside in 1851 and within fifty years the area was producing a third of the country's output of iron. The vast industrial conglomeration which they spawned contrasts sharply with the beauty of the hills. The Redcar constituency extends beyond the town itself north on to Teesside; within its boundaries are some of the most socially deprived areas of Britain: streets where youths practised handbrake turns in stolen cars until road humps were installed, where they claim even the milk-floats are armoured, where locals sometimes choose to compare their living conditions to those of Beirut. Bizarrely there is a degree of inverse pride about this. And although things have undoubtedly improved in recent years on the estates in South Bank and Grangetown, many of the social advances of the post-war years have yet to be widely appreciated here.

But Mo's new constituents immediately appreciated her. She has, since her election, been widely credited for having secured a considerable advance one way and another for the constituency of Redcar – just as she promised she would. 'I'm going to fight very hard,' she had told a group of old ladies, as recorded on the BBC film of her campaign. And of course she did. She has a sincerity that shines out of her and it worked for her here, as it still does. She won her first general election with consummate ease, more than doubling the Labour majority and increasing Labour's proportion of the vote from 40.6 per cent to 47.3 per cent.[3] Considering the circumstances, this result wasn't bad at all, and she was to prove a phenomenally successful constituency MP.

As soon as she was elected she hurled herself into proving that she

191

had meant what she had said, trying, at least, to deal with the many problems with which constituents immediately confronted her. She did indeed return to see those whose votes she had requested. She learned the map of the constituency like the back of her hand, better certainly than many of her staff. She knew every street. More impressive still, she never forgot an individual and, of course, being Mo, she always remembered everybody's name. Not surprisingly, after years of benign neglect, they liked this in Redcar. 'People just took her to their hearts,' said her old friend Vilma Collins[4], a member of Redcar and Cleveland Borough Council. They brought her their troubles and she was straight with them. They liked her no-nonsense style, her lack of pretension, her ineffable sense of fun. She behaved like a real person.

On one occasion, she had dropped a friend back home at a junction in Grangetown late at night and a passer-by mistakenly thought she was a taxi driver. He climbed into the back of her car, giving an address as he did so, and rather than pointing out his error she drove off. They started a conversation and a few minutes into the journey he recognised her voice and was quite naturally horrified at his presumption. 'You're all right. I'll drop you off. I'm going that way,' said his MP.

By such means she very quickly established herself as a first-class populist politician. Everybody in the constituency thinks they've met her. 'I can't count the number of times I've heard people say: "If I get no satisfaction I'm going to see Marjorie Mowlam",' said her friend John Pallister.[5] It was a popularity she built quickly and, ten years later, when she became Secretary of State for Northern Ireland, her standing naturally grew even further. They were proud of her in Redcar. There were those who said, in 1997, that she wouldn't be seen any more now in the constituency because she had rather more compelling dates in her diary, but it was not the case. She came to Redcar just as often, and held her surgeries just as frequently as she had before. She possibly didn't stay for so long, but that was understandable; she was, after all, about the business of resolving the longest-running political problem in the United Kingdom and what could be more important than that?

People actually used to apologise when they came to her surgery, feeling that their problem was insignificant and that really they shouldn't be bothering her. Didn't she have enough to cope with, poor pet?

The journalist Simon Hoggart gave a flavour of her popularity in Redcar in an article[6] he wrote in the run-up to the 1997 election, after her treatment for a brain tumour had been revealed. 'She has acquired something near the aura of a saint,' he reported. '"It was a mugging yesterday," her agent told me. "She hardly set out in the high street before the crowd came round her. She couldn't move".' Hoggart went on: 'If she doesn't know them, she hugs them. If she does know them, they get the full treatment, consisting of hug, followed by warm arm clasp, then the Mowlam forehead lowered on to their forehead in order to establish eye contact, almost literally . . . We met a man who got the full treatment because she had written to him two years ago. His dog had died and he had written asking what to do.' Now that's successful, hands-on, pavement politics.

But such success comes at considerable personal and emotional cost both to Mo Mowlam and to her staff. She is a difficult person for whom to work. She makes enormous demands of herself and therefore expects the same of others. That does not necessarily make it unpleasant for her staff but it certainly creates pressure all round. She *expects* people to perform in ways that can sometimes seem unreasonable. 'It's a nice job to have,' said Keith Legg, her agent in the constituency since 1995. 'She's an incredibly difficult person to work for. She moves the goalposts all the time. She gives you an instruction and then when you've delivered on it, she says no, she didn't want that. And no, she doesn't apologise; she never thinks she's wrong.'[7] He speaks from experience and respect. He thinks that his Member of Parliament is an exceptional and unusual person. He has not made the mistake of trying to be personal friends with her, which is a wise move since, as one of her intimates said, 'I don't think she's very good with people who are close to her.'

The fact that this popular and saintly woman who is regularly mobbed on the streets of Redcar can also get very angry when she doesn't get what she wants from her staff can also be confusing and difficult. 'She's either shouting and screaming and bawling at you to get you to do things or she's all over you like a rash,' said Keith. Humour is one way to handle it. There was an occasion when two of her staff were steering clear of her when she was letting rip in the office. As they stood looking out of the window at the blinding rain lashing in over the North Sea one apparently said to the other, 'So you didn't manage to sort the weather, then?' Brian Roberts, who was formerly the leader of Redcar and Cleveland Council, said that he used to 'shut the hearing off like' sometimes because of disagreements between them. There was, for example, the long-running row about the closure of the Redcar Baths, which Mo fought defiantly – and ultimately unsuccessfully – to keep open. 'I got a good towsing on that one,' he said.[8]

The word that is used time and again in reference to Mo by people who know her well is that she is 'driven' – partly by the impetus provided by her background, partly by her profound political beliefs and partly by fear of failure. 'I don't think she wants to fail at anything she does,' said her agent. She is also focused and she is relentless in the pursuit of a given target. She often hounds people in order to achieve what she wants. She cannot abide not being provided with the answers she seeks, with progress on a given problem. There is a road into Redcar – approaching the town from Darlington, where Keith Legg often used to collect her from the London train – which runs past a development project called the Kirkleatham Business Park. For some time Keith avoided ever choosing this route. He knew that if he did, she would demand to know why there had still not been much action on the site, and that it was he who would have to answer for this failure. 'Nothing has been done there, Keith,' she would announce, displeased.

'She's the hardest working MP in the country and always has been,' Brian Roberts said.[9] Nagging, working hard, not accepting no for an answer are all positive virtues and very useful in a politician. The electorate, voters, people – all want answers. Local authorities, civil servants, councillors, officials – all need to be chased and hounded. That way lies success, and while some people resented her relentlessness, it paid off in political terms and in public popularity. It is said in Redcar, within the Labour Party, that she could stand for Parliament without the benefit of any party label and still win the seat. That is some compliment in a place associated with such a traditional vote. In the 1992 county council elections in Grangetown, a staggering 89 per cent of those who voted gave their support to the Labour Party.

For all this personal success, life in Redcar has not been easy by any means for Mo Mowlam. For one thing, she inherited a divided local party, which was very difficult for her, particularly at the beginning of her parliamentary career when she was unacquainted with the lie of the political landscape in the constituency. There were two distinct camps within the party and a great deal of residual animosity from the past. Supporters of Paul Harford, who had been cheated of the selection for Redcar by Jim Tinn's carefully timed resignation, were confident that the new MP wouldn't last, that they would get her out by the next election and secure the seat for their man. The left-wingers in the party realised quite quickly that she was not going to be their creature and that made for more trouble. She had to tread carefully. She did so and the passage of time came to her aid. The internal political problems didn't exactly fade away over the years – for example, in the vote on the totemic issue of Clause Four of the Labour Party constitution,[10] which Tony Blair persuaded a special party conference to abandon in 1995, the Redcar constituency voted to retain the status quo – but her great strength which rendered her political position in Redcar totally inviolable – as it was also to prove within the Government – was her very unusual level of public support.

Some of the other difficulties that she has had in the constituency have resulted from various problems with her staff over the years, primarily because of the demands she made upon them. There is always a difficulty for any MP with a constituency outside London; he or she is required to be in London during the week but nevertheless has to bear in mind that he or she was elected to represent and help people in the constituency. In the first years after Mo's election, she ran her constituency affairs from Redcar. She had bought a tiny street house, at 49 Muriel Street in the centre of the town, just a couple of blocks in from the sea and installed a local Labour Party member, Judith Miller, there as her secretary and PA. During the week she lived in London and, before acquiring her own place in Kennington, she briefly shared a flat in Dolphin Square, near to the Houses of Parliament. Her friend Hilary Armstrong had inherited from her father. The two women also shared a pocket-sized office with a handkerchief of a window on to an inner courtyard in the Commons. From here, early every morning, Mo would ring her office at 'home'.

Every week, in the small hours of Friday morning, she would drive up to Redcar. She would leave London at 2.30 a.m., arrive in Muriel Street at 5.30 a.m., have a few hours sleep and start her constituency appointments at 9 a.m. 'She'd break her neck to come back and do it because she didn't want to let anybody down,' Judith said. 'She was hard sometimes. She's a perfectionist. She had to have everything done. She never stops until everything is done. She's just the same I would think now.'

She has always been restless. Keith Legg was the chairman of the Education Committee on the County Council when she was first elected and he remembered how irreverent and informal and *different* she was from other people. Other people sat at the table and talked. She was always getting up to fetch a piece of paper, to find an ashtray, to make a phone call. She would get up from a meal to make a phone call, without saying anything to the others present; she would just go away for ten minutes and come back and join in where she left off. Her mother said she would get out of the bath at 11 p.m. and sit wrapped up in a bath towel on the stairs insisting: 'Don't say anything. I've just got to ring someone *now*.' Mercifully she did have an ability to catnap, when she was exhausted, as she often was. She used to go to sleep on Keith's shoulder when he collected her from the London train at

Darlington, and her mother recalled how Mo would arrive home completely exhausted – yet two hours later how she could be re-energised.[11]

Meanwhile, Judith was working away in the upstairs front bedroom of the little house in Muriel Street with a photocopier, a filing cabinet and an old portable electric typewriter. She and Mo got on well. Mo was extrovert and generous, warm and friendly and she gave Judith a great deal of self-confidence. 'I did things I'd never dreamed I'd be able to do when I was working for her,' Judith said. 'She makes you do things you don't think you can. She'd say: "Of course you can! Just get on and do it".'[12] However, the work was overwhelming. 'It was horrific,' Judith said. 'These stacks of mail just kept on arriving.' Mo's election had immediately prompted an avalanche of post from hopeful constituents and it continued so to do. Every time she went out she would meet people in the street who would tell her their problems and she would always urge them to write to her.

'One of her qualities is that she's a very good advocate,' said Keith Legg who understands this all too well. 'She's not driven by self-interest. She will take up anybody's problem. She doesn't find it easy to say "No" to people, though she can be firm and say there is no point in someone coming along to the surgery again. She doesn't make outrageous claims to people either. She'll say: "I'll take it up. I'll do what I can." She can be absolutely wonderful and she does have the ability of making people feel good about themselves. She wants to please people, I think she's desperate to please people, because she wants you to feel good about her. She does take it to incredible lengths sometimes.'

Mo had office help in London, too, and used university politics students to ease the workload in her Commons' office, but it was clear that she needed more assistance in the constituency. It got too much for Judith after a year or so; she was finding it too difficult to manage her own domestic life because she was overwhelmed at work. The job wasn't nine to five – it was evenings and weekends as well.

By the time Judith left, Mo had already brought in some temporary help and another assistant, Jean McCourt,[13] all of whom struggled valiantly with the post and the problems. Mo had also met Kath Taylor, who was running a small book franchise business in the area, and asked her to come and see if she could make any sense of the constituency operation. They had an antiquated computer by this time, two filing cabinets – because Mo still never threw anything away – but there remained mountains of filing and a backlog of mail. And more arriving with every post. Kath agreed to do what she could. It took some sorting. Eventually she made some sense of it all; Kath was there to stay and the two had become very good friends.

Mo's mother Tina was also on hand to come and help with the house and her daughter's clothes when required. To their mutual pleasure, Mo's election to Parliament marked a new phase in their relationship. Her mother was quite converted to Labour politics by this time but never had any hesitation in telling her daughter if she felt she had got something wrong. 'My mother has become more political,' Mo herself said in 1998.[14] 'She used to phone me with a list of things that were wrong and needed to be put right.' When Mo was first elected, Tina used to walk her dog in the park where she would meet other dog-walkers. They would discuss the state of the world. 'Dogs are a great leveller,' said her daughter, relating this. 'She would come back and tell me what people thought and, more often than not, she was right.'

Kath Taylor loved working for Mo, which she did for five years. She would help with the surgeries on Friday night and Saturday morning, and she would accompany Mo sometimes to events around the constituency. They worked hard but they had fun sometimes. They would have a drink together on Friday when work was finished and they developed a close and significant friendship. They teased each other about their weight, particularly as Mo began to put on the pounds at Westminster, and they once went together for a weekend to a health farm. 'We were exhausted. We had all the health checks and they told us we weren't going to do anything,' said Kath.[15] They shared the intimacies of their private lives, too. Kath was married at the time with children, while Mo was ricocheting around emotionally in a somewhat racketty fashion.

They even went clothes shopping once or twice. Mo has famously never cared about clothes. When she was first elected, her dress was as unconventional as her persona. Mo, the new MP, would often turn up to meet people like councillors wearing jeans, T-shirt and trainers. It did cause a few raised eyebrows, but she was so good at what she was doing, meeting constituents or party members, putting people at their ease, that she was instantly forgiven. Later she recognised that she needed to pay more attention to what she looked like, although she hated having to do so. Her mother and her sister would sometimes buy clothes for her and send them to her.

When Kath tried to help with this irksome business, they went to a very smart ladies' dress shop in Durham. Mo had been on gruelling business at Durham Jail that day and the strain had left them rather giggly with the relief of tension that came afterwards. They were larking about and as a result they found themselves being patronised by the rather proper assistant in this shop – until this assistant suddenly realised from their conversation that she had a Front Bench spokeswoman dressing for the House of Commons on her hands.

The dress problem was to become worse. After the 1997 election when Mo became a Cabinet minister and the demands upon her appearance were obviously even more compelling, she partly resolved the problem by buying three versions of the same plain black or navy suits and keeping one in London, one in Redcar and one in Northern Ireland. She would even involve her security policemen in choosing her outfits. She would go to Harrods – to the 'Plus Sizes' department because she had by this time put on a great deal of weight – and, as ever, charm the staff and make new friends among them. But she was completely uninterested in the clothes they attempted to persuade her to buy. She has also shopped regularly from the ready-to-wear collection designed by Peter Lewis Crown for Lachasse in South Kensington. She professed that she couldn't care less about what she wore but it is evident that she does perhaps take rather more care than she sometimes makes out. She doesn't like fussy clothes or anything that is decorated. She likes plain colours: blues and hyacinth and pinks and what the trade calls 'snuff' colours.

'She has still got very small feet and legs and beautiful skin and a very clear image of herself and likes to dress within that framework,' Peter Lewis Crown said. 'Her clothes have to work for her and be the background for her.'[16]

Some time before this period she had even made one attempt at being 'folletted', as it was known. Barbara Follett[17] and her millionaire novelist husband Ken were in the vanguard of 'Labour luvvies', the rich and famous who supported Neil Kinnock's attempt to shake up the party's image. Barbara had offered her informal services to Front Bench Labour MPs on dress and style and colour co-ordination, which had become increasingly important with the televising of Parliament. Famously, for example, she advised Robin Cook to wear 'autumnal colours' to complement his red hair and beard. Some Labour MPs were extremely dismissive of such top-dressing and derided those involved, but Mo decided to seek advice in 1992. The day after the election, she went with Kath and some others to the Folletts' imposing house at Cheyne Walk on the Chelsea Embankment and they drowned their sorrows at the outcome of the election in champagne, drunk, for some reason, from a china teapot. Whatever advice she received, Mo later described herself as one of Barbara Follett's more impressive failures.

Despite her protests to the contrary, it does seem probable that she cares quite a lot about how she looks. 'She enjoyed her attractiveness,' said one of her former boyfriends. 'She had an earthy quality and she liked her attractiveness and deployed it. Her real attraction was her personality. She was a good-looking woman. She had great legs, good hair, nice face – but really all of that was in a way secondary to her vivacity. She must mind a lot, she must mind an awful lot.' He meant about how her looks had changed.[18]

The problems associated with her health, which led to her dramatic change in appearance, were all still in the future when Mo and Kath were friends. And the friendship worked for a long time. Sometimes they had rows, but mostly they used to laugh. 'We laughed and laughed. We laughed until we rolled on the floor.'[19] Kath treasured the closeness of their friendship. Mo has many friends and is much loved, and yet she has difficulty confiding in anybody. 'You couldn't get any access to an inner life,' said one ex-boyfriend, citing this as the reason they split up. 'Being insecure, having anxieties – she must have had all of those things but didn't bother anyone else with them.' She did have a very good friendship with Kath, however, and her friend was there for her when she *did* endure a painful emotional upheaval. This was one of the more difficult periods of her difficult life, the course of her love affair with the journalist Colin Hughes.

They had met in the House of Commons, where Colin Hughes was on the political staff of the *Independent*. He was a clever and talented journalist. He was also married – to the journalist Nicci Gerrard, with whom he had two young children. Mo was already on the Opposition Front Bench by the time they met. It was by all accounts a coup de foudre and they started an affair. It was, quite predictably, going to be complicated and cause a lot of hurt. Nicci Gerrard intuitively sensed it. 'He went home one night and she could smell another woman on him,' someone said, speaking figuratively.[20] Within a few weeks of her discovery, the couple were divorced. Everybody involved was, eventually, one way and another, wounded.

Mo had asked friends how she should handle things because she was very troubled by the potential fall-out. The response was that if there was no way that the divorce could be put down as an uncontested action, there wasn't much she could do in the way of damage limitation. On the other hand, it wasn't the first, nor last, such affair: divorces involving Members of Parliament and/or lobby correspondents and occasionally even both at the same time are not unknown. This didn't make it any more comfortable for anybody. 'Will it damage my career?' she asked, privately. Someone suggested the 'Duke of Windsor option', meaning that they should choose an unlikely location for their divorce, on the grounds that there are lengths to which the British press will go in pursuit of a good 'story' but they are often also lazy. And so the divorce was listed in a Reading court, somewhere obscure to all their lives; the grounds of divorce was Colin Hughes' adultery, with Marjorie Mowlam cited as the co-respondent. Fortunately, the advice proved sound and the divorce itself went largely unnoticed, except by those close to the eye of the storm.

The night he left his wife, in November 1989, Colin got on a train and headed north. He rang Mo in Redcar and she picked him up. It was a passionate and dramatic love affair and her friends described her as obsessed. One said that it was like an adolescent love; another, with a degree of irony, called it 'the love story of the century'. From all accounts it worked for both of them, at least to start with. Everyone said that Colin adored her: 'besotted' was the word her mother used. 'He used to sit and gaze at her as if she would melt if he took his eyes off her,' she remembered. For her part Mo was very protective of Colin and didn't want to let anybody else near him. He was precious and he was hers.

There was, however, a problem with his job. Just before his marriage ended he had undertaken to go to work in Washington. There was a vacancy for the number three position in the newspaper's Washington office and the chief US correspondent, Peter Pringle, had been in London in October to decide who should be appointed. The Foreign Editor, Stephen Glover, wanted to send Hughes, while the Editor, Andreas Whittam Smith, had promised the job to Sarah Helm. Pringle decided that Hughes should go. Hughes told his colleagues that his wife had also organised work for herself in DC, and he went to the States on a recce and found a house that would be suitable for his family. But then his circumstances changed utterly. By the time he arrived to start the job in January 1990 the marriage had already ended.

Few people at Westminster had known about the relationship, which the couple did not publicly parade, and it was suggested by some within the *Independent* that he had been sent to the United States because the editor thought it was less than ideal for a political correspondent to be having an affair with a member of the Opposition Front Bench. The newspaper was in its early idealistic phase and was currently running the advertising slogan: 'The *Independent*. It is. Are you?' This interpretation of events is quite wrong, however. His transfer had nothing to do with his private life and in reality being in Washington made everything intolerable.

It was less than ideal trying to conduct a love affair across the Atlantic. What made it worse was that Colin had the additional anguish of missing his children. He was jumping on planes to return to Britain whenever he could, and sometimes Mo would do the same, suddenly disappearing to Heathrow for a weekend in Washington without announcing her absence. This caused a few political problems when she was mysteriously unavailable and unaccounted for, but luckily her friends who knew, or found out, what was going on discreetly covered for her. The situation was insupportable. Colin was excessively miserable in DC and deeply unhappy at all this confusion around him. Shortly afterwards he astonished his colleagues by asking to be brought back to Britain as soon as possible. He made this request within weeks of having started the job. It led to considerable teethsucking in the City Road and in the Washington office, but after some internal debate it was agreed that it could be arranged.

It still took time. When Mo got the time and opportunity, during the parliamentary summer recess in 1990, she went to Washington and stayed as long as was feasible. She was a great hit with the other journalists, who swiftly recognised her as a rising star of British politics. But her stay was marked by an illness. She was clearly suffering from strain and overwork and she was very ill with an undisclosed ailment that her friends passed off as a mystery virus. And there must have been strain within the relationship. They discussed marriage and she very much wanted to have a baby. It has been suggested that one reason why the relationship failed was because she was insufficiently aware of how much Colin missed his children and how important they were to his life. An acquaintance who witnessed some of this at the time said that she was 'child-blind'. This was quite wrong.[21] On the contrary, Mo, recognising how much Colin did miss his children, wanted very much to have a baby precisely for that reason.

And the pity of it was that after all this heartache the relationship did not endure. Although it effectively collapsed while Mo was in Washington, they continued to try to make it work. It was touch and go. Back home in Britain, in the autumn of that year, Colin had been given the more mundane job of Education Correspondent. She thought the relationship was over at the time of the Labour Party conference that year and had to be cajoled into picking herself up and making herself perform at Blackpool. The couple weathered that and stayed together for another few months but then he left.

When they split up they quite understandably agreed not to discuss these private matters; nor have they. Nevertheless the version of events that has been published is somewhat inaccurate. It suggests that most of the commitment to the affair was on his side; that Mo was taken aback when he left his wife; that eventually she ended it. 'She couldn't cope with him being so pathetic,' one of her friends said. 'He used to drive her mad: he didn't want to go to the pictures or do things and have a life. He wanted to be at home with her.'[22] Her mother said: 'I think he was insanely jealous because she was so popular. He wanted her all to himself.'[23] Tina thought Colin was 'a great spoiled baby', and she added, 'I was mighty relieved when he departed. It was never mentioned until she said one day: "I've been helping Colin find a flat and he's left."'

What does seem to have been the case is that she cared for Colin a very great deal and that at the time it seemed to her that this was the love of her life. She was emotionally committed as perhaps she had not been before. They discussed marriage in very precise terms and she was desperately upset by her failure to conceive. And what hurt her more than anything was that Colin left her. 'She was devastated when that relationship ended,' one friend said. He lived alone for a time before finding someone else, whom he married shortly afterwards.

'He saw through her.' That was the comment of someone who understood Mo and although it sounds unkind and unnecessarily cruel, it was not meant in that fashion. It was an assessment of the fact that she is so much more complicated an individual than she may appear and perhaps that is precisely why she did have such an 'untidy' love life for so long. Other former boyfriends repeatedly refer to something along the same lines. She is a deep person and an intensely private one – yet that is so much in conflict with how she appears. The warm, cheerful, open, honest persona is a real one. She is that person. But there is another more profound person there, too, and sometimes it is difficult for anyone who is close to her – or who wants to be close – to reach below the surface to the next level. One former boyfriend related how he found himself completely exhausted by dealing only with her at the surface level. He saw her performing and he admired it, yet he became discomforted by the spectacle. 'Every situation she got into she would create an audience for herself.' His disquiet was that he felt himself to be merely part of the audience.

Those who did understand what had happened with Colin Hughes mostly felt regret and sympathy. The Labour Party conference in the autumn of 1990 was difficult for her, to put it mildly, because as well as being bereft, she had all the difficulties of her Shadow post with Gordon Brown to handle too. It was a bleak time. There would be blue skies and happier days ahead, when she would find a new partner and a relationship that really did work with Jon Norton, whom she later married, but it must have been very hard to believe at the time that anything like that was possible.

Jon Norton was peripherally involved in Mo's life for some time before they really got to know each other. He was a Labour-supporting City banker and a fund-raiser for the party, and in order to promote interest in the alternatives to Thatcherite economics he ran a discussion group for a number of like-minded people called the Smithfield Group, which met in a crypt in St Mary Le Bow in the heart of the City. The group would invite relevant MPs or economists as guests to their meetings and on one occasion Mo Mowlam attended as the Shadow City spokeswoman. They became friendly in a casual fashion and were undoubtedly very useful to each other at a professional level. It was helpful for someone with Mo's brief to have access to a supportive group of this nature and similarly it provided Jon with a direct line to Westminster. He had a considerable interest in public affairs and was also an active republican. One of his friends said that he had ambitions to find a parliamentary seat for himself at this stage; when he and Mo started living together he put them aside and involved himself in her career.

When Mo and Jon met properly it was at a dinner party. By this time Mo had picked herself up emotionally after the disastrous break-up with Colin Hughes. She had a brief fling with an old friend, an academic from Newcastle University whose marriage had collapsed, but the mutual consolation involved did not take them anywhere much – although they had both hoped it might. Jon is said to have fallen in love with Mo at a dinner party because she made him laugh so much.[24] Jon was married to the journalist Geraldine Bedell when he first met Mo in about 1990, but in the spring of 1992 the marriage was collapsing. That was not common knowledge and a friend who went to a dinner party at the home of Jon and Geraldine, at which Mo was also present, remembered noticing how 'she and Jon were getting on like a house on fire.' The friend added: 'She was really racy and her skirt was creeping up her tights and I remember thinking at the time: "Gosh, she's really after him".'[25] In fact Geraldine Bedell had already fallen in love with another journalist and political policy analyst, Charlie Leadbitter, and she left Jon for him at the beginning of March 1992. Coincidentally, Jon and Geraldine and their two children, Henrietta who was eight and Freddie who was four, were due to spend that very weekend with Mo in Redcar. The rest of the family came without Geraldine and a week later Jon moved in to live with Mo in Dolphin Square.[26]

Jon loved helping Mo to try to unwind at weekends, walking with her on the beach, helping her restore and improve their house, building a fireplace and cooking for her. He put some order into her life. But the main help he gave Mo initially was financial. And she needed help. She was short of money to run her offices and operate on the Front Bench at the level that she wished and she decided that one solution could be to set up a trust with money provided by Labour-supporting sources. The Mo Mowlam Research Fund was established to help her finance her office staff. There was a joint bank account, although she could not herself sign cheques; the two people with access to it were Norton and Mo's assistant in Redcar Kath Taylor. It was meant to resolve the niggling office administration problems, but as the years went by the troubles actually got worse. According to one of her MP colleagues it was partly because of the amount of work she generated for which she obviously needed considerable back-up. But, said this friend, 'She tried to have too many people and didn't pay very well.'

When Jean McCourt became ill with cancer, another young woman, Chris Scott, joined the staff in Redcar as a part-time typist. She stayed for over six years and still claims to have the record for length of service. Chris and Kath ran a good office: efficient, conscientious and well-mannered. And there was a good team spirit: they were all committed politically and they were all working towards the same end; Mo was the front person, a keen and enthusiastic politician doing a great deal of work which she was able to achieve because of the behind-the-scenes help. By now they had got another computer and the letters got answered. People did not get formulaic responses either; Mo was insistent about that.

It had, however, got rather crowded in the front bedroom in Muriel Street and Tina Mowlam was worried, probably with good reason, that the weight of two people, two computers, two filing cabinets and the photocopier was too much for the floor of the little house. And then there was the paperwork. The office was turning round four hundred constituency cases a year on behalf of an MP who wouldn't throw anything away. It was getting ridiculous. A local businessman, Alan Brundell, who ran a shop in Station Road, slap in the middle of town, came to the rescue. He offered to let the flat above his shop to Mo at a reasonable rent. It was a good offer and a great relief. There was a big room for the office, lots of space, a kitchen, and the flat had its own entrance with a buzzer and a voicebox. The latter was particularly attractive to Kath and Chris since, because of Mo's policy of being accessible to her constituents at all times, anybody could walk in to the offices. The women, who were there on their own all week, had felt increasingly vulnerable in Muriel Street because of the occasional unpredictable oddballs that inevitably turned up. The buzzer on the door was just what they needed. Mo transferred the office and in due course found the house for herself for which she had been looking.

She had wanted to live directly on the seafront since she arrived in Redcar and she had looked at a number of properties. She found her ideal quite simply. Someone with whom Kath was acquainted was selling and Mo liked the house immediately. It is easy to see why: it's a pleasant four-bedroomed, double-fronted terraced house looking straight out to the sea and with a small garden at the back. She moved in there in 1991 and gradually did it up, living in only a couple of rooms for some time. She had a wallpaper stripping party for Labour Party members once. Tony Blair gave her his old kitchen table in varnished pine.

The troubles at the Redcar office continued to develop. As the workload increased, the strains inevitably began to show. Mo expected an enormous amount from anyone who worked for her and was sometimes irritable when things did not get done. As her responsibilities within the Labour Party hierarchy and on the Front Bench grew she needed to spend more time in London, which put more pressure on the women in Redcar. Kath and Chris had nine children between them and many other things going on in their lives and Mo became anxious that they were not performing as well as they could. She would complain, for example, if she telephoned and found that there was nobody in the office in Redcar. She also became increasingly concerned about keeping in touch with all that was happening in the town and worrying that her staff knew about issues with which she had not been kept acquainted.

Chris believed that Mo's personality changed. She had been a friend to them both but now she was asserting her position as their employer. 'We pulled her up on it, both of us, to keep her feet back on the ground,' Chris said.[27] 'There were times when she lost it, she didn't know where she was because of the work that she has. Originally she was a really kind person, she really was, I would argue with anybody about that.' The trouble in her view was control. 'She wanted to be seen to do everything herself.' Chris said. It was understandable, Mo being Mo, but she was making unreasonable demands on herself. And there were ongoing financial problems. Kath had argued that Chris should be paid more, but because there was a limit on the money available Mo said that this could be achieved only by altering the balance between the two women's salaries; Kath would have to accept less in order to pay Chris more. Eventually Kath decided that the time had come to move on and she gave in her notice in the spring of 1992. Mo helped her find another job and she left six months later. But arrangements in the office then became even more complicated and chaotic.

A number of people replaced Kath on a short-term basis, including her ex-husband, Ken Taylor, a local councillor from whom she had recently separated. He did the job for six weeks but that did not do much for what remained of the friendship between Mo and Kath. Chris became involved reluctantly with doing some of the PA work during the periods when there was nobody else to do it, but by now her responsibility was for casework and she did not wish to take on the PA work. She was also upset when Mo decided that they would save time and effort by sending standardised letters to constituents, something she had never done before. Chris objected to this on the grounds that Mo had built up her reputation with a personalised touch in dealing with her constituents. 'She had got to the point where she felt she'd got a big enough majority and she could lay off the other side of things – that's how I felt and it was a big issue with me because there had been a big effort setting up that personalised touch.' Eventually, Mo decided to downgrade the Redcar operation and run her main office in London. Her research assistant, Nigel Warner, who had initially worked for her and another MP, starting this job shortly after she went on the Front Bench, took responsibility for all her research work in London. When Labour moved into Government in 1997, he became a civil servant and has been one of the crucial supports she has had in her political career.

Mo moved the Redcar office into the ground floor of her house on the seafront in the spring of 1995. While this was a practical solution, it was handled badly and became messy, although it was still some time before matters would come to a head. When Mo changed the arrangements between her offices Chris had had to accept a pay cut as her responsibilities were nominally reduced. There had been murmurings in the town suggesting things were not going as well as they could in Mo's office and word had got around. Chris got a telephone call from a union official at the Transport and General Workers' Union suggesting that it was in her interest to join. It was a tricky situation but she joined the union, along with another member of staff, Shaun Adams, who worked in the office for just under a year, and had also had his pay cut. Then, just before Christmas 1995, they both lost their jobs and they contacted the union to negotiate a severance deal on their behalf. There was a little local publicity. Chris Scott, whose pay had been reduced from £12,000 p.a. to £9,000 p.a., was awarded £3,000 under the deal, and Shaun Adams, whose pay had been reduced from £5,000 p.a. to £4,000 p.a., was awarded £2,000. It was an unpleasant incident, a highly unfortunate one for any Labour MP and a sad end to the friendship between Mo and Chris, who was greatly upset by everything that happened.

When Keith Legg was hired in 1995, in the midst of all this trouble, he was careful to maintain a relationship with Mo that was always strictly professional. Mo still proved to be a difficult employer, but the office was restored to an effective and efficient operation within time. Her demands did not diminish and she trod on a lot of toes. It is said within the Labour Party in Redcar that she has not been very careful about keeping her friends there. A number of people who felt that they were close to her, consider that they have been dropped as her national and international status has grown. There is a feeling that she has found more glamorous company and a sadness that she had less and less time for some party members who thought that they deserved a bit more of their share of the credit. These sorts of sensitivities are always to be found within any local political organisation; what hurt her political pals in Redcar was that they had thought she was different.

None of this made any impact on her personal popularity with the man and woman on the Redcar street. *They* still thought she was wonderful and, in a way, this accentuated the hurt of these former friends. It was as if she didn't need them any more; her political status increased steadily, so that she could do no wrong, and she knew that her majority was unassailable. They did not wish to diminish this; most were simply sorry that she had moved on without ever really saying goodbye and thank you.

By the time these changes were noticed it was evident that Mo was beginning to run her life in a different way. It was not that she was any less occupied with work – on the contrary – but Jon Norton had entered her life in 1992 and had given her an important new focus. Unfairly perhaps some people blamed him for the change they detected.

She and Jon lived in his house in Cleveland Road, Islington, until Mo became Secretary of State for Northern Ireland in 1997, at which point for reasons of security they moved into a flat in South Eaton Place in Belgravia, previously allocated to Michael Howard as the Home Secretary. They didn't like it. It was a modern building attached to a police station, there was nowhere for his children to play, excessive security and it didn't have a decent view. The crunch came on one occasion when Jon came home in the middle of the night, didn't have the appropriate identification and the police wouldn't let him in. They decided to move back to Islington where they remained until late 1999, after Mo returned to work in Whitehall as the Cabinet Office minister, when she was given a 'Grace and Favour' apartment in Admiralty House and the house in Cleveland Road was put up for sale.

Mo and Jon married on June 24 in 1995. They were nagged into it by Jon's children. His divorce, on the grounds of irreconcilable break-down, had gone through just about as amicably as these things can be managed. Geraldine Bedell was the petitioner but only because both parties decided that there was no need to put more money in the lawyers' pockets and she was prepared to do the paperwork. They had qualified for a divorce in 1994 after two years' separation, but no one was particularly bothered about immediate action because they were all busy people and their circumstances were congenial. The divorce when it happened served to regularise an existing arrange-ment but the prospect of marriage did make Mo extremely happy. They were clearly very much in love with each other.

According to due form, Jon had a stag night. It was a dinner at Manzi's, the fish restaurant near Leicester Square, and there was one rather odd aspect to this event. Mo's boyfriend from her university days, Chris Pye, with whom she is still friends, had recently returned to London after living in the US and had met and liked Jon. But they had met only once, so Chris was really very surprised a few months later to be invited to this dinner with the likes of the novelist Ken Follett and the late journalist and broadcaster Vincent Hanna. 'It seemed weird to me,' he said. 'Here am I a close personal friend of Mo's and although Jon and I got on fine, I couldn't work out why I was being invited to his stag party with lots of people I didn't know who didn't know me. I couldn't work out whether Mo had said to Jon: "You'd better invite that Chris Pye you know" or whether Jon had done it because he liked me, but I felt very warm about it – very pleased to be asked. I had a very nice evening with people I had never met before.'[28]

Mo scarcely told anybody at Westminster about her impending marriage, although she couldn't resist telling one or two pals and she was clearly very excited. There was one moment when her joy and delight spilled over and she just couldn't keep it to herself. She kissed a surprised Michael Mates, a Conservative MP, in a House of Commons lift and whispered in his ear that she was getting married in the morning.

It was a happy day. The ceremony at Middlesbrough Register Office was attended by only their close family and a few friends. The bridegroom had prepared a wedding lunch back at their home; they spent the afternoon at the Redcar Races and then they went back to the house again to drink champagne and eat the fruit cake baked by Jon's mother. They would have just over a year of marriage before life, for several reasons, began to get very complicated indeed.

CHAPTER 10

'As a politician I know what I am doing'

Westminster 1992–1994

The political disappointment of Labour's fourth successive election defeat in 1992 that was felt so keenly by everyone on the Opposition Front Bench was particularly unfortunate for Mo Mowlam. There had been real expectation within the Labour Party that at last the Conservative's domination of government might be brought to an end. They had a weak leader in John Major, an increasingly divided party and the opinion polls indicated a profound desire for change. If Neil Kinnock had become Prime Minister Mo Mowlam would have been entitled to expect an influential post in his government. It was not to be. The election took place on a bright spring day and up until the last it seemed likely that the Labour Party was on course for victory. 'The sun is out – and so are the Tories!' Kinnock boldly told a radio interviewer on the afternoon of the election. But he didn't believe it. Those who knew him well detected that he was already aware that he was beaten and when the votes were finally totted up in the early hours of that miserable April morning, a shattered Neil Kinnock took personal blame for the outcome and determined on an act of expiation by resigning the Labour leadership. This was not good news for the ambitious MP for Redcar. A change in leadership had obvious implications for her own political future. Now she would have to learn to adjust her expectations.

She had been and remained a close and trusted friend of Kinnock's. She was part of his entourage and she had made herself indispensable as a link between him and the membership of the Parliamentary Labour Party. 'She was genuinely part of the process of trying to get support for what Neil was doing with the party,' said a member of his team.[1] While the inevitable election of John Smith as successor to Kinnock would prove a setback for Mo, the work she had done and the networks she had established in her first parliament nevertheless proved useful.

She had made friends early on with another MP of her generation, Adam Ingram, who was elected for East Kilbride in 1987 and who was Kinnock's Parliamentary Private Secretary from 1988 until Kinnock's resignation as party leader. The unpaid post of PPS is most usually explained as that of a minister's parliamentary bag carrier. An MP appointed to this role is expected to act as the political eyes, ears and nose of the minister or, in this case, the Leader of the Opposition. Adam Ingram therefore occupied a significant role within the PLP and in alliance with Mo contributed to the restructuring of Westminster's party Left: what might be termed, amid the burgeoning party organisations, the 'Sane' group of Labour MPs. 'She and Adam Ingram got on very well,' said the same Kinnock staffer. 'They were an important political element in the development of the neo-Tribunite forces in the PLP.'

They had a number of areas of mutual interest, both political and personal. Mo had been a Trade and Industry spokeswoman and Ingram was a whip until 1992, then became a member of the Trade and Industry Select Committee. It helped that they decided also to share research assistants for a time, employing a succession of people who would work for them both – a common practice that enables

MPs to eke out their resources by each paying half of a salary. Mo had by now set up the Marjorie Mowlam Research Fund to channel individual donations for research purposes and she received contributions from the Rowntree Foundation and from union sources. Nigel Warner, who has remained on Mo's staff since then, was the last of these shared assistants, performing this dual role until 1993 when Ingram was appointed to the Opposition Front Bench. Their friendship also linked Mo to a wider circle of younger Scottish MPs, including Henry McLeish, Calum MacDonald, Lewis Moonie, Alistair Darling, who were all also elected in 1987 and shared a common interest and view of politics and the future of the Labour Party. This was helpful for Mo, too. She has always been widely credited as a highly efficient political networker and she was establishing her reputation in this respect at this time. It was not without a degree of self-interest: she was also in the running for the Shadow Cabinet.

'She's a great networker,' said one of her friends. 'She'll phone people; get people on side; make them offers they can't refuse – she's great at motivating people for the common cause.' Another friend, praising the application of her networking skills on political canvassing, described her as 'a serious political bean counter'. The same man added: 'She was very likeable. I don't think anybody should underestimate that in politics.' He was right. She was likeable – and widely liked – because she was straightforward, friendly and funny.

She was even liked and appreciated by members of the Conservative Party, including her own 'pair'[2], a rising star in the Government named Michael Portillo.[3] He found her good company, co-operative and straightforward. As a minister with a lot of other commitments, he was dependent upon her goodwill for getting away from the Commons when he wished to do so and she didn't mess around by keeping him unnecessarily when the Labour Opposition wasn't planning to spring an unexpected late-night vote. 'Sometimes she would just do it with a nod and a wink and sometimes she'd just walk up to me in the lobby and say 'Good night' – and I'd know I didn't need to stay,' he said.[4] It was a great advantage for any minister to have an obliging pair and he greatly appreciated it.

'She was bright and easy and rather original,' he recalled. 'She was a new sort of MP – very informal, relaxed, very happy to talk to the other side. She had an irreverent, cheeky manner about her which was very attractive. We got on fine. I don't remember that we discussed substantial matters of policy but we used to tease each other a bit about what was going on in the other's party.' He called her a 'good-humoured Gatling gun' once. She attended his fortieth birthday party at the Spanish Club in 1993, the same night Norman Lamont, who was also present, was to mark by later resigning as Chancellor of the Exchequer. Portillo was particularly impressed when, early on in Mo's parliamentary life, she lost a front tooth and yet persevered undaunted on a Commons' committee on which they were both doing business. Mo has a number of false, or crowned teeth and she had a problem. 'Anybody else – a man or a woman – would have made their excuses for a couple of days. She just pressed on. It was gutsy and it was unusual.' It was typical Mo, a modern Mrs Doasyouwouldbedoneby, someone who was prepared to do what was necessary, whenever required, without needing to give any more thought to implications.

When asked in 1992 how she relaxed, she replied with typical *élan*: 'I lie back and think of other people climbing Munros'.[5] Years later people still quoted her approvingly, but it was actually an unexpectedly tricky question for her, as she is not very good at relaxing. In *Who's Who* she cites travelling, swimming and jigsaws as her hobbies. More revealingly, she once disclosed: 'I do nothing to relax, which is my biggest handicap in life. I've no outlet. Before I got in here I lived a reasonably normal life and went to the pub and played darts and walked and had a reasonably balanced existence. But since election it's unbalanced and addictive and counter-productive in the end.'[6]

In that summer of 1992, in addition to winning friends with her wit, she also displayed her developing skills as a parliamentary political operator. One such instance concerned the decriminalisation of cannabis. In a little-noticed incident she revealed a degree of the political understanding that has served her so well over the years. She had agreed to sign a petition calling for the use of cannabis to be legalised, which was to be published as a full-page advertisement in *The Times*. However, the legal use of soft drugs is a controversial issue and she clearly realised that a great many older members of the PLP might not share such a liberal view and she pulled out. Like almost anyone of her age, Mo had smoked marijuana when she was at college. It was not in any way a remarkable thing to have done for someone who grew up in the 1960s and perhaps for that reason signing the advertisement did not initially seem of much moment, let alone unwise. The advertisement was published exactly twenty-five years after a similar appeal on the pages of the same newspaper, famously organised after the arrest of Mick Jagger for possession of pep pills, which had led to the legendary *Times* editorial headed 'Who Breaks a Butterfly On A Wheel?'.

When the advertisement – organised by Release, an organisation founded to give advice on drugs and on the law – appeared[7] it contained 198 names of public figures who were prepared to be identified with this cause. The name of Marjorie Mowlam MP was not among them. 'I think she thought better of it in the end,' said Caroline Coon, the founder of Release. 'She did this very regretfully and we have her blessings.' Ms Coon, who herself always had an acute political sense, then added, 'I guess she wants to be in the Shadow Cabinet.'

Even so, Mo didn't make any secret of her experimentation with cannabis in later interviews after she had become famous and thus a subject for close examination by Fleet Street's acerbic profile writers. She had smoked joints at Durham, she readily acknowledged, but she didn't like it. 'It didn't strike me as a useful use of my time,' she said.[8] She was clearly being perfectly open and honest – and as she also explained later she was 'much more into sport so that's what I stuck to'[9] She knew the score, though, and she was smart enough when questioned by a *Daily Telegraph* interviewer before the 1997 election to dodge a question about whether she was one of the rock 'n' roll generation who smoked dope. 'No, not in this article today, I'm not. No, no, no, not for *Telegraph* readers,' she said. 'I am a sixties child in other ways. I travelled around. I lived.'[10] She herself is undoubtedly extremely careful not to be associated personally in any way with illegality, but among her friends are people who move in circles where marijuana is certainly smoked and cocaine snorted.

Having previously been so candid, it must then have come as something of a surprise in January 2000 when she was faced with a front-page headline in a broadsheet Sunday newspaper over a story claiming that she was under pressure 'to come clean about whether she has ever smoked cannabis.'[11] By this time she was the Cabinet Office minister with a portfolio including responsibility for the Labour Government's campaign against drugs, so her personal involvement was relevant. But it was scarcely front-page news, particularly as the most damning fact the report was able to produce was that her old friend in Iowa, Claudia Beyer, remembered once seeing Mo at a party with a joint in her hand, although she said: 'I didn't see it touch her lips.'

Mo dealt with this in a straightforward fashion by giving a television interview pointing out that she had never made any secret of being 'a child of the sixties' and that she had already said that she had tried marijuana but was not a part of the drugs culture. 'I said I tried marijuana, didn't like it particularly and, unlike President Clinton, I did inhale,' she said.[12] This was not enough to satisfy the newspapers and although no one appeared to take seriously the suggestion that her 'admission' put her Cabinet job under question, the incident did necessarily give rise to a raft of articles and comment and headlines. It coincided with the problems Mo encountered when she returned to Britain from Belfast, but it was actually more an example of the arbitrary nature of the trade of journalism than an orchestrated attempt to damage her position as a minister.

The origin of the story was not, as ascribed by at least one newspaper, as 'someone who was with her at Iowa who went to a newspaper and said that she saw her handling drugs at a party'.[13] Rather, after Mo had been given responsibility for the drugs issue on her return from Northern Ireland, someone in the *Daily Mail* hierarchy thought it worth attempting to find out if there were any witnesses to her having dabbled with soft drugs as a student. The reporter assigned to the story spent a great deal of time and effort tracing her student past, but failed to find anything more damning than Dr Beyer's recollection, and so the *Daily Mail* apparently decided that the story was not worth publishing. But then the reporter in question moved to the *Sunday Telegraph* where a different view was taken. It may not have been much of a story, but it was interesting and it set a few hares running when it was published.

But Mo was not new to the see-saw life of a politician. Back in 1992 Neil Kinnock's resignation marked a setback to a career that was until then straightforward and promising. According to her friend the actor Michael Cashman, who became a Labour Member of the European Parliament in the 2000 elections, she tried to dissuade Kinnock from going. 'She was among a few of us who lobbied Neil really hard not to resign as leader,' he said. 'Mo and I were among a small group who really wanted him to stay on, but he was adamant.'[14] He would not have been receptive to such entreaties. Although he had seen it coming, Kinnock was psychologically destroyed by the 1992 defeat. He had found the previous winter extremely difficult and had already contemplated standing down some time before the election campaign, to allow the party to fight it with a new leader already in place. His was a personal tragedy: he had done so much to shake up and revivify the party and yet in the end it was his leadership and his own personality that was widely identified as the source of the party's ignominious defeat. When he was first elected Labour leader in 1983, cheerfully accepting the dreadful inheritance of that time, he had told one well-wishing friend: 'If we don't win the next election it won't be my fault.' And it wasn't. But a great deal had changed by 1992 and given the political circumstances, it was not surprising that Kinnock took the rejection by the electorate as a matter of utter personal humiliation. Nothing would have persuaded him to stay. He was not even prepared to remain in office until the autumn in order to allow the election of his successor to proceed in an orderly fashion.[15]

But the circumstances of Kinnock's resignation guaranteed John Smith a shoo-in. And whatever her approaches to Kinnock, Mo had already allied herself with the Smith campaign in April, very shortly after the loss of the election and she later voted for the winning team of Smith with Margaret Beckett as his deputy. It would in fact have been unusual if she had not voted in this fashion: the outcome of the election was a foregone conclusion and Smith easily saw off his only challenger, Bryan Gould, defeating him by a massive majority. Yet in typical fashion, she had also let Gould know that it wasn't personal. They had worked together in 1989 when she was his deputy as campaign co-ordinator for that year's European elections and he recalled her as a good colleague and, in his words, 'a nice person'.

He was also impressed with her approach to the differences that naturally arise in politics, what Neil Kinnock among many others has described as her 'inclusive' qualities. Gould explained: 'There are some politicians who are very aware of the boundaries of what they think and what somebody else thinks. They will establish what you think and if you're not where they are, they will say: "Oh well, we obviously disagree on this, or on that . . ." But there are others who look always for the common ground, who say: "We agree on this, so maybe we agree on other things as well." Mo always struck me as one of those politicians who reach out to people, try to work with them and find common ground.'

He was particularly touched by how she acted in the 1992 leadership campaign. He remembers: 'We were all doing head counts as to who was going to vote for whom. She decided that she would vote for John Smith rather than me but sent a message via my researcher saying: "I'm going to vote for John but I still think you're pretty good." It was an illustration that she didn't make enemies easily.'[16] Was it also calculating? Although Smith was the obvious winner, Gould was not at that stage written out of the future script. It is more likely that it was just Mo being Mo, as usual recognising that little is lost by being generous, that what goes around comes around.

When the time came to dish out the jobs, however, it didn't come round for her this time. John Smith did not choose to promote her. After her valiant efforts in the City of London – Lunching for Labour or the Spring Roll Offensive as it was dubbed – in what had been a very successful, high-profile, economic posting, she would have been justified in expecting at least an equivalent Shadow responsibility. What she was given was the post of spokeswoman on Women coupled with the Citizens' Charter, a portfolio which involved covering one area of policy that did not even merit a ministry and another that was widely derided as a public relations initiative and a political nonsense.

Little wonder then that she emerged from the Leader's office in 'floods of tears' after learning of her appointment. She had been in there a long time and other candidates for Shadow office were banked up, waiting to learn their fate from John Smith. Mo's tears are not often witnessed but they were on this occasion.[17] She must have protested vigorously, but it was to no avail. After the tears came anger. She was furious – as she made plain later when she telephoned her personal assistant, Kath Taylor, in Redcar. 'The - - - - - have given me Women!' she wailed.[18] Interestingly she used the plural – no doubt because she had little hesitation in blaming not only Smith but also Gordon Brown. Her adversary was now safely installed as the new Shadow Chancellor and she was sure he had persuaded John Smith that she should not be given an important job because she posed too much of a threat to him.

She may well have been partly right. Gordon Brown was determined to do what he could to keep her from another economic post or even a post with economic implications, like a spending department. 'Gordon wouldn't let her within 100 miles of any economic portfolio,' said one close observer. 'She was never going to get any job that Gordon Brown didn't want her to have,' said a Shadow Cabinet colleague. 'Gordon's not comfortable with women around him – and certainly not if they challenge him,' said another minister by way of explanation.

That was a serious enough disadvantage, but John Smith, meanwhile, was said to have adopted a hands-off approach, distancing himself from any of this sort of in-fighting. Mo now found herself without a powerful friend at the top of the party. According to another Shadow Cabinet observer there was a further aspect to her relationship with John Smith that would prove difficult for her: the new Leader had a different view of society – and a woman's place within it – to that held by Mo. This person said: 'John was quite old-fashioned about women. Part of the colour of his politics was about respectability. He was a Scottish barrister with a wife and nice daughters and Mo was way off that spectrum. She didn't behave in the manner he felt women should behave – particularly on the sex side of things, casual sex, that sort of thing which she was very often about. He wasn't approving. That's not the way people like John Smith lead their lives. He found her a bit frightening and threatening.'[19]

Despite this view, there is plenty of evidence that John Smith liked Mo personally, as he liked anyone who proved themselves to be competent and hard-working. It was her bad luck that one reason he chose her for the Women's job was precisely because she wasn't an all-guns-blazing feminist, and he believed therefore that she would be a far better advocate, being demonstrably more reasonable and pragmatic than someone who was more aggressively committed. That point aside, Smith would of course have been influenced by Brown's insistence on a distance between him and his former junior spokeswoman.

Mo had lots of chums in the PLP, particularly chums who were chaps, but they were not in a position to help her here. And she wasn't going to get much support for being side-lined from women colleagues in the parliamentary party. For one thing, the Women's post was *meant* to be an important responsibility; after all, the party had been committed to the establishment of a Ministry for Women. The trouble was that there were other priorities in party politics and even committed feminists in the party knew that the issue did not have the political importance they felt it deserved. Besides that, although Mo has always described herself as a Socialist and a feminist, she was not in a position to claim sisterly support, since she had not specifically identified herself with the feminist wing of the party. She was much more involved with her men friends in the mainstream and they were not too keen on what *Private Eye* derisively described as the 'wimmin's' issue either. Furthermore, the stance that Mo took on positive discrimination in the party's internal elections, which was a hot political issue, was predictably skilful, but while she boosted her own position in consequence, she failed to endear herself to her assertive feminist colleagues such as Harriet Harman.

Under a change of roles in 1989 the number of MPs directly elected to the Shadow Cabinet by members of the PLP had been increased by three and at least three votes were required to be cast for women candidates to validate the ballot paper. This was designed to ensure that there was a respectable proportion of women in the party's front ranks. It also, intentionally, enhanced the chances of any woman candidate and when Mo first stood for the Shadow Cabinet in 1992 she was elected, tying for sixth place with Harriet Harman and Chris Smith, all elected for the first time and all with 135 votes. Both of the others had sat throughout the previous Parliament, so it was a very respectable result for someone who had only been in Parliament for five years. She and David Blunkett were the only two of the 1987 intake to make the grade, and he, too, had something of an advantage, because of his prior membership of the party's National Executive. There were now five women members of the Shadow Cabinet – four of them elected, plus Margaret Beckett who was automatically included as deputy Leader. It looked good for the party to put forward such an image, particularly in contrast to the paucity of women in the

Conservative Cabinet, and so building on this advantage the party decided to increase the number of dedicated women's votes to four the following year. That proved a step too far for many of the politically unreconstructed misogynists of the PLP.

As the journalist Andy McSmith described it: 'This produced a reaction of the tearoom, and a highly effective campaign of revenge against the women most publicly associated with calls for positive discrimination. Since they had to vote for four women, a large number of MPs deliberately "dumped" their votes on women candidates with no real hope of getting on.'[20] Mo Mowlam was identified as 'sceptical or hostile towards positive discrimination', according to McSmith, and thus likely to benefit. Bryan Gould recalled: 'I'd never seen that she was ambitious. At the time there was quite a lot of agitation about positive discrimination in the Shadow Cabinet elections and it was people like Harriet Harman who were making all the running on that. Mo was one of the most obvious beneficiaries of voting for women but she was seen as being in the second rank. She didn't seem so much focused on it.'[21]

She wasn't and she consequently did extremely well in 1993, increasing her vote, moving up to fifth place overall and securing the most votes of any of the women elected in what is, effectively, a popularity poll among MPs. Harriet Harman lost her seat and while John Smith still kept her on in the Front Bench team, it was obvious to others that Hatty and Mo were not the best friends on the river bank.

There was a distinct feeling among some of her women colleagues that Mo had used this situation to secure her own advantage, that she paraded her matey relationships with the lads to good effect for her personal position but not to defend the principle of positive discrimination, still less to defend her sisters. One said: 'She benefited from the positive action proposals but would never come into conflict with the lads by speaking up for it. Her position was: "Vote for me because I'm a lad and I don't agree with all this positive action stuff." She'd hang around at the bar and do things with the men that made her a male-friendly option to the feminists.'[22] She was also held to have treated her post as spokeswoman on Women's Issues with a complete lack of interest, which upset some colleagues who thought her behaviour inappropriate. The same woman critic said: 'She made it clear that she regarded the job with contempt. But it is important to stand up for women. If you're given that job – even if you don't want it – you owe it to women in the country to make it seem as if you're interested. To her it was demotion, not worthy of her.'

Obviously there was a degree of needle involved here. Mo did not make much of a splash in this post – few noticed her contribution, such as it was; fewer still remembered later that she had even occupied the post. She did visit the House of Commons rifle range to inspect it as a potential site for a possible creche in the Palace of Westminster but that is almost the only recorded public evidence of any activity on her part during the year or so she would remain there. She gave an interview to the *Daily Mail* in August after her appointment, earning herself a full-page slab of useful publicity, but there is scarcely a word devoted to her aspirations for her new position.[23] She did tell Lynda Lee-Potter that when she got the job her mother was 'ecstatic' and 'was just in tears with happiness', but given that Mo herself had been in tears of disappointment, it seems likely that her mother's emotion was engendered rather by her daughter's recent election to the Shadow Cabinet than by her new Front Bench responsibility. She alluded to her own inclusion on the list for selection as the candidate for Redcar as being a result of Labour's policy for putting a woman on every shortlist. 'I went along more as a favour to the party than any belief that I would get chosen,' she said, managing at the same time both to understate somewhat her approach to her own selection and any enthusiasm she may have felt for getting more women into the House of Commons.

In 1993 she did support positive discrimination in favour of women in the selection of Labour candidates – a controversial policy which was subsequently challenged in the courts and judged illegal, but which still resulted in a dramatic increase in the number of women fighting winnable seats in 1997. Mo was in fact very much in favour of getting more women into the Commons, but she had a strongly egalitarian view. Her main interest was getting more Labour MPs of either sex into the Commons.

She has always believed very strongly in individual rights: having been, for example, a strong defender of the case for equal rights for gays and lesbians. 'Her commitment to that is as strong as her commitment to anything else,' said Michael Cashman, who with his partner Paul Cottingham, a member of the Labour Party staff with responsibilities for fund-raising, is among Mo and Jon Norton's intimate friends. 'There are certain people within the Labour Party who believe in equality for some – that's not socialism. If you're a socialist you believe in equality not for some, but for everybody. That's my guiding principle and certainly one that Mo shares.'[24] She has a number of gay people in her circle of friends. Her fellow Cabinet colleague Chris Smith has been a friend for years. They met when she was elected and their relationship developed when she was in the Shadow City job and Chris Smith was a junior spokesman at the Treasury. It was fuelled by a mutual dislike of Gordon Brown. Later Mo would stand up for her friend when he was Social Security spokesman against Brown as Shadow Chancellor in a long-running bitter Shadow Cabinet fight about excluding 18-year-olds from Child Benefit. During their years in Cleveland Road in Islington, she and Jon lived near Chris Smith and his partner and they socialised as a foursome. Mo and Chris speak weekly on the telephone.

Mo has been outspoken – and brave – in supporting the case for lowering the age of consent for homosexual men. In 1994 when the first attempt was made to introduce equality and reduce the age of consent for homosexual men to 16, she was one of those to put her name to the amendment tabled in the Commons. There was a large and high-profile press conference at Westminster, which Mo attended, before the debate actually took place and it helped whip up a great deal of public interest. After the vote – in which MPs defeated the age-16 amendment, but reduced the age of consent from 21 to 18 – a large and angry crowd of gay and lesbian activists gathered outside St Stephen's, the public entrance to the Palace of Westminster. Douglas Slater, a former clerk in the House of Lords and a member of the homosexual pressure group Stonewall, recalled: 'After the vote, I went to St Stephen's and there was a riot outside. It was the night after Derek Jarman had died. I said: "Somebody has got to go out and speak to them!" And Mo said: "I will". It was a big crowd and they were howling. I remember grabbing a megaphone from one of the policemen and I held the megaphone while she made a very courageous speech.'[25] She apologised to them for the votes of those of her colleagues who had contributed to the outcome. 'There was an enormous crowd and it was pretty angry,' Angela Mason[26], an official of Stonewall who was also present, confirmed. She was very impressed with Mo's courage.

Mo was not fazed. She had done almost exactly this before all those years ago in Newcastle-upon-Tyne when she confronted the hundreds of angry students who had failed to gain access to the E.P. Thompson lecture. She didn't duck it now and that straightforward approach made a strong impression on those present. In consequence she became a bit of a heroine with the gay and lesbian community. Four years later, in 1998, she was made Woman of the Year by the gay newssheet, the *Pink Paper*. 'She's always had great standing in the lesbian and gay community because she's always stuck up for us,' said Angela Mason. Another of her personal friends is John Miskelly, who chairs Stonewall, and when she was Northern Ireland Secretary she found time to attend one of the organisation's equality shows in order to present an award to a gay group from Northern Ireland.

But then she has always found time, whether for causes in which she believes or to help friends. She is the walking exemplar of the thesis that anybody who wants something done should ask a busy woman. She is always prepared to pitch up at a primary school for a pal's child, or to talk to someone's class of university students, or to help with a political campaign. While her arrangements have always been somewhat chaotic – until she had police protection and was escorted everywhere she was always late for meetings or meals with friends –

fellow MPs knew that she was someone who could usually be counted upon to stand in if another speaker cancelled. She astonishes her friends and acquaintances by the extent to which she will seek to look after their needs, often at the expense of her own time and privacy. She packs her own programme and uses time to the maximum effect: when Michael Cashman was selected as a European candidate in 1998 for the Midlands, she said to him: 'Right, I'm doing a whole day in Coventry on 13 November. I want you to be my guest and accompany me.' She took him with her in her car everywhere she went, introduced him to everybody, said to them in effect: "This chap's all right" and then took him back to her sister Jean's, and put him up for the night on the sitting-room sofa.[27] Because she was personal friends with her former protection officer Adam Richardson, she startled the local populace in West London when she suddenly bowled up at his children's school pantomime in Chiswick, signing autographs and glad-handing her way around the school hall.

'Why does she bother?' a woman who has known her for many years asked rhetorically: 'because somehow, somebody might be of use.' This observation wasn't meant critically, but points to Mo's desperate insecurity which is assuaged by feeling that she is useful to other people. 'She's not a complete person,' said a colleague who knows her better than most. 'There's something missing there.' Sometimes it looks as if she lives life vicariously, as if she is more concerned about other people's personal lives than experiencing her own. She shares her time with others, but not her deep feelings. She clams up about her own problems and her inability to confide makes it difficult in turn for those who regard themselves as close friends. One such political friend described how during a particularly tricky spell in her time in Northern Ireland 'I would occasionally see her and ask how things were and she'd say: "Oh it's hell" but she'd know that she was not telling me anything.' This friend went on: 'At that time she was back into asking questions and not giving anything herself – that's the way she normally behaves in a political situation. It means that she still can't trust you enough to discuss what has gone on with you.'

Another friend said almost exactly the same: 'I'm not sure that she doesn't in a sense try to conceal feelings and fears too much and that's what puts her sometimes under a lot of stress.' This woman pointed out that when Mo became ill in 1997 she handled it with immense courage in public. 'In terms of personal relationships it was different – and it was exactly the same when her mother died – she wouldn't talk about it or address it.' And when this friend tried to persuade Mo to unburden herself, all she would say was: 'I don't want to talk about it. It upsets me too much,' and change the conversation.

But she is never too busy to drop somebody a hand-written note in a personal crisis. If a friend at Westminster is ill or suffers a bereavement, the sympathetic line from Mo will be among the very first to arrive. Even to those people with whom she doesn't always see eye-to eye, she will hold out the hand of human sympathy. When Peter Mandelson was obliged to resign from the Cabinet just before Christmas 1998 over his home loan, Mo Mowlam was one of the three of his ministerial colleagues who was immediately in touch to express condolences (the other two were Frank Dobson and David Blunkett, followed shortly afterwards by Jack Straw). Then she took him for a highly visible breakfast in the Savoy Hotel to demonstrate her personal support.

Her kindness is not always so public. After she became a Cabinet Minister she met the proprietor of a Mexican bar and restaurant in West London through a neighbourhood connection with Adam Richardson. This man, John Wasilko, had also suffered from a brain tumour and Mo befriended him. His restaurant is not far off the main route from central London to Heathrow airport and every so often on her way to catch a plane she would drop by and have a margherita with him. 'I love her,' said John Wasilko. 'She's the most amazing woman I've ever met.'[28] He recognises they're not intimate friends, but they're pals all the same and in between her visits they will talk on the telephone from time to time. She takes his calls. He calls her 'Mo-Mo' and one year he gave her some bottles of tequila and margherita mix for her birthday. She rang the next day to thank him for the headache she had in consequence.

Another woman who knows her well, away from politics, observes: 'Her charm should not, I feel, be interpreted by anybody into thinking she's a soft touch. There's a core of steel and I think she could be very ruthless if it was required – and in a sense quite self-consciously so. It may be because of the lousy background? You know – you have to either sink or swim and while swimming you may have to flag down a lifeboat which is on the way past.' According to this source, part of her strength is that she would do 'whatever it takes' in any set of circumstances to achieve her desired end. 'She is tougher than any man if required.'[29]

She was prepared to do whatever it took to get Labour elected. But she also wanted the Labour Party to help itself. 'We've got to respond to people's aspirations,' she said in her 1992 interview with Lynda Lee-Potter. 'The aspirations that the Labour Party had in the forties and fifties about comprehensive education meant that I was able to change my life. In the nineties I don't think we do respond to people's aspirations very much.'[30] Given that the wounds of the recent election were still, really, unbound, she was clearly correct about the last point, a view that she held strongly. But there is another point to quoting this comment and that is that again, as is often the case, what she said reflected a picture of her own life which was slightly askance from the reality.

Not much. The mirror just wobbles a bit when she holds it up. It wasn't entirely accurate to cast herself as a comprehensive girl-made-good as a consequence of her education; after all, she was someone who had passed the Eleven Plus and gone to Chiswick Girls' Grammar, where presumably she would have remained had her father not been moved when she had only just started secondary school. By the same token she has often referred to her father as 'a Post Office worker' and has mentioned him working in the sorting office – which he must doubtless have done at some point in his progress through the bureaucracy he joined as a boy on a bike. Nevertheless, however unintentional it may be, she gives the wrong impression by calling him a Post Office worker when his last job in the organisation was as the Assistant Head Postmaster for the city of Coventry. It is perhaps part of the problem of being a chameleon, of trying always to be someone who can fit in with the social circumstances whatever they may be.

Although she didn't try very hard to fit in with being Shadow minister for women's issues, she nevertheless makes the most of it in her official biographical material giving the appointment more substance than it perhaps deserved with an airy reference to 'Shadowing the newly created Office for Public Service and Science'. She also entitled herself at one stage, in July 1993, as the Shadow Minister for Citizens' Rights, which had a good ring to it. Even though this was something that she believed in, she had known immediately that she was saddled with what she regarded as effectively a non-job and the reality was that there wasn't much to do. She therefore put the time to very good use by working on her public image: travelling around the country, visiting constituencies on 'citizens' charter business' – which could mean whatever she wanted it to mean – and back at base in Westminster stoking up support for her own position in the parliamentary party.

Mark Fisher, who had been the Arts spokesman for the previous six years, was her junior spokesman and they got on very well together. 'It wasn't much of a brief for Mo. There wasn't much for her to do,' he confirmed. 'Most of Mo's work that year was making sure she got back on to the Shadow Cabinet. She took it incredibly seriously. It was really important how many votes she got and she put a huge amount of thought into it and spent time planning it – particularly that first year it was a big factor in her life. She had seen other people get on the Shadow Cabinet and then slip off. She hadn't got on as a result of a piece of luck and having got there, she wasn't going to slide off. Underneath all that joking and fooling she's a very serious person.'[31]

They became good friends. Fisher was going through a tricky period in his personal life and Mo was swiftly established as his confidante. She was a wonderful listener, genuinely interested and concerned in what was going on and ready to offer sympathy and help. He liked her very much and appreciated the way in which she became involved. 'She loves people confiding in her, she likes being involved,' he said. 'Those are her huge strengths: she can make you feel like a close friend and get very involved in your life terribly quickly.' He also remarked that she was not judgmental, she didn't take a high moral stand, as others would.

This was an aspect of her character that Harriet Harman would later come to appreciate when she ran into a storm of criticism in 1995 over her choice of secondary school for her children. Mo was the only prominent member of the party who was prepared to go on television and defend an overwhelmingly unpopular political decision. 'Harriet did what she thought was best for her boys,' Mo said on *Newsnight*. It was what she believed; she didn't judge other people for what they decided to do in areas of their lives that were nothing to do with politics. However, she did get fed up at being asked to do things that others would refuse. It was Tony Blair who asked her on that occasion to go on television and expose herself to a grilling by Jeremy Paxman. According to a colleague, she told Blair, 'Yes, I will do this for you – but Harriet would never do it for me.'[32]

The year passed, a quiet one professionally for Mo, although as she was in the early months of her relationship with Jon Norton there was plenty going on in her life. She exuded happiness. Jon seemed to give her ballast to balance her life in a way she had previously lacked. He also tried to teach her to relax, which she said made her a better politician.[33] He was a good cook – not altogether good news from the point of view of her weight – and it was a relief to have someone to go to home to, someone who believed in her. There had been big, empty, unacknowledged wastelands of loneliness in her life and, most recently, the aftermath of her love affair with Colin Hughes had not been easy. Several of her friends speak of the emptiness there had previously been at the centre of her life, relieved only occasionally by a boyfriend who would usually be of slight importance. Her own deep reserve, which most people didn't recognise, meant that she was a woman with hundreds of friends but no real intimates. Now at last she had a man who mattered to her.

Jon was someone to travel with, too. She loved to travel and that first summer they spent together they went to Greece for a holiday; afterwards they went abroad as often as they could. Mo was always an adventurous traveller: she had been to South America with her boyfriend Dan Sammons just before she left the US; once, in 1982, she planned a five-month sabbatical in Turkey – although that didn't come off because her mother was ill; she took her mother to China in the Easter holidays in 1985, and she had travelled often with friends.

An apparently successful holiday, early in her parliamentary life, was with Peter Mandelson. They had become friends through the early years in the Kinnock office and were good chums for a spell. Mandelson recognised her as someone who was going places – politically, that is. 'It's more interesting that Peter went on holiday with *her* than that she went on holiday with Peter,' said one man who is particularly good at reading the runes. They went to Spain and stayed in paradors, sharing lots of merriment. Their friendship survived the holiday, but thereafter not for very long at Westminster. There seemed to be no very specific reason why they later ceased to be friends, but their relationship certainly fell away shortly after he was elected in 1992 as the Labour MP for Hartlepool, very close to her own constituency. Initially he would come and visit her frequently when she was at home in Redcar at the weekend. It didn't last. The visits soon stopped.

'Once he got in to the Commons, Peter was just busy totally undermining her in the North,' said someone else who watched all this. 'He was siding with everybody against her and being public about it. Peter is very good at being friends with people and then stabbing them in the back – Gordon [Brown] for example; he was friends with Gordon a lot longer than he was friends with Mo.' One of Mo's friends thought it was about political rivalry: Mandelson knew that Mo Mowlam has some indefinable quality and it was outside his control. Other prominent members of the party were not in the least surprised: 'Everybody falls out with Peter,' one said. 'She was hostile to Peter because anyone who has any dealings with Peter becomes hostile to Peter.' Another said it was because he suddenly became very self-important: 'He started inhaling all the assumptions of his importance.' Yet another attributed it to his innate Machiavellian instincts. 'She doesn't trust him at all,' this person said. Nor, it seemed, he her: 'Peter said to me that she was "unreliable" which is quite a damning phrase in Peter's lexicon,' said a friend of his.

There were two definable political reasons for disagreement. One was proportional representation, which Mo Mowlam supported. One year at the Labour conference she agreed to speak at a meeting in favour of PR and, according to her assistant Kath Taylor, there was 'a major bust-up' between Mandelson and Mo during the festivities at Northern Night, the area party for MPs and activists. 'He said it was politically wrong for her to have done it,' Kath Taylor reported.[34]

A more domestic dispute was the establishment of unitary authorities in local government. Mandelson had used his maiden speech to support the claim of the local authority in his constituency of Hartlepool to be restored to the independent status it had lost years earlier when it was merged with the new county of Cleveland. There was now a proposal to abolish Cleveland County Council and he and Mo were on opposing sides. It could scarcely have been otherwise as her local party was dominated by county councillors, fighting to avoid abolition, and his by district councillors, seeking autonomy. When Mo Mowlam used an adjournment debate in the early summer of 1993 to defend the case for Cleveland, she found herself interrupted by Mandelson an astonishing ten times in a couple of minutes as he sought unsuccessfully to oblige her to give way. An atmosphere of considerable bitterness lay behind the exchanges recorded in Hansard.[35]

The bad feeling between them would increase as the years passed. She said once that whenever she sat behind a bowl of red roses on a party platform – an innovation introduced by Mandelson – she longed to hurl them into the crowd.[36] Even in the summer of 1998 before her position in Northern Ireland had been seriously undermined and she was still riding high as Secretary of State, her old friend from Durham, Chris Pye, witnessed an unforgettable exchange between them. They were all at a party given by Waheed Alli, the multi-millionaire television tycoon and Labour peer, at his home in Sussex. Pye and his wife and Mo and her husband were eating together when Mandelson wafted by and said: 'Hello, Mo – how's it going?' Pye said: 'It was all very jovial but he hated Mo and Mo hated him. It was obvious. There was a real sense of dislike there, false brightness hiding dislike I felt. Then he went and she said: 'Oh - - - -'[37] The insult was vulgar and offensive and heartfelt.

Another parliamentary friend with whom she went on holiday was Betty Boothroyd. This time it was a friendship that was later to prove very important and helpful to her. They had got to know each other through Commons' committees when Betty Boothroyd was one of the deputy Speakers. The impromptu holiday came about when Mo, as the Shadow City spokeswoman, was due to visit Hong Kong to discuss policy issues during a recess. Betty Boothroyd was going on holiday to Sri Lanka, one of her regular haunts, and suggested that her young friend made a stop-over. 'She turned up and it was absolutely super. I adored spending time with her there, showing her round, meeting my friends there – all of whom loved her. I regarded her as the younger sister that I'd never had,' Betty Boothroyd said.[38] 'I do remember her arriving without a swimsuit – for a place like that! She was quite slim and could buy them on the spot so we got her a wonderful bikini in which she looked gorgeous. There wasn't a quarter of a yard of material in that. She looked lovely!'

Mo's ability to arrive for a holiday in the sun without a bathing costume was entirely predictable. 'Fundamentally she appeared to suffer from a total lack of organisation,' said one of her friends. 'She had the scruffiest desk in Westminster, her handbag was a mess, her outward appearance – anything physical to do with her in those days was a complete shambles. But on the important things, the things that mattered, on that she was completely organised, there was nothing dizzy or left to chance. She knew who to sit with in the Smoking Room. She planned constituency visits with an eye on keeping in with the colleagues. On the one hand she was physically shambolic and chaotic; on the other, in her mind, she was organised and effective and she knew exactly what she was doing with her life and her career.'

By this means she managed to construct an interesting and complicated set of alliances within the party, people on whose votes she could count for election to the Shadow Cabinet. It included some women MPs, some MPs from the North-east where her own seat was located, some from Scotland via her friendship with Adam Ingram, and a sprinkling from people who just liked and admired her. And it paid off at Westminster in the autumn of 1993 when she increased her vote and her position in the annual political beauty contest. She got 156 votes, just four fewer than Gordon Brown in fourth place and ahead of Tony Blair who was sixth (although the vote was of course distorted to an extent by the requirement to vote for a minimum of four women). She also got a move: John Smith gave her responsibility for shadowing what was then termed the Department of National Heritage.[39]

It was once again not a job that she, or anyone else, would regard as mainstream. She knew little about the policy issues involved as she admitted frankly in private. 'Right, I know absolutely nothing about this. Tell me about it,' she said to one of her friends who had some expertise in the field. She also contacted her friend Michael Cashman to talk through some of the issues. She wasn't particularly interested in the subjects, but it was something into which she could get stuck in. The brief covered the arts, broadcasting and the press, the new national lottery, museums and galleries, libraries, sport, leisure and tourism. Her job, as in her previous City portfolio, was to clear the decks of all

Labour's old policy baggage. It was much more of a real job than she had previously had and she readily took it on, but as Cashman said: 'It didn't challenge her. She's a doer and there's very little to fix or do as an Opposition politician.'

The Department had been established after the 1992 election when David Mellor, who became the first Secretary of State, managed to persuade John Major to create a new ministry with a Cabinet seat, conveniently bringing together a number of topics in which he happened to have a personal interest. Bryan Gould was appointed as the Shadow spokesman by John Smith – a serious demotion for him which led him to resign from the Shadow Cabinet later in 1992 and subsequently to leave British politics. He was replaced briefly by Ann Clwyd and Mo took over from her. There had not therefore been much of an opportunity for anybody to establish a distinctly Labour approach to an area of policy which contained a number of potentially controversial and sensitive aspects – not least the party's portrayal in the press.

She had three junior spokesmen: Mark Fisher, who moved with her and who was once again the Arts spokesman; Robin Corbett, who specialised in the Media; and Tom Pendry whose area was Sport. She was completely frank with them about her approach: she did not care much about any of the subjects involved, but she wanted to know enough to keep her back covered. She admitted her ignorance and laughed about the fact that she had never been to the opera. She was not bothered about the detail and did not wish to understand the intricacies of, for example, Public Lending Rights. She was anxious about how the policy of the Department would affect local authorities and she was very concerned about broadcasting and the relationship between the Labour Party and the media in general. Apart from that she was happy to let her junior spokesmen take care of the small print. 'I'll tell you what I want to do and you can do the rest,' she said.

What it came down to was that she intended to deal with matters that had a high media profile and attracted public and political attention. She recognised that her best and most effective option was to be seen to be busy, particularly after the inactivity of her previous job. She was clear and quite ruthless about this and everything worked well as long as her colleagues accepted as much. She planned to take the credit when it was due because they were a team and she was the leader of the team. If they didn't like it – well, tough.

'She was much clearer and more straightforward than a lot of other people,' said someone who watched what happened. 'Life would be a lot simpler if others adopted her approach. There aren't many people in politics who work well with teams but Mo is an absolute exception. She makes it plain that she's the team leader and is scrupulous about team meetings. She likes to know what other people have to say but always likes to have the last word – to my mind she is the model of somebody to work with in a group.'

Shortly after her appointment she told the *Guardian*[40]: 'With this new job I have to read all the arty-sporty sections I used to throw away.' And she was quite unapologetic about this statement when she gave a subsequent interview to the *Observer*.[41] 'I am not going to paint a picture of an opera-going, theatre- and orchestra-visiting individual which I am not.' After all, the transport spokesman was not expected to be a train buff, she pointed out. 'As a politician, I know what I am doing and where I am going politically and strategically.' In fact she rather enjoyed the experience of having her eyes opened about some aspects of the brief with which she hadn't previously been familiar and she quickly mastered an appropriate populist line.' For most people watching TV and playing sport is what the heritage and culture of this country is,' she said to Andrew Billen in the *Observer* article, having also made the point that when she got the chance she watched *The Bill*, *Between The Lines*, *Have I Got News for You*, *Gladiators* and *Blind Date*. And supported Middlesbrough football team.

She has the common touch, an instinctive political sense that is the antithesis of spin as this interview illustrated. She rejected pretension disclosing that she chose to spend her spare time in the same manner as much of the rest of the population. Mo has a natural gift in this regard, which is not to say that either she is unaware of it or she doesn't cultivate it. For she does now and she did then. She once said of herself: 'I can't sing, I can't dance, I can't write, I can't spell – but something I can do is get on with people.'[42] She continued to travel around the country in this job, visiting arts centres and sports facilities and television companies. She displayed these consummate personal skills and built further upon them.

Her technique as one witness observed, is simple: 'to exude masses of energy and interest and to make sure that she knows everybody's name. She will make sure, even if she only has a sandwich, to go in and thank the cook. She will make sure always to do the things that other people wouldn't do – speak to the girl on the desk, the girl at reception, the cook. When you saw what she was doing, it was almost funny. But as a result nobody ever forgot her and everybody loved her. And then, to put the final icing on it, as soon as she gets back from anywhere she will send a thank-you letter, three or four for every trip, handwritten: "Dear X, That was great. Thank you." It wasn't much, but it was enough and it was good manners – and it had a magical effect. People never forget: "D'you know? That Mo Mowlam – she wrote to me!" She just is magic. She does light things up when she goes into a place.'[43]

As well as endearing herself to the public, she made some important policy starts. She began preparing a policy on privacy law, which she wanted balanced with legislation for freedom of information – influenced by an unsuccessful attempt by Mark Fisher to introduce such legislation by means of a Private Member's Bill. She got involved in the Campaign for Press and Broadcasting Freedom and with the various issues surrounding the politics of BBC and independent television. She became involved in future broadcasting policy and impressed her junior colleague Robin Corbett, who said that she tackled the subject head-on: 'not just knobs and buttons but how to approach the new technology'.[44] She talked a great deal about 'accountability', a matter on which she appeared to impress Andrew Billen. 'For all the absence of heights in her cultural hinterland, Mowlam displays a clear mind and a frankness. They may yet arrive at a credible alternative cultural policy,' he wrote.

What was not reported, or even known, was that in the few months she occupied the post she went on a charm offensive with the country's newspapers and the big-deal media moguls. Some of them she knew already. She had, for example, become close friends with David Montgomery, the Chief Executive at the Mirror Group since 1992 and their relationship was to prove very important when she moved to the Northern Ireland office. She also got to know the former editor of the *Sun*, the infamous Kelvin MacKenzie, a man famed for despising all politicians with the single exception of Margaret Thatcher. Or so it was believed. It turned out that Mo and MacKenzie also got on well – astonishing some others, as David Seymour, the long-serving political leader writer at the *Mirror*, observed a few years later.

At the post-election Labour conference in Brighton in 1997, David Montgomery was to host a small supper upstairs at English's, the famous seafood restaurant, after the annual Mirror Group cocktail party and he wanted Mo Mowlam to be invited. Others present included *Mirror* reporter Sheree Dodd, who later worked for Mo as a press officer, Mo's research assistant at that time, Anna Healy, the Labour peer, Bernard Donoughue, and one of the group's editors, Bridget Rowe. Seymour was told at the last minute that MacKenzie – by then working for MGN – wanted to come as well and he was horrified by this. He sent an advance party to the restaurant to ensure that their guest of honour knew and was forewarned. Seymour said: 'I was really nervous and proposed to say to Mo: "Look I'm sorry but we'll do what we can to keep you apart." When I got to the restaurant there were Kelvin and Mo at the end of the table chatting away. They talked all evening. I saw her the next day and she said she had known him for years because they had been on a television programme together in Southampton once. "He's an absolute pussycat," she said. "Full of insecurity." He was like putty in her hands. And there it was: The Mo

Mowlam Pied Piper Syndrome. That's why Kelvin had wanted to come to the dinner because he was in love with Mo, like everyone else.'[45]

Connections like this were important for a revisionist Labour Party which recognised that a significant proportion of its difficulties continued to be the way in which it was publicly presented. People like David Elstein, then the Head of Programmes at BSkyB,[46] and the late David English of Associated Newspapers – people, that is, who would not normally have any connection with the Labour Party and who had spent at least the previous decade avoiding so doing – were now aware of the need to adopt a new relationship with a changing Labour Party. Besides, they were all taken by the charm of the impressive new Shadow spokeswoman. She had drinks with Rupert Murdoch – not itself a remarkable event, but this was only a relatively short time since the Labour leadership, under Neil Kinnock, had refused to give press briefings attended by employees of News International. She also set up what proved to be a very successful conference about these issues, held at the QE2 conference centre in Westminster and sponsored by various newspaper groups. However, at the time it did not get much attention because it took place during the Labour leadership election in 1994, arising from the sudden and unexpected death of John Smith, an event that would change the whole structure of the next generation of politics in Britain.

CHAPTER 11

'If I have to become po-faced then I suppose I will'

Westminster 1994–1997

The interlocking plates of policy and personality which under-pinned the whole surface of the Labour Party shifted as a result of John Smith's second and fatal heart attack on the morning of Thursday, 12 May, 1994. Nothing would ever be the same again. Tony Blair was in Aberdeen and heard of the Labour leader's tragic heart attack via a telephone call from Gordon Brown. Mo Mowlam was at Darlington railway station, changing trains for Hull, en route to the launch of a policy document. She was with her junior spokesman Mark Fisher when she heard the news and she had no doubt about what to do. She turned round and got straight back on the London train, leaving that day's engagements to Fisher. She was visibly very upset. Despite their differences she was very fond of John Smith. And she knew she needed to be in London.

She was in her office on the second floor of 1 Parliament Street, on the same corridor as Tony Blair, in next to no time. Shortly after-wards she joined her friends Charles Clarke and Adam Ingram and Kinnock's former economic adviser, John Eatwell, in Blair's outer office.[1] They gravitated towards Blair's office partly for geographical reasons, but there was also perhaps an instinctive awareness, too, of what lay ahead. There was nothing conspiratorial about their presence there. They were all shocked and wanted to talk to other colleagues. The night before had been marked by a glamorous fund-raising dinner at a Park Lane hotel attended by most of the party's leading figures. John Smith had made a speech and Ingram had been sitting drinking with him afterwards. But as this small group struggled to come to terms with what had happened, they were immediately aware of its implications. Adam Ingram, for one, said that he realised within half an hour of learning of John Smith's death that he would be supporting Tony Blair as his successor. It was a recognition that dawned gradually on many politicians and journalists throughout the day.

As Andy McSmith explained in 'Faces of Labour', there was some grumbling afterwards that Blair's candidacy was pushed forward as the choice of media commentators and that this was partly true – but it was also because he was inescapably the obvious choice.[2] In the two years since Kinnock's departure a number of Labour MPs had made common cause by gossiping idly about the chances of either Tony Blair or Gordon Brown succeeding to the leadership in circumstances then unforeseen. Blair's career had already perceptibly overtaken that of his close friend Brown, something they both wryly acknowledged without quite understanding why. As has been widely chronicled elsewhere[3] the events of the next few days before Brown's agreement not to stand for the position led to some fundamental realignments in the leading ranks of the Labour Party, notably with the fracture of the relationship between Brown and Peter Mandelson. They would also have implications for Mo Mowlam.

She wanted to be the campaign manager for Tony Blair. She identified him as the next Labour Party leader to the *Belfast Telegraph*, in 1992. Now she expected to be the person who would make that happen. According to Blair's biographer John Rentoul, she described herself to journalists that day as the person running the campaign. It was, he wrote: 'a role she had privately ascribed to herself on the day of John Smith's death.'[4] It was not to be. Decencies were nominally being observed: John Smith's funeral was held on 20 May, eight days after his death, and it was agreed by the Shadow Cabinet that a period of mourning should subsequently be allowed and no candidates announced until after the European elections on 9 June. But despite this there was, of course, an immense amount of political activity already under way. When Blair returned to London on the afternoon of Smith's death, two other Shadow ministers, Peter Kilfoyle and Jack Straw, had called at his office – in addition to Mo Mowlam and Adam Ingram – and there seems no doubt that he had already decided to run. He had hesitated over running for the deputy leadership in 1992, but he did not make that mistake again. He played his cards close to his chest, but the talk about him wavering was nothing but nonsense according to one adviser who saw him the following morning: 'I have never been in the presence of a man who was so sure of his own destiny.'[5]

Although some, like Peter Kilfoyle, were under the mistaken impression that the campaign team was not formed until after the funeral – he having received a call from Blair on 21 May asking him to join it – the bones of the team had in fact swiftly been formed practically within hours. Blair wanted Jack Straw rather than Mo to run the campaign as he immediately made clear. He wanted her to play a key part, he said to those he consulted on the morning of Friday the 13th, but he didn't want her in charge. His view was that Straw would be 'a safer pair of hands' than Mo and he also believed that he would be less likely to stir up antipathy from the Brown camp – where Mo was not only unpopular, but detested. Blair's understandable objective was to keep everybody on side, which was one reason why, when Gordon Brown's position was eventually resolved and Peter Mandelson became secretly associated with the Blair campaign, it was important for his involvement to remain undisclosed.

In reality, Mandelson was involved from the moment Blair rang him from Aberdeen to report Smith's heart attack. The two of them also conspired in an extraordinarily Machiavellian manoeuvre to try to make Gordon Brown feel better about what Blair now saw clearly was going to happen. It had always been understood between them – or Gordon Brown *thought* it had until then – that Brown as the senior and more experienced would have the first crack at contesting the leadership when an opportunity arose. Blair now knew that whatever Brown decided to do, he was going to go for it, and he could see that he would win. According to one of those involved he therefore deliberately connived with Peter Mandelson in placing at least one newspaper report to boost Brown. An unwitting agent of this was the journalist Patrick Wintour of the *Guardian*, a close observer of Labour politics and one of the journalists at Westminster trusted by Mandelson. The source reported: 'Patrick Wintour had been away on holiday until the Monday after Smith died. He immediately wrote a story suggesting that Gordon Brown was in a strong position and should not be written off as a potential candidate. It was Tony's idea: to build Gordon up so that when he was knocked down – i.e. when he realised that he couldn't win – he wouldn't feel so badly about it. Everyone understood that Blair would win, but it was still important to make Brown feel that he was great.'[6]

Straw took a day or two to decide not to run as a candidate himself – or to see how the land lay before he committed himself – while Mo was described by one of her friends as being both annoyed and irritated by what was going on. 'At first she said: 'I'm not going to have anything to do with the campaign committee. I won't even be on the committee! I'm not going to be in Jack Straw's shadow.' But in the event, she did do it. I think Tony probably won her round because he was very good at that sort of thing.[7] She spent the week busily seeing others who would be crucial.

She did, however, also demonstrate in the course of that week perhaps what Blair had meant about 'safe hands'. Two days after Smith's death, she travelled by train to campaign in the Eastleigh by-election to be held on 9 June. The Conservative minister John Patten was on the same train and in the course of a brief conversation Mo made a jesting aside about how Blair was concerned about whether there would be enough space for his family in Number 10. It was a typical Mo remark: accurate, as it eventually happened, but not meant to be taken seriously and certainly only intended as a private, good-humoured exchange between parliamentary colleagues. Patten was due to address a Conservative audience later that day, however, and repeated what she had said, expanded in such a way as to make her seem presumptuous, Blair complacent and the Labour Party insufficiently sensitive about their recently buried leader. One Labour front bencher is said to have suggested that the real question was whether Number 10 'would be big enough for Mo Mowlam's mouth.'[8] It made some political capital for the Tories for a few days – although Patten was actually taken to task by at least one of his own side for the discourtesy. But it was an episode that didn't do Mo many favours. 'It was a throwaway line, a joke, but she was labelled as the soul of indiscretion as a result,' an MP friend said. 'That became part of the "Myth of Mo" – that she was too undisciplined to be given too responsible a job.'[9]

There was a similar kerfuffle a few months later when she wrote an article for the *Mail on Sunday*. 'My Plan to Move the Queen to a "People's Palace"', it was headed, with the explanatory sub-head: 'Shadow Heritage Spokesman claims selling off two royal homes could create a modern residence.'[10] It became known and was widely ridiculed in the tabloid press as her attempt to give the Queen a Conran kitchen. In retrospect, the article was clearly unwise, perhaps because of the way in which it was worded, but it was a well-argued case for helping the royal family come to terms with modern Britain in a manner which assisted the country's heritage and was of benefit to British craftwork and the taxpayer. It was this last point that had prompted the piece in the first place. It was, arguably, set in motion by

Gordon Brown. The Shadow Chancellor had told members of the Shadow Cabinet that they had to find ways to cut their budgets. According to one of Mo's team, they were all being encouraged to think of new ways to spend such money as was at their disposal and Mo took this edict seriously. Her plans were radical but not unreasonable and demonstrated an encouraging readiness to re-think policy. It caused a great deal of fuss and as she later told the journalist Martyn Harris, with a somewhat exasperated tone, 'If you can't float ideas and have a dialogue we are in a pretty sad state.'[11]

She acknowledged in the interview with Harris that sometimes she was thought to speak too freely. In the only reference to her in his book about modernising the Labour Party, Philip Gould described Mo during this leadership campaign as 'a politician who always spoke her mind regardless of the consequences'.[12] He would presumably have expressed that opinion personally to others, like Blair, at the time, but it would have had little effect on her. Talking to Harris she said, with obvious feeling, 'I don't want to become an enclosed, two-sentence person. It *bores* me that there seems to be nothing between *Celebrity Squares* on the one hand and being a po-faced git on the other.' Later she added that she hoped she didn't have to change her style 'but on the other hand I don't want to damage my party. So if I have to become po-faced then I suppose I will.'[13]

It was light-hearted, all very jokey, but in retrospect it reads rather darkly for it was a tragic interview between two people who didn't know that they both had brain tumours. Martyn Harris died just over two years later. A year after that Mowlam was comparing herself to a children's cartoon Tellytubby and joking that she had become 'Po-Mo'.

The irony about all of this free-thinking and expression was that it was being so human that made her attractive and therefore precisely why Blair wanted her in his campaign. A member of the campaign team said: 'I often suspected that it was Mandelson who said to Tony Blair: "These are the people you must get on side" and that Mo was one of them because of her sheer popularity and her easy-going touchy-feely ways. And because she can speak to people.' A friend of hers was more explicit: 'She was quite important because she was representative of the Left within the party – not in the way that John Prescott was, but left of Tony Blair. She got on well with the working-class lads in the PLP because they saw her as one of the lads who drank, swore and told dirty jokes. That would be quite a valuable way of getting a lot of intelligence about what was going on in the party. Besides I think Tony liked her and respected her.'

Blair was very shrewd about exactly whom he needed and why. And that included being choosy about those whom he didn't need: Charles Clarke, for example. Kinnock's former head of office, had personally identified Blair as the next party leader at the time of Smith's election. He offered help to the Blair campaign with which he was strongly sympathetic, yet was excluded because he was seen as being too closely linked with his former boss Kinnock. He told friends that at one stage he was even invited to attend one event upon Blair's successful election only to have the invitation humiliatingly withdrawn. His old friend Mo Mowlam was quite offended on his behalf. She thought it was a lack of valuation of his real talents, a problem she was beginning to find out about in regard to herself. Clarke is streetwise, highly competent and a smart political operator – as was proved by his remarkably swift promotion within the Government after being elected to the Commons for the first time in 1997.[14]

Someone who was on the inside track was another friend of Mo's, Peter Kilfoyle, the MP for Liverpool Walton. He had a politically significant importance to the project because he represented the traditional northern working class within the Labour Party and yet was a politician who also recognised the need for modernisation. He was an Opposition whip until Blair became leader and thus very attuned to the political mood. He backed Blair, whom he saw as the man most likely to win the next election for the Labour Party because he would appeal to the floating voter of middle-England. Blair respected him and indeed, in 1992, apparently wanted to elicit

Kilfoyle's view about whether he should stand then as deputy leader under John Smith. A greatly puzzled Kilfoyle had been invited to dinner by Blair at the Vitello D'Oro, a restaurant behind Church House in Westminster. It was an unusual event because Blair didn't normally socialise in this fashion and didn't even know the names of nearby restaurants when he suggested the meal. When they met, Neil Kinnock was giving a farewell party for his staff at a nearby table and, in the event, Blair said nothing of any significance. Kilfoyle went home to bed without a clue about the purpose of the meal. He didn't then know that Blair was privately agonising about whether to enter the contest and Kinnock had advised him not to do so. Whether it was the outgoing party leader's presence that night which prevented Blair speaking his mind is conjecture, but with hindsight Kilfoyle told friends he was certain that the other man meant to ask his opinion about whether it would be a good idea.[15]

The deputy leadership campaign in 1994 gave rise to a big disagreement and Mo played a part in it – one which would have given her satisfaction as it involved slapping down Gordon Brown. Both John Prescott and Margaret Beckett were running for the posts of leader and also of deputy leader. If Tony Blair won he wanted John Prescott as his deputy. He was 'old' Labour and would be very useful in terms of the wider party. Prescott got on with Blair, whom he favoured over Brown. 'I prefer Blair because at least you can have an argument with him and disagree,' he once told a member of his staff. 'Brown always pretends he agrees with you and stabs you in the back when you aren't looking.'[16] Gordon Brown, who was trying now to empower his future status as Shadow Chancellor, didn't want Prescott to be the deputy, however. He wanted the former incumbent Margaret Beckett. An insider explained: 'He thought Prescott had some wacky ideas and would meddle all over Gordon's patch. Beckett would be tame and do nothing and it would be obvious to everybody that the *real* deputy leader was Gordon.' On the day that nominations were closing Brown went on television without consulting anybody and announced that he was nominating Beckett. There was consternation in the Blair team at this blatant attempt to bounce the outcome by giving the impression that they also wanted Beckett. Blair was angry. Straw was furious. Mo privately berated Brown with her usual impeccable building-site vernacular.

The insider explained: 'She was allowed to go on TV as one of Blair's campaign team and say she was nominating John Prescott. She was licensed to do that. She would have done that, anyway, but she had arranged to do interviews with the BBC and Sky so Tony was quite happy that she should say that because Gordon did what he had done without consulting or being authorised by him. By that stage Tony had decided he wanted John as his deputy: Philip Gould said that Blair/Prescott would be better than Blair/Beckett because nobody knew who Margaret Beckett was.'[17]

The other bizarre aspect of the Blair campaign, as is now well authenticated, was the supposedly secret role of Peter Mandelson. Initially Mo was among those who did not know that Mandelson had decided to support Blair – at what proved to be the cost of his friendship with Brown. A friend of hers rang her at the outset. According to him she said, somewhat inelegantly, 'Me and Jack are going to be the campaign managers', at which this man expressed amazement that she would put herself in double harness with Peter Mandelson. She then snapped back: 'If you've got any hard evidence for that let me know – because if he's in, I'm out!'[18]

It wasn't only Mo who disliked Mandelson. Everyone in the Blair team recognised that he should be kept at arm's length because his widespread unpopularity within the PLP could only cause harm to the Blair vote. The insider quoted above said that Blair's assistant, Anji Hunter, specifically denied that Mandelson was involved. According to John Rentoul, in the week after Smith's death Mo herself threatened to sue an unnamed newspaper if it reported that Mandelson was working on Blair's behalf.[19] It may have suited her to continue to pretend otherwise, but at some stage she certainly knew what was going on.

Mandelson has told people that it was 'nonsense' to suggest she was ignorant in this respect, not least because he spoke to her daily on the telephone.[20] Peter Kilfoyle, whose job was counting heads among Labour MPs, had no idea of Mandelson's involvement until the victory party at Church House, when Blair paid his famous tribute to the mysterious 'Bobby'[21]. He was heard to ask a friend later: 'Who's this Bobby?'

Tony Blair, the new leader of the 'new' Labour Party, was comfortably elected with an overall 57 per cent of the vote and a handsome majority in all three sections of the party's arcane electoral college system on 21 July 1994. He went on holiday shortly afterwards, leaving Mo Mowlam in her position as National Heritage spokeswoman for the course of the summer. She appeared to have begun enjoying it. She played football for the Labour Party against the press at the Blackpool conference – Sport was of course part of her brief – and she had tackled media policy. In the *New Statesman* in September she wrote a detailed analysis of her approach, easing the party's traditional prejudices into the clothes of the 'new' Labour wardrobe. 'Our aims as socialists have not changed but the methods of achieving them have to change as the real world changes.'[22] That may have been aimed at enhancing her vote for the party's National Executive Committee, for which she was standing for the first time that year, but if so it didn't help. When the results were announced at the party conference she was the second runner-up in the constituency section, behind Ken Livingstone, with 35,045 votes. One reason for her failure, it was suggested, was because of her article about selling Buckingham Palace, but it would have been remarkable to have been elected at her first attempt. She was, in any case, elected the following year with 53,578 votes, assisted by a rule change designed to increase the number of women members – the sort of positive discrimination that she later, typically, described as 'Bimbos for Bambi'.

Her setback in the 1994 NEC election was a disappointment, but it was nothing to what lay ahead. Within a few weeks she discovered that this real world of politics meant a change for her, too, and it came very much against her will. There had been rumours during the summer that she was heading for a new Shadow job: one suggestion was Education and Employment and another was Northern Ireland. On 21 October, after the Shadow Cabinet elections in which she came ninth with 124 votes, Blair told her that he planned to make her the Shadow spokeswoman on Northern Ireland. She didn't want it. She resisted and aggressively so. She told him that she wanted to stay with National Heritage, that the policy was at a crucial stage, that she needed to see it through. She held up the rest of the Shadow Cabinet reshuffle. Chris Smith, who was expecting to replace her at Heritage, as he eventually did, spent all day cooling his heels as the recalcitrant Mo Mowlam stormed in and out of the leader's office. Some said three times. Some said five. On the final occasion, Tony Blair asked her if she wanted to be a member of his Front Bench at all and she knew that she had lost.[23]

'She saw that it would mean going into the Government as the Northern Ireland Secretary and she didn't want to do it,' said one friend. 'She was absolutely furious,' said a colleague. 'As a major political ally of Tony's she should have been given a major portfolio – something like Health, Education or the DTI, a significant medium-range portfolio, rather than what she regarded as a Cinderella position. I think that she had been badly treated and she felt that Tony had not been forthright.'

It wasn't that she had no regard for the significance of Northern Ireland. Her objection was because the job of Northern Ireland Secretary was out of the main domestic political arena and she so much wanted to be a part of what was going on. 'She was very, very angry,' this man went on, 'because she thought being *put*' he used the verb deliberately, 'to Northern Ireland' was a denigration of her qualities and her talents – which, of course, it was.'

In retrospect, in view of the extraordinary personal success that she would realise in Northern Ireland, it seems that her anger was misplaced. Northern Ireland was to become the cause that her political career had previously lacked. But it was the driven woman in her who used to lie awake at night when she was first elected to Parliament and worry about getting on who was incensed. 'She wanted a serious job and she would see Northern Ireland as being side-lined,' said another ministerial friend who also bumped into her in a Commons' corridor during the reshuffle. But no one could have told her anything that day. 'She knows what she's doing. It's all because of the family and because being driven was what kept her afloat. Tony was trying to say something different about it, but she didn't see that.' She couldn't have known then that her political instincts were entirely right: it was indeed another post away from the mainstream which would keep her – probably intentionally – at a remove from the heart of the Blair project. She was bitterly disappointed. It was, coincidentally, Peter Mandelson's birthday on the day that she was appointed. Trafalgar Day.

One reason she was so dismayed by this appointment was because of what she believed it said about her relationship with the new leader. Apart from the hiccup over who ran his election campaign – which she later put down to having been stitched up by Jack Straw – they had always got on well. Despite the adjustments she had to make, they continued to do so as least until the 1997 general election. But she could now recognise that she was not as central to 'new' Labour as she may have thought she was. She had her advantages, her personability and her popular touch, and Blair would be happy to use them, but she was still being kept at a distance. Once again it came down to the influence of Gordon Brown. 'He doesn't like people who think for themselves and she was never going to get any job that he didn't want her to have,' observed a Shadow minister referring specifically to the outcome of this reshuffle.

One of the defining differences between Tony Blair and Gordon Brown however is that Blair regards the ability of any individual colleague to be more important than her, or his, personal loyalty.

Brown of course takes exactly the opposite view, judging loyalty as a price above pearls, let alone political competence. Blair admired Mo's abilities: her energy and candour and he was very serious about the task that would lie ahead for a future Northern Ireland Secretary in a Labour Government under his leadership. Before he became Prime Minister he had a small private dinner at which an expert on the Irish question was present and in the course of the meal he casually dropped the name of Mo Mowlam into the conversation. His guest recalled: 'I remember him saying: "Do you know Mo Mowlam?" and I said: "Yes, I think she's wonderful. Wonderful! And she goes down wonderfully." He said: "That's half the battle, isn't it?" and I said: "No, not really, because people like Jim Prior[24] went down well . . ." I don't think he realised at that stage how important Northern Ireland would become for him personally as a symbol of his success or failure.'[25]

However, he had correctly identified her political skills, which he obviously thought were what would be needed. He would commend her facility for being forthright, her lack of arrogance and how natural she was. 'Mo is Mo. You take her or leave her pretty much as you wish,' he said in a television tribute[26] to her at the time. Only in retrospect does it seem somewhat double-edged. She spoke to everyone on equal terms and was no more differential to the party leader than she was to anyone else. She always told him exactly what she thought, not, as so many politicians do, what she thought he would like to hear and he rated that. He also appreciated the fact that she had independently recognised the need to modernise the Labour Party.

Ron Rose, a political dramatist and left-wing activist involved with the Arts for Labour organisation, claimed some responsibility for drawing Blair's attention to Mo in the first place. Rose was a friend of Blair's father-in-law, the actor Tony Booth, and encountered Mo Mowlam through her political activities at Northern College, Barnsley. During the 1987 election campaign, he and Booth stayed overnight at the Blairs' house and he remembered telling Tony Blair that he should look out for this Mo Mowlam who was unexpectedly fighting Redcar, that she was 'great'.[27] But in fact Blair and Mowlam had already met when he had visited Northern College as a speaker in the mid-1980s; ambitious as she was herself, she would have recognised the potential of this swiftly rising young Shadow spokesman who was so highly regarded by Kinnock.

She did have some influence in the Blair office during this period. After Blair's election as leader, Mo contacted Tom Sawyer, an old acquaintance she had met through Bob Fryer of Northern College. Sawyer was the regional secretary of the trade union, NUPE[28], in Newcastle-upon-Tyne, and now, somewhat to his surprise, she suggested that he might consider working for Blair. The new leader needed someone in his office who was of the Labour movement, she said. A meeting was arranged between the two men, which led to the surprise appointment of Sawyer as Labour Party general secretary[29], the most senior official in the party bureaucracy and the person with the unenviable job of managing the National Executive Committee. From this point on, while still pursuing her Front Bench commitments in Northern Ireland, she began to play a significant part in Labour's internal political reforms.

She had been made a member of the party's new constitutional commission set up in 1993 and had been active on John Smith's behalf in supporting One Member, One Vote in internal elections. She was enthusiastic about the revision of Clause Four, Blair's first big test of his power within the party, and despite clashing with her own con-stituency wrote a joint letter with her researcher, Nigel Warner, endorsing the change. In 1995 when the political world went into recess she was made the party's summer campaign manager and that autumn she replaced Jack Straw on the National Executive – he having only been elected for the first time in 1994. That would have caused her some satisfaction since they do not get on well. He has been extremely angry with her at times, blaming her for briefing the press against him, and has told friends he regards her as disloyal.

Now she was on both the two key party bodies, the NEC and the Shadow Cabinet[30] and she had a foot in the leader's office. 'I saw her as my greatest ally on the NEC and I'd go to her for advice and support. I'd say: "How do you think this would play with Tony?"' said Tom Sawyer. 'Tony's office had a very high regard for Mo up to the election. At that time she was a very respected colleague who could bring something new and fresh. He felt he needed her because she gave him street and party credibility. She was very loyal and very hard-working.' 'She's very very loyal, but she likes to be included. If you include her and make her feel part of what you're doing then I think her loyalty is almost unlimited.'[31] This final point would have a lot of bearing in future on her relationship with Number 10 when Labour took office.

During this period before 1997, Labour embarked on a dramatic series of changes in its structures and rules. It also established something called 'Party into Power', a programme intended to manage the tricky relationship between the party activists, the party organisation and a possible future government. After 1997 it became 'Partnership in Power'. Previous Labour governments had always suffered as a result of the strain between ministers and the demands of the more left-wing grass roots, as represented on the NEC and at the party conference. It was part of the modernisation project to reshape this but in a fashion that did not compromise either side. It changed the Labour Party. It took a great deal of work and Mo did more than anyone, according to Sawyer. 'Mo was the only member of the Shadow Cabinet who was prepared to give up a lot of time flogging through the internal change – which was enormously important, even if no glamour was attached to it. She was the only one on the Shadow Cabinet who was prepared to do anything. She didn't take the traditional route of saying: "I'm a great wonderful person" and then spend all her time with journalists, but she rolled up her sleeves and got on with the nitty gritty. She used to come into the office and say: "Tell me what you want me to do."'

She was the person who would 'go on the box' and defend difficult changes – such as, for example, women-only short-lists of parliamentary candidates – and, according to Sawyer, she was good at it. She was convincing. It was partly because she was also adept at getting people on side. The intrepid journalist Ann Leslie, a friend since the days of Mo's relationship with Laurie Taylor, remembered once going on BBC Radio 4's *Any Questions?* with her when the issue of Hong Kong passport-holders was topical. When they talked at the dinner for the panel which precedes the live broadcast they correctly guessed this topic would be raised; Labour was in favour of giving a right of entry to the UK to British passport-holders in Hong Kong. 'Mo said to me: "How can I defend the indefensible?" I laughed and said: "I'm sure, Mo, you'll find a way." And she said: "I think I'll need your help." When the programme went out, in an odd way, between the two of us, she was saved from defending the indefensible. If she'd been somebody else I'd have slammed into her about Labour Party policy – but I let her get away with it. There were big strokes and kisses afterwards.'[32]

Although she was outspoken, she also exhibited sensitivity when required. Sawyer remembered her coming into his office shortly after his appointment, when they didn't know each other particularly well. She threw her handbag on the floor, kicked off her shoes, put her feet up, pulled out her cigarettes and said, almost automatically: 'D'you mind?' Sawyer can suffer from bad bronchitis, which is exacerbated by cigarette smoke, and he murmured that in fact yes, if she didn't mind, he did. He was impressed by the speed with which she changed course.

A number of members of the NEC, assisted by external advisers, formed a series of task forces, set up at the end of 1995, to look at various aspects of what was under way and to try to reassure the party that its democratic interests were being appropriately protected. Mo had her own group – on party and government relations – and her old friend, Bob Fryer, who was one of the outsiders brought in to help, recalled how keen she was on achieving a new modus vivendi. There were a great many meetings and Mo was heavily involved.

'She was very, very important,' in Fryer's view. 'One of the reasons why she was seen as a really valuable member of that group was that it was understood that she had relatively easy access to Tony Blair. Her contact with him was not because of her membership of the Shadow Cabinet but because of her personal contact, which went back quite a long way. It was understood that she could raise difficult issues with him if necessary. Tony Blair wanted it clear that people were elected by people – and a Labour Government couldn't have a special accountability to party conference and the National Executive in a way that the rest of the country felt excluded from that relationship. He wanted the nature of the relationship changed and the assumptions behind it.

'She was a strong member of the National Executive, probably the most senior member in party terms. She was popular with the party already. She was in the Shadow Cabinet. She could get to see Blair when she wanted. She was known to adhere to the line that the way forward was not simply to dilute the party – that this would be not only unacceptable but politically inept. All of this added up to a feeling that Mo was a very important member of this group.'[33]

According to some a few strains did begin to show. There was already an awareness within the parliamentary party that the leadership was evolving into a troika – with Blair relying on Brown and Mandelson, without sufficient reference to others and what they were doing. One example came within an area of Mo's responsibilities: she chaired the NEC Youth committee. In this capacity, she had overseen a research project, with assistance from policy specialists within the Labour-supporting Institute for Public Policy Research. She then discovered that none other than her old adversary Gordon Brown had embarked on a similar programme, also using researchers from the IPPR but coming to different conclusions. In consequence, she and Peter Kilfoyle, by then an Education and Employment spokesman, wrote a joint letter to Brown pointing out the dangers of a lack of liaison and asking him to do them the courtesy of consulting them in their respective capacities, so that the party's work in this field could at least be co-ordinated. He failed to respond. Mo was said to be 'cheesed off' and the extent of her antipathy to the Shadow Chancellor began to surface publicly.[34]

She had a great deal with which to contend. She was extraordinarily busy. She visited Northern Ireland every week. She had endless NEC responsibilities and she was working at a phenomenal rate. She and Jon married in 1995 and it was a commitment that naturally mattered greatly to her; she wanted to get the balance between her professional and personal life right as well as managing the relationship with his children. At the same time she was contending with her ongoing staff problems in Redcar, while at Westminster she got an official slap over the wrists for failing to register a £21,000 donation from Mirror Group Newspapers to pay her researcher. As ever, she was trying to give up smoking and yet Jon was cooking her delicious meals so she was putting on weight. She was worried about that. 'She clearly wasn't very well,' Bob Fryer said. 'She wasn't just tired, she was exhausted. But she would brush aside any comment with "Well what do you bloody expect?"'

In September 1996, during the parliamentary recess, she became ill. It was glandular fever, or so she told the very few people who knew about it. She retreated to Redcar, on her own, and behaved in a most untypical fashion. Her house on the Redcar seafront has her constituency office in one front room and her library, containing mostly academic books, in the other. A conservatory runs across the back of the house, extending the width of the wide hallway and a comfortable rear sitting room. On the other side at the back is a pine-clad kitchen with the pine table the Blairs gave her years ago. It is a four-bedroomed house and one of them doubles as her private study and she has a desk there looking out to sea. Throughout the time that she was there she remained upstairs – at least during office hours, while her agent,

Keith Legg, and the two other members of staff, Eileen Johnson and Judy Moore, were in and out of the constituency office downstairs as usual. It is understandable that being ill, with people working in her home, she would want to retreat to her own private quarters. But uncharacteristically she didn't want anyone else in Redcar to know that she was there and that she was ill. She didn't want anyone to know that she was vulnerable. Eileen and Judy took her food. Keith kept out of the way. When she decided that she was better she went back to London. It was a curious episode.

One of Mo's many political friends is the Labour baroness Margaret Jay. Over the years Mo had stayed at her home in the west of Ireland, and Jon Norton and Margaret's husband, the medical professor Michael Adler, had become friends as well. At Christmas 1996 Mo and Jon visited with Jon's children but there was no suggestion that Mo had any indication she might be ill, although there was much talk about her giving up smoking.

It was typical of her not to say anything. She knew she was ill, though. She had been suffering from a pain in her left arm for months and over Christmas it had got worse. There was a tremor in her hand as well. She had been meaning to do something about it. She had even made two appointments and cancelled them, pleading pressure of work. Now, from Ireland, she rang her assistant Kate Williams, asked her to make another early appointment – and returned to the festivities. On Monday 6 January, as soon as she was back in Britain she saw her doctor. She was referred to Charing Cross Hospital for tests for a brain tumour.

She has disclosed very little. She was alone when the doctor told her about the existence of the tumour, the size of a small orange above her left temple. She was very frightened, and she had to wait a week before learning of its provenance and her chances of survival. When reassured, after waiting those few dread-filled days, that she would live, she just got on with it: with the terrible treatment and with the rest of her life.

261

She told Tony Blair – in a matter-of-fact sort of way, he said. She wanted to continue working if that was all right by him and it was. She told Jon and Henrietta, his elder child, and then they went out to see the film of *Evita* as they had planned. Her assistant Kate Williams also needed to know. Kate, the daughter of the playwright Colin Welland, had become a close friend in the three years she had worked for Mo, organising her diary in London and Northern Ireland, and she would have to drive Mo to hospital every weekday for the gruelling sessions of radiotherapy. The treatment lasted from January through March and the steroid treatment went on through April.

The hospital had offered Mo the choice of having treatment straight away or waiting until the autumn when the election was over. She took the immediate option. It was extremely tiring. The political atmosphere in the run-up to a general election is always very febrile and there was still a great deal of work to do – work she had to do herself because she hadn't told people that she was ill. Many suspected it, despite her claiming afterwards that nobody had noticed. She boasted, in her memorable appearance on the *Parkinson* show, that it was only when she was sitting alongside the rest of the Shadow Cabinet at the launch of the manifesto that it was remarked that her appearance had altered. That was not true. Many people had been aware of her dramatic weight gain after she started taking steroids. When her friends asked her about it, she just shrugged them off. It was also apparent that she was wearing a wig. Although she had had her own hair cut before it fell out in handfuls in order that it should match her wig – or wigs, she had at least two because, she said, she kept losing them – she still looked profoundly different. 'She *says* that nobody noticed she'd put on six stone and had a wig!' said one colleague. 'I asked her: "Are you all right?" and she said: "It's just I've given up smoking."' As ever, Mo was not prepared to confide in anybody. When she bumped into Margaret Jay after their discussions at Christmas, she would laugh and say: 'See what you've made me do by giving up smoking!'

Bill Doult, the lobby correspondent for the *Evening Gazette* in

Middlesbrough, one of her 'locals', was one person who noticed and even wrote about it in his column, two months before the national press. It was drawn to his attention by Michael Bates, the Tory MP for the Langbaurgh constituency, next door to Redcar. 'What a transformation!' Doult wrote. 'Gone is the friendly bouncy crown which the Redcar MP has sported for as long as anyone can remember. In its place is a new streamlined Mo with what might almost be described as a sleeked pageboy cut.' So startling was the change, he added, that he almost failed to recognise her. Amazingly, what he also didn't recognise or apparently suspect was the reason. He went on to report the suggestion that her 'stunning new appearance' was a Labour tactic to entice the Ulster Unionists to support them in a division.[35]

One person got it right. The Speaker of the House of Commons, Betty Boothroyd, was very troubled when she saw her friend on the Opposition Front Bench. She recalled: 'She looked terrible. She looked grey, dishevelled. I have such great admiration for her – apart from love for her – and I didn't like to see her looking like that.' The Speaker immediately sent her a note asking her to come and see her in her apartments forthwith for a talk.

'I said to her: "I know you well enough to say: what's wrong with you? You're not looking good. You're not presenting yourself as well as you can and you're doing yourself a great injustice," and tears welled up in her eyes and she said: "I've told nobody else this, other than Jon and Tony Blair, and I haven't even told my mother but since you're challenging me like this . . ." and I felt brutal because I was challenging her . . . "I don't know, nobody knows, whether it's malignant and I don't know what to do." I felt dreadful that I'd been so abrasive with her. So she opened up then and told me. It was the early days then when she didn't know.'[36]

Mo explained the nature of the 'horrendous treatment' at Charing Cross Hospital, which she had to have every day. She had a geographical problem as the hospital is the other side of London from her home in Islington and she couldn't drive herself. All she could do was try to rest in her office. 'There's nothing anyone can do about this,' she said, hopelessly. Betty Boothroyd's response was immediate. She offered Mo a bedroom in her private flat, above Speaker's House. 'Whenever you've been to hospital, whenever you're tired, you come here and you rest here. You have a bedroom here.' After that, during the day, or whenever she wanted to do so, Mo would slip through the office that connects the Speaker's formal apartments with the Commons' Library Corridor, take the lift to the private flat and go to 'her' bedroom to sleep. The Speaker's housekeeper, an indomitable and very kindly woman named Roseanna, would wake her with a cup of tea at whatever time she requested. It was one of the things which helped her to get through.

She was, she told Betty Boothroyd, worried about the press. She was anxious about photographs. She suspected that someone might deliberately try to bump into her and knock her off balance to prove that she was wearing a wig. She had even thought that some of her MP colleagues might try that, too. She was steeling herself for the ordeal ahead: 'I'm going to tell them,' she resolved to her friend when the election was about to be announced. Her timing was prompted by the launch of the party manifesto on 3 April. Her appearance in the public parade produced a predictable amount of comment. The *Daily Express* ran a 'Then' and 'Now' pair of photographs under the headline 'Why are so many of us afraid to give up smoking? Ask Mo Mowlam. She's the Labour front bencher who put on 2 stone in just 3 months – and doesn't it show.' The *Daily Mail*'s Lynda Lee-Potter wrote the infamous column in which she compared Mo with 'an only slightly effeminate Geordie trucker'. The odd thing was how nobody suspected the truth. Mo put out a statement the next day. She was about to become a national heroine. Shortly afterwards, she mentioned how she'd always been rather fond of Geordie truckers and that confirmed it.

CHAPTER 12

'Discipline before desire'

Northern Ireland 1997–1999

W hen Mo Mowlam arrived in Belfast in the warm spring sun-
shine of Saturday, 3 May 1997 and walked immediately into
the main shopping area to glad-hand her way among the people on
Royal Avenue and Donegal Place, nobody could ever have guessed
that she had been appointed to a job that she did not want. In the busy
months before the general election, before her brain tumour was diagnosed, she had prepared diligently for this post. She had impressed her
friends and colleagues, even those who knew her well enough to know
how disciplined she was, with her degree of application. One of them
came across her once studying a calendar she had compiled containing
all the dates and anniversaries of historic and political consequence in
Irish history. She had visited Northern Ireland almost weekly in the
two and half years she had shadowed the job in Opposition, and ten
years previously she had also been a junior spokeswoman for 18
months. She had come to love Ireland and the Irish. In what is a relatively small society she now knew a great many of the people who
mattered. She also knew lots of the unimportant people. And they

mattered to her, too. She was probably one of the best prepared people ever to be appointed Secretary of State for Northern Ireland since the introduction of direct rule. None of that made any difference to the fact that she would have preferred another job in Government.

Hers was one of the last appointments to be made, on the Saturday morning after the election. A journalist from Northern Ireland suggested to her on the Friday night that she was on her way to Belfast. She said: 'How do you know that? I know nothing.' She was insistent but non-committal. 'I don't know,' she said repeatedly. When she was, at last, called in she clearly failed to persuade Tony Blair to offer her an alternative, just as she had in 1994. She must have known that it was a lost cause. She met a friend at the taxi rank at the Members' entrance to the House of Commons shortly afterwards and she told him what her first job in government was to be, but it was only when he looked into her face that he saw the disappointment in her eyes. The word he used to describe her was 'crestfallen'. After that she never let it show and nobody ever guessed. One of her colleagues believed that it was she who had deliberately trailed the suggestion prior to the election that Jack Cunningham was going to get the Northern Ireland portfolio, in the hope that it might then actually happen. If it was the case, it was in vain.

She was already a politician who had won hearts and minds throughout the United Kingdom for her personal courage. Within a year she would be propelled from the platform of politics in Northern Ireland into international celebrity. A year after that, ironically enough, she would be fighting to keep the job.

She first got the taste for the fun and the flavour of Irish politics in the winter of 1988 when she attended a weekend conference of the British Irish Association in place of her senior spokesman, Kevin McNamara. The BIA was established in 1972 as a forum to improve understanding between Britain and Ireland and had evolved into an organisation through which influential politicians, civil servants, journalists and diplomats were able to meet and exchange views in private, formally and informally. Informal Irish discussions normally involve both music and alcohol and so it proved on this occasion when Mo Mowlam came to Ditchley Park, the historic house near Oxford where the conference was held. Marigold Johnson was the BIA secretary. She recalled what an impression Mo made that evening, when the isolation of Ditchley and the snow on the ground outside obliged most of the sixty people attending the conference to spend the Saturday evening together.

'There was a long night to come and everyone was quite sober, standing and chatting, and she was a great success, really enjoying it. It was a particularly friendly gathering of people and everyone wanted to sit next to her, everyone wanted to talk to her. She didn't appear to know anybody. She was very kind and enthusiastic, participated in everything, and just got on well with everybody.'[1]

John Boyd, a distinguished diplomat and then a Deputy Under-Secretary at the Foreign Office, played the piano.[2] John Hume, the leader of the SDLP, sang, and the Unionist MP Ken Maginnis recited a ballad about Northern Ireland. Mo was sitting on a sofa next to the distinguished Irish journalist Mary Holland. 'Well I never thought to hear people singing at a BIA accompanied on a grand piano by the head of the Foreign Office playing for Irish singing! I couldn't have believed it!' Mary Holland said, laughing. And Mo declared: 'I think I'm hooked! I think I'm hooked on Ireland.' There was, said Marigold Johnson who overheard this, a sense of shared pleasure that they had all helped her fall in love with Ireland.

Yet she also recalled Mo saying how interested she was in working in the Treasury, that she liked the idea of dealing with the economy and the City. When Mo went to be City spokeswoman the following year, Marigold Johnson assumed that this bright and interesting young politician would lose interest in Ireland. Yet despite her later attempts to evade the job, Mo Mowlam actually *was* hooked. There are very few British politicians of either of the main parties who have been appointed with a Front Bench responsibility for Northern Ireland and have not in consequence earned themselves a lifetime's emotional commitment to the case.

Mo kept in with the Irish question. Seamus Mallon, who was to become Northern Ireland's Second Minister, distinctly remembered meeting her for the first time – as, interestingly, so many people do. He related to Linda McDougall, the television journalist, how Kevin McNamara introduced them over a cup of tea and how, when Mo left, he had said: "'My God, where did you get this one?" Because she really was vivacious, she was jumping out of her skin, she wanted to get on with the job, she wanted to find out everything in the first ten minutes. He said: "Don't worry. She's good".'3

During this first period of her appointment to the Front Bench Mo also attended another BIA conference, in September 1989, this time at a Cambridge College. Among those invited was a 44-year-old auburn-haired law lecturer from Queen's University, Belfast named David Trimble. His presence caused some interest. At the session he attended he spoke impressively and there was a feeling that he might be representative of a new and more forward-looking Unionism. He and Mo met and Marigold Johnson took a photograph of them shaking hands in the quad. Perhaps she had a sense that their histories would entwine.

When Tony Blair won the Labour leadership in 1994 all his political energies between then and May 1997 were directed at one end: winning the next general election. He did not focus on the Irish question. He had decided that he would support the Conservative Government, which had given top priority to the pursuit of a peace process and had achieved significant progress with the Downing Street Declaration of December 1993. He had lunch at the Irish Embassy a couple of months before the 1997 general election and said: 'I know people criticise me in Ireland, criticise me for maintaining the bipartisan policy with the Conservatives. But I guarantee you this: that if I'm elected, I'm going to make a difference in Northern Ireland.'4 Belfast was in fact the first place he visited when he was elected.

But when he first became leader Blair's motivating factor was not to frighten the voters. When the first IRA ceasefire was called in August 1994, Kevin McNamara was still the Shadow spokesman. It was the middle of the holidays and Blair's office rang McNamara's home to tell him not to say anything in response to the breaking news; the leader of the Opposition was going to handle this one himself. One caller to the leader's office in the morning was told: 'Tony is not saying anything until he hears what the Prime Minister says, because our polls are showing us that on this matter John Major is doing very well indeed.'[5] And so it proved.

That was only one of a number of signs that McNamara was likely to be moved. He had been the spokesman for six years and had been promised the Cabinet post by Kinnock if Labour won in 1992. But Blair wanted a new emphasis and McNamara, as a Catholic, was perceived as being 'too green', too sympathetic to the nationalists. When Blair called him in during the autumn reshuffle he was fairly brutal. 'I don't want you in my Cabinet,' he said. To the surprise of Blair's office, McNamara just said 'Fine' and got up and walked out. He was hurt by the abrupt dismissal, but he left before Blair managed to offer him another post as he had intended. McNamara later told friends that he was too identifiable as 'old' Labour and didn't look the part for the new model Labour Party – 'because I'm fat and bald and green'.[6]

The beauty of the choice of Mo Mowlam as his replacement, as seen by several of those closely involved, was that she was bright, able, persuasive, radical and she appeared to carry no ideological baggage. And there was something else: she was a woman, the first to be appointed to this post and later the first woman Secretary of State. It was a time when Northern Ireland society was facing a great deal of change, in its economy, in the collapse of its heavy industry and in the whole fabric of its society. Someone else who was disappointed not to get the job was the Labour MP Clive Soley, himself a former Labour Northern Ireland spokesman, but magnanimously he thought Mowlam an inspired choice because the shock of obliging Unionist Northern

Ireland to do business with a woman politician might actually accelerate the process of change.[7] It was to prove an immensely important aspect of her appointment. 'The North of Ireland was used to grey men in grey suits coming and doing a grey job for a grey period of time,' said Seamus Mallon. 'No grey suits with Mo. She came attired as she usually did – in what she could find at the last moment.'

Even at the beginning the Unionists were discomforted by this very tactile woman. Clive Soley related how he was walking up Whitehall on one occasion when he saw Mo and Ken Maginnis coming towards him. 'He was walking down towards Parliament Square with Mo by his side and Mo had her arm around his shoulder. Now Ken, like most Unionists, was the sort of man you didn't touch in public – unless you were all drunk and then you put your arms around in the usual macho male bit – and he was walking along looking uncomfortable and then he looked up and saw me coming towards them, probably grinning broadly. He began to lean away from Mo, so there was this increasing angle with Mo trying to hold him back with one arm still around his shoulder and him desperately trying to get away from what he probably regarded as the embrace of the devil – and the she-devil at that.'

According to Soley, who was still very much involved in what was going on, Mo came into the job with no illusions about the Unionists. She carved out her own approach to policy, a reinterpretation that was to put to one side the question of a united Ireland, to focus on negotiation and movement and not to worry about what happened afterwards until that much had been achieved. It was pragmatic and sensible for a party in opposition, he said. Jack Straw was trying to change the party's approach to the existing anti-terrorist legislation – 'new' Labour did not want to be seen as soft on terrorists – but Mo was effective in preventing the party being too simplistic about it. There was a case for some change but she argued also for the restoration of civil liberties and the proper use of the law. She also understood the importance of London and Dublin working in unison and she personally established a strong and effective relationship with the Irish Government.

There was a further aspect to the bi-partisan approach Labour adopted that was extremely important. This was that Clive Soley, who had maintained his contacts and his interest in Northern Ireland, was acting as a secret and unacknowledged emissary between the Conservative British Government and the leaders of Sinn Fein. From February 1994, through 1995 and up until at least February 1996 when the ceasefire broke down, he conducted a series of highly confidential meetings to assess the possibilities of moving the peace process forward. After Mo Mowlam had been appointed, she knew exactly what was going on; she was aware of everyone Soley met and everything he learned. It must have been of great assistance to her as an exercise in the obscurities and the sophistications of Northern Ireland politics. It also meant that she was often ahead of the Government in a comprehension of what might happen *next* in a highly volatile situation.

Soley's notes for a meeting with the Northern Ireland Secretary, Sir Patrick Mayhew, on 8 March 1994 give some explanation: 'Sir Patrick Mayhew is very keen for me to continue my "initiative" but anxious that I should not be seen as a message carrier. I urged him to reopen contacts but the Government is clearly reluctant to do so. I also suggested he reiterate "no veto" on political progress by the Unionists. He is happier with the latter but makes the point that if Unionists didn't participate there may be little point in continuing talks. Agreed I will see Sinn Fein leadership but not report back unless I had something specific, e.g. a date to end violence. Meanwhile I will inform John Smith.'[8]

As it turned out, neither the Prime Minister, nor John Smith, nor subsequently Tony Blair wanted to know anything about this exercise. Sir Patrick asked to see Soley a week later. 'He had told the Prime Minister who said we should have no contact. Sir Patrick made his personal view clear . . . Gave assurance that I would not talk about passing messages. It's a pity, Sir Patrick Mayhew is really trying and willing to take risks but the Prime Minister is politically too weak. (Sir Patrick Mayhew told me that personally he thought I was doing the right thing.)'[9]

At one point Mayhew went to see John Major and Mowlam went to see Tony Blair in order specifically to achieve an important possible step forward that looked possible because of Soley's talks.[10] There were obviously immense political dangers involved, however, on both sides. From Blair's point of view he did not want to risk being involved with something that might fail – better by far that if anything was ever revealed it could be put down as Soley's fault, the results of an over-enthusiastic politician acting beyond his remit. Soley said that in retrospect he understood the caution. 'At the time I thought this is stupid why can't we grab it? I was thinking the mileage in it would be a statement saying: "Yes, this is the peace – and a Labour MP has given it to the Government."' It was very risky.[11]

Soley's notes make fascinating reading. Five days later he landed at Belfast and was collected at the airport by Dennis Donaldson, who chaired Sinn Fein West Belfast. At the Sinn Fein press office he had talks with two of the party's prominent figures, Gerry Adams and Mitchel McLaughlin, and they discussed the current sticking points in what the governments in London and Dublin were seeking to achieve. Soley wrote that Adams, 'who claims he cannot speak for PIRA[12], was drafting a paper and this will be made known to HM Govt (via John Hume[13] in Dublin) . . . They will keep me informed. I said I think it might be best if I started to clarify now because they might get a dusty answer to the document he is drafting. I made it clear I was not nego-tiating or passing messages but that I might be able to move things along at a later stage; if appropriate and if I had something positive to say. Memo: 1) See Sir Patrick Mayhew and discuss; 2) Draft "speech" setting out what I think would clarify for <u>all</u> Republicans; 3) Discuss with Sir Patrick Mayhew; 4) Discuss with Mitchel McLaughlin.'[14]

Throughout his notes of his meetings – which took place variously in Belfast and Dublin, in his own office and elsewhere in the House of Commons, at conferences and in the Northern Ireland Office – Soley shows how the parties were agonisingly inching forward in an atmos-phere of mutual distrust and suspicion. As the possibility of the first

IRA ceasefire approached, he met Mayhew. 'I told him that both Gerry Adams and Mitchel McLaughlin recognised how he and the British Government had moved with the Downing Street Declaration and Patrick expressed some surprise and relief as he feared they didn't recognise it but I also pointed out that the leadership view was not the most typical of their supporters and there was still a deep distrust of the British. He surprised me by saying he knew that and that he also knew that a lot of distrust was rooted in the attempt by the British Government in 1973/4 – I presume he meant the Whitelaw talks. He was very explicit that it was designed to "trap" Sinn Fein and that it had failed and had thus done enormous damage. I told him that I had pressed SF very hard on the need for a significant period of "peace". Anything less than six months and it would be very hard to find anything positive to say at all. I had told Mitchel McLaughlin that if there was no ceasefire at all then even I would be inclined to "give up and go and watch telly"! Mitchel replied that he would pass that on but that we should understand that they were trying to get SF to take a "responsible position", but that there were different views. I also told Patrick of my statement to SF that if there was a ceasefire of some type then at least it created a base camp from which I and others might be able to plan other moves. He said that was very helpful to know.'[15]

There are a number of obvious reasons why Soley's talks were so significant and also why they could not be disclosed at the time. One of these relates specifically to Mo Mowlam's appointment as Secretary of State in 1997. Because she knew everything that was going on, she was exceptionally well-placed and informed when she took office, and her insight helped her make an extremely important contribution to the process that eventually produced the Good Friday Agreement: she was responsible for drawing the Republican movement into the negotiation. Her successor as Northern Ireland Secretary, Peter Mandelson, would say later that this was 'her great mission'.

The whole peace process was stymied by the obvious weakness and vulnerability of the Tory Government, limping as it already was towards the end of its over-extended period of office. Indeed, at one point Soley and his contacts discuss the impact of the replacement of John Major, should it happen. After talks with Mitchel McLaughlin, Soley wrote: 'I expressed my fear that if we are waiting for a stronger British Government we could then end up with a weak Sinn Fein. I therefore suggested the attached proposal as a way forward. I will see Sir Patrick Mayhew but also Jim Prior. If I can get some positive indication from them then maybe we could buttress John Major's position with support from people like Jim Callaghan and possibly Maggie Thatcher. Mitchel says dialogue is needed for leadership of Sinn Fein to show the doubters that the British are serious and that things are moving forward. He will come back with an answer within 10 days.'[16]

In retrospect, Soley's own view – not expressed in any self-serving fashion – was that his 'initiative' undoubtedly helped Mayhew personally to move the process forward. The hypocrisy was that the Tory Government wanted this series of talks, which later also involved some Unionists, to continue; they were just not prepared to acknowledge that they were even taking place.

'Secretary of State wanted to reconfirm that I was not negotiating or carrying messages and I again said that I saw it as telling SF what the British political perspectives were, including the Labour Party's, and that I wanted to hear their perspective. Clearly they know that as a parliamentarian I can talk to many people of influence and I have told them that but I don't go beyond that. He said that it was "extremely useful to have this window" and left me in no doubt that he wanted me to continue . . .'[17]

Yet Mayhew did use Soley. There are a number of examples of times when he was anxious to hear what Sinn Fein thought of various developments and others when, obliquely, he also sought to convey messages. 'Patrick also stated categorically that the NI office had not bugged the talks as alleged by SF. He gave me his word on that but as I hadn't really questioned it I think he just wanted me to do all I could to knock any suggestions on the head . . .'[18]

A further reason why these talks were significant was because of the way in which, after the general election when Labour had taken office, the Conservative Front Bench chose to interpret the idea of the supposed bi-partisan approach in the House of Commons. There were not many who knew of Soley's 'sole role', but Mo Mowlam, once in office, assumed that some word of the extent to which Labour had co-operated in opposition must have been conveyed to the now Tory Opposition. Despite this, she found her position consistently undermined by the Shadow Northern Ireland spokesman Andrew MacKay – to such an extent that on several occasions she gave serious consideration to releasing details of Soley's mission in order to embarrass the Tories and point up the contrast in their approach to the meaning of 'bi-partisan'.

Oddly enough, it was also partly as a result of Soley's activities that the Conservative MP Peter Temple-Morris[19] crossed the floor of the House of Commons after the 1997 election and joined the Labour Party the following year. In 1996, as it seemed inevitable that the ceasefire would end, Soley wrote to Mo Mowlam to report that he had learned from both Temple-Morris, who was closely involved as a backbencher in Irish affairs, and from the then Minister of State, Sir John Wheeler, that the Government was acknowledging that the process was unlikely to continue. Soley went on:

'Peter Temple-Morris is very depressed and tells me the Government is, in effect, "shutting down the process". He attended a recent meeting of Tory MPs at which Sir Patrick Mayhew described the Mitchell Report[20] as "a load of bollocks" and further "we are going to try for elections, but they may go back on violence; they probably will and if they do we have got to throw all the blame on them". This meeting was a few days before the February 9 bomb[21]. Peter Temple-Morris thinks the Government knew there was likely to be a renewed outbreak of violence, though when I last saw Sir Patrick Mayhew at the beginning of this year he was clearly optimistic there would be no such return to violence – though he accepted there was a risk of the IRA splitting.

'I think since then the Government have made a conscious decision not to push the Unionists too hard in order to guarantee their parliamentary support, and that if this meant taking the risk of renewed violence it was one they were prepared to take. I don't want to come to this conclusion but it is hard to read the situation in any other way.

'Following my talk with Peter Temple-Morris I approached Sir John Wheeler for his view. I started by saying that I feared the ceasefire was over, that we could go back to the old pattern of violence but that the Unionist para-militaries may also bomb Dublin if the IRA campaign were to focus on Britain. I had hoped that he might reassure me this was not the Government's view, but he said he agreed with me, though not necessarily about Unionist retaliation. He seemed to imply some division in Government ranks . . .'

Soley goes on to describe Temple-Morris's problems with his party and writes: 'there may be a possibility of persuading him to resign the Tory Whip.' This had been 'implied' in some of their conversations. Soley had also asked him if he would be prepared to talk to Tony Blair about Northern Ireland and Temple-Morris had agreed 'because he was so appalled by what was happening.'[22] Soley invited Mo to raise this delicate matter with Blair, and in consequence Jonathan Powell, the Opposition leader's ubiquitous Chief of Staff, came to meet Temple-Morris with Soley over a meal in Chinatown. Temple-Morris is a man who is very fond of Chinese food. He and Soley had met originally to discuss these very sensitive issues at the Chinese restaurant in the old County Hall building, just across Westminster Bridge from the House of Commons. But Temple-Morris became very uneasy about meeting there because it was uncomfortably close to Westminster. Soley switched the venue of their assignations to restaurants in Soho's Chinatown – where arguably they attracted rather more attention as there were relatively few non-Oriental customers. It was as a result of this that Peter Temple-Morris decided on his own future and the course of one little bit of political history was set in train.[23]

The extent to which Mo Mowlam was prepared for her new job meant little to the people on the streets of Northern Ireland when she arrived there. It was the woman herself in whom they were interested. And she was an instant, extraordinary success. She went out and hugged people, anyone she could get her arms around, as a way of expressing her embrace of the community. They were astonished. People in Northern Ireland aren't naturally tactile, they are a northern race, chilly, more reserved. Hers was a different style to anything anyone here had encountered from a politician before and, according to the community worker May Blood[24], it brought a new dimension into the place. The people of Northern Ireland had been used to thinking of the Secretary of State as someone remote, up in Hillsborough Castle, or behind the forbidding faceless walls of Stormont.

The approach worked. People liked her. 'She arrived in Northern Ireland at a time when we needed a hug,' said May Blood. At the top of Royal Avenue an excited journalist dropped his microphone and she picked it up for him. Even Ken Maginnis conceded once that when she was an Opposition MP and stayed with him and his family for a couple of days 'she was good fun'.[25] A Unionist who has a British Labour politician to stay in his home and describes her as 'fun'? A Secretary of State who picks up a reporter's microphone? These things were previously unknown.

Her very personal approach gave rise to an immediate stream of anecdotes. If you hadn't been kissed by Mo in Northern Ireland, it was said, you must have been running very hard in the opposite direction. The phrase 'touchy-feely' came into use – the dreaded phrase as it became and not only because it was very soon exhausted with overuse. Probably it was always inevitable that, eventually, this exceptional popularity Mo Mowlam enjoyed at a personal level would be used against her by the enemies she created at a political level. It was unavoidable because she challenged Northern Ireland, she confronted it – its establishment, its politicians, its institutions, and its people; she confronted them all with their own shortcomings. It was just as she had challenged people all her life: friends, colleagues and the local Labour parties. It was just that this time, here in Northern Ireland confronting the prejudices born of 600 years of history, the challenge was on a somewhat larger and infinitely more dangerous scale.

And her popularity carried its own danger for her closer to home, too. It was never going to be a source of undiluted delight to her political enemies, or even her colleagues, at Westminster. She was once asked at a press conference in Castle Buildings at a time when everything was going well and her personal credibility was at its height, what her best moment had been in the course of the successful negotiations before the Good Friday Agreement. Typically she didn't answer the question as put. One of her ministers remembered: 'She said that the worst moment was the day the opinion polls said that she was more popular than the Prime Minister – and it was the day the Prime Minister was arriving in Belfast.'[26]

For now, though, in 1997, all was going well for her. The political situation was in a state of major flux and the arrival of a new Labour Government with a powerful mandate for change and a charismatic Secretary of State was a vital new ingredient. The scale of Labour's overall majority was obviously an important element – and was a surprise to the MP for Redcar. A friend who spoke to her during the election remembered her forecasting a majority of forty. However, for Mo Mowlam herself, two and half years after this triumph, it did not end happily. She would leave Northern Ireland against her wishes and having been in some ways humiliated. Yet there are many people – and they come from every possible persuasion – who will say that the progress that was made during her exceptional tenure would not have been made without Mo Mowlam and, indeed, was made possible only because of the very individual nature of her character and personality. As Chris Patten[27] put it: 'I think there are a few jobs in politics where personality matters and Northern Ireland is one of them.'

Perhaps it was her tangible humanity? The fact that she was so demonstrably, visibly vulnerable? When she was the Shadow spokeswoman people remembered how she used to be driven around, her feet, as ever, on the dashboard – exactly as in Chris Hutt's car when she was a teenager. When she got wherever she was going she'd take off her shoes, put up her feet, pull out the cigarettes and everyone would relax and think what a relief to meet a real person for a change. Now she didn't have the cigarettes any more, but she had something much more powerful: her very presence was a visual reminder of her illness, her courage and her indomitability.

And then there was the wig. Her newly appointed junior ministers arrived in Belfast on the Monday after the election, 5 May 1997. Paul Murphy and Adam Ingram were the two Ministers of State, Tony Worthington and Alf Dubs[28] the two junior ministers. Ingram was her old friend and Murphy, who had been a Northern Ireland Shadow spokesman in 1994–95, had been surreptitiously studying the brief again before the general election with a view to an appointment back in Northern Ireland. They all arrived at the same time and there was an atmosphere of tremendous excitement and euphoria as they relished the Labour victory and delighted in their own appointments. The job was obviously daunting but the horrid realities had not yet set in. When they went to see their new boss they found the Secretary of State trying her office for size and sitting there completely bald. She had decided that the people who worked with her had to get used to what she looked like with no hair. It was a shock. It was only when he saw her looking like that, one of them recalled, that he realised how seriously ill she had been. Until that point her own courage had disguised the reality.

One person who had helped Mo prepare for government was a Tory Northern Ireland minister, Richard Needham[29]. He confirmed how well informed she was: 'She knew a lot more about Northern Ireland than anybody else coming into the job,' he said. She had very skilfully created a network of cronies, informers and friends and this gave her much greater confidence. More importantly, he said: 'It gave her the power to take decisions. Most people who went there got swamped by the system and did what their civil servants told them. Her position allowed her to take initiatives and do things which no other Secretary of State would have dared do – and that was very, very important in taking the whole thing forward.' He described the age-old process whereby civil servants, with views set in concrete, tried to hobble their ministers by unnecessarily marking papers 'confidential' and 'secret' merely in order to prevent their contents being discussed outside.

When she was in office Mo Mowlam was greatly criticised within the civil service of the NIO: she never took decisions; ignored the boring minutiae in pursuit of something more politically glamorous, like perhaps a five-second clip on the main evening news bulletin. She was said to take a broad brush approach and not be bothered with the detail. She suffered hugely from damaging leaks from within the department. The Northern Ireland civil service, like everybody else, was being challenged by her approach and its staff was unsettled and didn't like it. The leaks were intended to undermine her and the peace process. Often they were based on fairly innocuous papers, but just by reaching the public domain they became more significant and thus made life for the Secretary of State more difficult. 'The civil service in Northern Ireland is out of control,' one distinguished member of the Protestant community said. 'They operate against everybody except themselves. The Labour Government have had to take account of the normal psychology of the people who have been running Northern Ireland for the last thirty years and don't want to give up power.'[30] On taking office, however, as soon as she could she secured a team of senior officials with whom she was comfortable and whom she trusted. There were three in particular – Bill Jefferies, the political director, Jonathan Stephens, the assistant political director and her private secretary, Ken Lindsay. To some extent they provided the bulwark that she needed against the leaks. It was still difficult, though.

Even her most enamoured supporters – and there are many – would not say that she was an exemplary minister in all respects, for she was not. There was a series of problems, some more serious than others.

One was her language, which offended a great many people, particularly Unionists who expected ladies to be refined. Mo wasn't refined, she was vulgar and it could upset people. Allegedly, it even once upset Sinn Fein's chief negotiator Martin McGuinness. 'Secretary of State, I do wish you would stop calling me a bastard,' he said plaintively on one occasion. But she would happily call anyone the first thing that came into her head. At one level it worked because it made her appear normal, real, yet at another level was often a gross error of judgement.

Speaking of herself at this time, she provided one of the best definitions of her approach to her job and her performance in office. She told Steve Richards of the *New Statesman*: 'Being the type of person I am can be a plus and a minus. There's nothing I can do about being me, so they just have to live with it.' Asked by Richards what 'being me' meant, she went on: 'I will be direct, I will be straightforward, I will want to get things done. I don't sit back and wait for things to happen. So I'm a clear person in that sense. I'm a very up-front person. I can talk to people directly. One of the dangers in this job, with all the security, is that you can lose touch. But I can go down to the market place and speak to working-class people on either side and they say to me: "We want peace . . . for goodness' sake, keep going." So I have an ability to communicate and drive things. We've got to keep the momentum going. The downside is that my style is difficult for some men to handle. I've read that some Unionists say I enjoy "lovey dovey terrorist huggings". Well I've never knowingly hugged a terrorist in my life. But in the end I am what I am. It's me.'[31]

George Mitchell, the American senator who chaired the original negotiations and dedicated five or more years of his life to trying to secure Northern Ireland's peace, thought Mo's language was irrelevant. He recalled the story of how during the American Civil War when things weren't going well for the North, Abraham Lincoln tried a succession of generals before bringing in the legendary Ulysses Grant as the Commander of the Union armies. It did the trick. Mitchell said: 'Grant was known to be a heavy drinker and there were complaints to

Lincoln about his drinking. Lincoln said: "I don't know what he drinks but I'd like to send a case to all my other generals." That's what I feel about Mo's swearing. It didn't bother me at all.'[32] Mitchell regards Mo Mowlam as an outstanding public servant and is one of those who believed that the Agreement might not have been achieved without her. 'People say that there are lots of peaks and valleys in the negotiating process. The truth is that there are a lot of valleys and just a few peaks. Mo made the valleys bearable.'

Not everyone was so charitable. Mo's white-van-man mouth was one of the things used against her in a notable public tiff during her first year in office. Prior to the general election, when there was an assumption that Labour would win, Richard Needham was overheard by a journalist, at a party at the Irish Embassy in London, suggesting to Mo that one of her first courses of action should be to change the head of her press office in Northern Ireland.[33] She followed this advice and sacked Andy Wood in July 1997. He had been in the post for ten years and was angered and disillusioned by his dismissal. Wood marked the first anniversary of her appointment the following May with a bitter account of his brief period working with her which he liberally sprinkled with examples of her industrial language.[34] But everyone knew what she was like and they had got the Agreement by then.

Things were not always easy in her office. The staff were used to a different style, a more conventional approach to government – the attitudes taken by what Chris Patten described as 'men with pinched cheeks and little pinched Treasury minds.'[35] 'You could always tell from her protection officer's face what sort of day it was,' one member of staff said. When things were going to be difficult he would come in and grimace and everybody else picked up the warning.

She had a painting on the wall of her office called 'Discipline before desire'. She didn't like it; in fact on the contrary she disliked it. She had asked the curator of the Government Art Collection to tell her the titles of the paintings when she went to choose the decoration for her office and she liked the title. She used the painting as a judge of her visitors:

when people came in and said they liked it and complimented her on her choice, she would have a very choice way of describing *them* just as soon as her office door was shut behind their backs.

She hated bureaucracy and was not good at handling it. She got bored easily. She wasn't good at running meetings either, and some people in her office thought she wasn't systematic enough. The trick of a well-organised meeting, particularly in politics, is that there should be a clear objective, that those present should know the purpose and that it should be steered towards the outcome. This did not always happen when Mo was in the chair.

She was a very demanding boss. There was big trouble from her when people did not deliver information or fulfil requests she had made. She could not tolerate people who did not pull their weight or do the work or put in the hours. Hers was a very voluble style. She worked harder than anyone and she got exhausted. There was the travel, too, which was demanding. She would wake up in the morning uncertain in which of her three bedrooms – London, Hillsborough or Redcar – she would find herself. She was across the Atlantic and back again, too, when it was needed, as it often was.

She didn't look after herself properly, either. The treatment for her brain tumour had ended in July 1997, but it was still a traumatic illness, which she had suffered only just before taking on this gruelling commitment. She kept telling everybody, irritably, that she was fine. She got very bored with being asked constantly, 'How are you really, love?' and complained about 'this Mother Teresa attitude that people have towards me'. But one of her friends said, 'She had no strategy for her physical well-being. You have to stop at times, just to get rid of the tension. In her case I think it took its toll because she was on the go the whole time.'[36] She could recover her physical strength with a short break and, when she could be persuaded to do so, the difference was noticeable. But she didn't do it often enough.

And sometimes, perhaps because of this, she made mistakes. Prominent among these in the first few months was the issue that arose over the Garvaghy Road in Portadown. She had formed very powerful relationships with community women's groups all over the North. She felt that it was very important to listen to women. Her approach was summed up by one observer as: 'Never mind these old bigots and these old men in suits! I'm going to blow the cobwebs away.' Des McCartan of the *Belfast Telegraph* said: 'Mo is not a feminist, but a fighter for women in all situations and she believed that she should tap in to the women's perspective of what Northern Ireland is all about.' He added: 'Her vision was about stopping men dictating to the community at large, telling people: "You have to spend the rest of your lives in the shadow of guns." And she had a higher motive: too many ordinary people are suffering. We as a Labour Government must do something about that.'[37] Her solidarity with women was much appreciated by them. (When a local rugby player made an ill-judged and offensive comment about Mo Mowlam, describing her as 'the only known antidote to Viagra', he was obliged to withdraw his statement. 'The Women's Coalition threatened to collapse his scrum,' said one journalist.[38])

It was in the context of these beliefs that she met representatives – mostly women – of the Nationalist residents of the Garvaghy Road to listen to their views about the Orange Order march that traditionally passes through their area. They objected to the traditional Protestant parade through what is a Nationalist, Catholic community. She gave them her word that they would be informed of the decision taken on whether the march would be allowed. It was a misplaced pledge. The 'threat level' was constantly changing, the Chief Constable advised ministers and it was decided that the march should be allowed to proceed. There was no way in which the Secretary of State could fulfil her undertaking without putting lives at risk and she was faced with the alternatives of overriding the Chief Constable or going back on her word in a highly charged, dangerous situation where others' lives were at risk. She lost a great deal of street credibility and felt very bruised as a result.

Her relationship with the military was not text-book either. They acknowledged that her contribution was an individual one and that this was particularly because she was a woman. 'It took a woman to say, we're not going to live in our sectarian cages. There is common ground and we can find it,' said one serving member of the army. They were, however, disappointed. He gave this explanation: 'The military felt that she didn't understand the security situation. She felt that the security situation was negotiable and in the melting pot of things that could be negotiated away, bartered against progress. But you can't equate the military process with progress – you've got to equate it with the threat. It was also felt that she was a bit naïve, that she told Sinn Fein things that she shouldn't have known and if she did know them, she shouldn't have passed them on. We were uncomfortable about what she might do next. The most important criticism was that the military suspected that she saw us as part of the problem, not part of the solution. We had a feeling that she wasn't particularly interested in us and apart from her initial visits, she didn't come and visit us at all. She didn't really want to know what we were up to, or what our position was, or why we were doing what we were doing. We never saw her. She never came and said: "Hi boys, good to see you." She talked to local people and if she had made the same effort with us, come to the camp and broken protocol and put an arm round a squaddy, she would have done herself a power of good. Everyone knows she's genuine and a soldier can spot somebody who's a fraud at 500 paces but because we never got the opportunity a lot of suspicion stemmed from that.'[39]

This assessment gives a flavour of the complicated balancing act that Mo Mowlam had to perform during this first tumultuous year. It was the period which also saw the murder of the prominent loyalist Billy Wright inside the Maze Prison and her decision personally to visit the prisoners. It was a profound crisis and one of her officials told her that the news from inside the prison was bleak. 'She was quite quiet and then she said: "I shall have to go in." Nobody but nobody else would have said that.'[40] It was brave, but a desperately dangerous decision at every level. It worked, but it was risky. A prominent Ulster business-man said: 'It put everything on the line. She clearly displayed physical and moral courage the like of which had not been displayed by any other British politician since the Troubles began.'[41] She said: 'I am sure it will shock a lot of people, including my own mother,' but she was wrong about that. From Coventry, Tina responded: 'I wasn't in the least bit shocked,' she said. 'You can't just go on doing things by the old rules. They haven't worked. You have to take risks.'[42]

That was not the universal view. The Shadow spokesman Andrew MacKay criticised her: 'Those appalling pictures of the Secretary of State with yobs with tattoos undermined mainstream politics and undermined her position as Secretary of State.'[43] They did not have a good relationship and it would get a great deal worse. The Conservative Party was suspicious about how genuine the commitment of the Nationalists to decommission weapons was and therefore strongly and vociferously criticised the prisoner release programme that followed the Good Friday Agreement. MacKay claimed that she did not keep him informed, while she argued that he did not deserve to be informed if he did not uphold the bi-partisan approach. He responded that he wasn't taking lessons in bi-partisanship from her. After one of these exchanges in the House the two spoke in the Members' Lobby. 'She said: "If you carry on like this I'll take away the support that you get in the province when you visit." I just said: "You do that and I just can't wait for the press conference".'

According to his account she attempted on one occasion to appeal over his head to his colleagues. 'I suspect that never before has a Secretary of State asked to address the Shadow Cabinet. My colleagues were bemused and asked my advice and I said it would be churlish to refuse. She came along and was pretty heavily cross-examined by Michael Howard. After we finished, she left and everyone just burst out laughing.' The reason for this mirth was, apparently, what those present regarded as her risible performance, although the incident also provides a rather curious insight into Shadow Cabinet meetings.

These petty ongoing concerns were, of course, as nothing when compared to the main canvas. All Mo Mowlam's actions were against the backcloth of the negotiations. A further ceasefire had been declared within three months of her taking office, there was ever-increasing polit-ical pressure in Northern Ireland for further progress towards a permanent end to the Troubles and there were extraordinary public expectations. It was all heady stuff.

It was the domestic politics in the North that was the most difficult aspect for Mo Mowlam. She was one person who might be able to bring Sinn Fein into the peace process, but was regarded with under-standable suspicion by the Unionists. Richard Needham had given her one piece of advice. 'I told her: "You must love both sides equally. You have to love them. In a strange way, you really have to appreciate them – their culture, their humour, their differences. You have got to become imbued with what they feel and think. I don't mean that you have to like or tolerate them – you have to come to a view that both sides are right. *Both* sides are right. And if you can do that, over a period of time, even though you make mistakes – and you will make mistakes – if you really, really appreciate them, they will appreciate you".' Mo's problem was that she couldn't do it with the Unionists. She was honest enough to admit that to me before she became Secretary of State. She said: "I think I'm going to find that very hard." There are people you instinctively have an empathy for and people you don't and, in the end, that shows through.'[44]

Needham, unlike his colleague Andrew MacKay, was generous and unstinting in his admiration for his political opponent. 'People say that she is no good on detail, broad picture, etcetera. Of all the people I had opposing me she was certainly the most impressive. She may have been disorganised, but she certainly wasn't disorganised in terms of her argument, or her research, or in picking out the terms on which I was on the weakest ground. I always looked upon her as a friend – which doesn't often happen in politics – but she was formidable in terms of her professionalism, her work, her effort. She cared about it. You really felt she cared, Mo, you *knew* she cared about it. I don't think you can ask for much more, really, from a politician.'

The first political problem was back in Number 10. Clive Soley said that during the run-up to the General Election the relationship between Mo Mowlam and Tony Blair was 'pretty stormy at times'. 'Mo was trying to get Tony to sign up to the directions she was moving in and when Tony tried to pull in one direction and she in another, I think he would have pretty big arguments with her. Certainly in Government she would go off and say "silly so-and-so, he's doing this!" I think she was giving him hell at times, she had pretty splendid invective for him. But at the same time, and this is where Tony is probably under-estimated, he's good at listening and he was listening to her. That doesn't mean to say that he did everything she wanted because he didn't, but nevertheless it was all moving in the right direction. There might have been blood on the walls at times, but at the end of the day he was trusting her. When he came into the negotiation they basically appeared to end up in the right sort of position, even if Mo was reluctant or unhappy with aspects of it, there was never any indication of the sort of disagreement between a Secretary of State and a Prime Minister that could wreck the overall policy.'[45]

Shortly after the election things were going well for Mo within the Cabinet Room. One member remembered wondering if Blair had changed his mind about Mo. 'He seemed much warmer and more engaged about her than he had been. I thought: "He's decided there's a place for Mo. She's actually won her place." She was doing the business. People are quite utilitarian – it was what *she* could do for the Government. It wasn't from sentiment or a value base, it was about delivery.' Then it changed. I can't say that I actually noticed it in the Cabinet, but I was aware that it had changed.'[46]

What happened was that in seeking to pull the Nationalist politicians into the peace process, to bring them in from the cold and involve them fully in a democratic structure for the first time in more than two decades, she was suspected by the Unionists of becoming too close to them, particularly when she shook hands with Gerry Adams, as she memorably did in the summer of 1997. This was an event of momentous significance and about which she herself was very anxious. She sought reassurance from her staff afterwards, asking them if they felt she had done the right thing. It was because she knew there could be a political fall-out, but it was unusual for her to demonstrate such personal vulnerability by parading her fears and anxiety. 'She was tainted, touched with the Blarney,' it was said. By such action she was falling into a Unionist trap because of their strong suspicions that they were also being enticed into something which would oblige them to sacrifice more than they were ready to give up. At this point, because the Government was profoundly aware of how important the issue was for its own popular standing, officials from Number 10 and the Prime Minister himself became increasingly involved in the negotiations, thus effectively destroying the Secretary of State's credibility with the Unionists. In the course of 1998 Blair told friends privately that he had not realised before he took office how important the Irish question would be for him, as it had been for so many of his predecessors. Asked if he was hopeful, he said, 'Very.' He told one of his officials that the only thing that ever kept him awake at night was Northern Ireland.

He invested the matter with his authority. A Foreign Office official on the Number 10 staff, John Holmes[47], and Jonathan Powell, the head of the Prime Minister's Office, became actively part of the British team. The Unionists now had a direct line of appeal to Tony Blair himself. They didn't need to bother with his emissary any more, they wanted 'the big man'. At times Mo Mowlam was very angry. It is claimed that one way in which she responded was by 'sulking'. She wouldn't talk to the Prime Minister sometimes, refusing to take telephone calls from him. In public she denied that anything was happening with which she was not wholly in agreement, yet she knew she was being sidelined. 'Oh, he never speaks to *me*,' she said sarcastically of the Prime Minister at one stage. After he had succeeded her in the autumn of 1999, Peter Mandelson told one journalist privately: 'Tony Blair has been his own Northern Ireland Secretary for the last eighteen months.'[48]

At times in the run-up to the Good Friday Agreement, she was actually kept out of some of the negotiations. Irish officials were astonished at the high regard with which the Prime Minister held the opinions of his Press Secretary Alastair Campbell in comparison with those of his Secretary of State. Seamus Mallon was appalled to see her sitting outside the room where the negotiations were taking place, dealing with the routine correspondence in her ministerial red box. It was humiliating and hurtful and eroded her position in the political process. Others became very angry on her behalf. One of her friends, a businessman, said: 'Number 10 chose not to do what the Chief Executive would do in any company, which is to say: "Speak to the department head." He didn't do that, either through the pressure of the situation or lack of management acumen.'[49]

As events got more heated, more involved and more time-consuming, the Prime Minister was said to be spending 40 per cent of his time dealing with Northern Ireland. When one of the final sessions of talks moved to Hillsborough, the official residence of his Secretary of State, and lasted for three days and three nights, Mo herself spent part of the time reduced to the role of hostess, padding about in her bare feet, fussing around finding beds for people and making sure that they were fed. One round of talks at Stormont was 'very much a Number 10 operation' and it was graphically illustrated when the two prime ministers, Tony Blair and the Taioseach Bertie Ahern, emerged for photographs – without the Northern Ireland Secretary.

It would be wrong to interpret this as diminishing her part in the success that the Good Friday Agreement represented. All the parties to the negotiation, with the exception of the Unionists, paid her credit. A Dublin negotiator wrote privately of her contribution: 'She was a critical player. Her terrific people skills, her indefatigable stamina, her optimistic spirit were vital. There were many points at which failure seemed inevitable. Mo never gave up, nor would she leave anybody around her to do so.' In Dublin's view it was necessary for the prime ministers to get involved. 'It needed flattery and authority and the weight that their assurances could give,' the same official said.[50] The word from the inside was that John Holmes was very impressive and carried much of the early strain on the British side. Jonathan Powell, acting on behalf of Tony Blair, who became increasingly more involved as the months passed, was also impressive, a good negotiator and a good listener 'but a bloody pragmatist'. He was said to deal peremptorily with all the British ministers, not just the Secretary of State. She herself was professional, but it was clear that she resented the way in which her position had been usurped.[51]

A further complication was that while Tony Blair and David Trimble got on well together, Mo Mowlam and David Trimble most specifically did not. They were very different sorts of people. At one point they did not talk to each other for what one of his friends described as 'months and months and months'. That was clearly no way to do business. This friend said: 'I think in some ways he had to blame somebody for what was happening. He had to kick Mo to demonstrate to the rest of the Unionist community that he was in charge and he knew who was to blame for the diminution of Unionist power and the changes they were going to have to swallow – and Mo became the whipping boy. That finally became acknowledged by Mo and Tony Blair. Mo's attitude, very bravely, was that if I've got to be kicked around and beaten in return for a peaceful settlement then I'm prepared to do it.

'Where it went wrong, I think, is that it came down to a personal relationship. Instead of just saying in public, "She's the devil incarnate, etc.", David Trimble allowed himself to get emotionally upset by her. He could have remained cordial in private while saying, "I'm sorry I'm going to beat you up in public." I think he allowed it to spill in to his emotional life and that wasn't very pretty and Mo was understandably hurt and humiliated. I don't think she will ever forgive him.'[52]

Two significant factors that operated initially in Mo's favour were her huge popularity with the public and in the U.S. with the political establishment and the hugely powerful Irish American community. She had struck a note which none of her predecessors had ever previously sounded. The Americans thought she was simply stunning. She wowed them from the word go. Three weeks after the general election she was in Washington and they couldn't believe what they were getting. She had prepared them carefully: at a press conference with eight London correspondents of American newspapers and networks, she had whipped off her wig. 'I don't care about you lot,' she told them. 'I've had enough of it today. I'm in a mood.' They loved it and when she got to America, the people loved her. She had already established that she was an unusual British politician when she was the Shadow spokeswoman. Congressman Peter King, a supporter of Sinn Fein and a politician close to Gerry Adams, had once been denounced in the House of Commons for his views and he did not get on at all well with her Tory predecessor. He first met Mo in Washington in 1995. She was with a group of other British MPs. 'Hello, I'm Mo,' she said. 'I'm Patrick Mayhew in drag.'[53]

Now they said she was 'the missing ingredient', 'great', 'a sensation'. One commentator said: 'What people have been looking for here is a willingness to dive in up to your eyeballs. She's it.'[54] She told Senator Edward Kennedy where he was getting it wrong and he took it on the chin. In New York City she was a similar success. Adrian Flannelly, a distinguished and influential Irish-American broadcaster who runs his own radio shows and privately advises the Mayor of New York on Irish issues, was hugely impressed by her. She pulled off a typical Mo stunt: she waltzed into his radio studios on Madison Avenue to give an interview and all the telephones were ringing in reception; the next anyone knew a British Cabinet Minister was sitting behind the desk answering the phones. They thought she was unbelievable. There was a degree of suspicion, of course. Adrian Flannelly said: 'People either love her or they can't stand her. "The Boys"[55] don't like her – which is to her advantage.'[56] But most Irish-Americans are not signed up members of the IRA. For her this was real power.

And when she met the President and Hillary Clinton, she hit it off big time with both of them. Bill Clinton told staff she was one of the most remarkable women he had ever met. So did Hillary. Their personal involvement in pushing the Good Friday Agreement forward had a very great deal to do with their personal affection for Mo Mowlam. They both helped contribute to this, the world's big push for peace in Northern Ireland. It was something that everybody wanted, particularly anybody who had ever been on the case before. Chris Patten, a former Conservative Northern Ireland minister himself, explained why he didn't hesitate when Mo Mowlam rang him out of the blue in early 1998 and asked him to conduct the independent review of the future for policing in Northern Ireland. As it happened, he was in the US at the time.

'I think to her surprise I said: "Fine". She said: "Don't you want to talk to Lavender[57] about it?" I said: "Lavender will say 'Fine' too". Having said at every dinner party and other occasions, too, that I thought it was scandalous that the British political establishment didn't take Northern Ireland more seriously since it was our biggest domestic political issue, I felt I couldn't do more than put myself where my mouth had been.' Patten had an instinctive admiration for Mo Mowlam, although the fact that his review should be seen to be independent meant that he scarcely saw her while it was under way. He described it as the most emotionally gruelling job he had ever done. Even while he was at a distance from the Secretary of State, he came away from this experience with an understanding of Mo Mowlam's popularity with the people of the place. 'There are very few British politicians who make it with the British public so that when their name is mentioned, the public instantly applaud,' he said.[58] Mo Mowlam was one of them.

It was very much to Mo's personal credit that people wanted to turn out for her like this. When Hillary and Mo subsequently met in Northern Ireland the First Lady's timetable was very tightly structured. The period allocated for their conversation was over long before they had said all that they wished to say. Mo had mentioned that she hadn't had a chance to swim so off they went and completed their chat in the pool. After one visit, Hillary Clinton agreed to return to Belfast for a second, specifically as a favour to Mo. Shortly afterwards, when Mo was due to visit Washington, she was privately invited as a personal guest to stay in the White House. This is not normal protocol. Visiting Cabinet ministers usually stay with the British Ambassador, Sir Christopher Meyer, in his magnificent mansion a little further up Massachusetts Avenue. Mo had stayed there already and enchanted her fellow dinner guests, but this time she was put up in the Lincoln Room in the White House. Years before when she was living in the US and her mother was visiting her one summer, the two women had posed together, as all tourists do, on the pavement outside the fence at the bottom of the lawns with the White House as the impressive backdrop. Mo was twenty-something, slim, pretty and looked about 15. Can she ever have imagined – when perhaps she asked a stranger to take the picture of the two of them – that she would stay there, as an honoured guest, in the room where Winston Churchill had once stayed? Mo greatly enjoyed hearing that callers had been told: 'The Secretary of State is in Mr Lincoln's Bedroom.'

But all was not well in the White House during the time Mo Mowlam was Northern Ireland Secretary. The Clintons had serious domestic problems of their own. When the American Presidency was at the height of the crisis over the Monica Lewinsky affair, with the president facing impeachment and the very continuation of the Clinton administration in question, a desperate Hillary Clinton had dinner one night at the White House with three women friends. The three intimates who counselled her secretly that night were US Secretary of State Madeleine Albright, the Health Secretary Donna Shalala and Mo Mowlam. That was how close she was to Hillary.[59]

Before he became embroiled in these problems, Bill Clinton had already been impressed with Mo as a politician. Because of the power wielded by the Irish-American community, the Irish issue is important for American politics as well. A settlement was in the interests of everybody. But more than merely recognising Mo's particular talent, Clinton was also nice to her. At least one person noticed that he was rather more considerate to the Northern Ireland Secretary than Tony Blair was to his own minister. 'When Clinton comes over he puts his arm around her for the photographers. Blair cuts her out of the picture. He doesn't even realise he is doing it,' said someone who watched this happen on more than one occasion. This person also related how on one occasion a pot of tea had been provided and Mo went over to it and started pouring out cups of tea. The Prime Minister and the President were sitting down and it was Clinton who said to her: 'Come and sit down.' Mo replied, 'Oh, didn't you know? I'm the new tea lady around here.'[60]

The Good Friday Agreement, the 'imperfect peace', was achieved on 10 April 1998. It may not have been perfect in anyone's book, but that was partly the point: everyone was a little dissatisfied. What it did represent was a gigantic step for Northern Ireland. It was a triumph for those who helped achieve it and Mo got much credit, particularly with the public. She found time, when she got back to Britain, even though she hadn't slept for three days, to ring the Irish Ambassador in London, Ted Barrington, who had not been in Belfast for the talks. She knew he would value a call from her, however brief. They got on well. On one occasion at a meeting of the British-Irish inter-parliamentary organisation in York when they had needed to talk urgently, the only available place was a twin-bedded hotel bedroom. They both took off their shoes, lay on the beds and, with the official note-taker sitting between them, conducted their official business. 'These things wouldn't happen if Mo wasn't around,' he used to say.

But how long would she remain around? From Easter 1998 the political progress went forward haltingly and Mo's long-term future in Northern Ireland became increasingly shrouded by the mists that rolled in over the Irish Sea. She had a tough time in the summer. The bomb in Omagh was the hideous centre of it. But for Mo, devastated by the deaths of innocents, it was a cruel summer in other regards. The first stories started circulating that perhaps she was not up to it, that her health was bad, that perhaps her judgement was not what it had once been. Paul Murphy, one of her Ministers of State, dismissed the rumours. 'I suppose some people were envious that she was so immensely popular,' he said. It was complete drivel that she couldn't handle detail and there was misunderstanding about the fact that she quite rightly delegated work. She was, after all, running Northern Ireland as well as everything else that was going on. 'I have never seen such a workaholic. She would constantly be thinking and talking about it. She would ring me at eleven or twelve at night.' He described her as one of his closest friends in politics and was incredibly impressed by the manner in which she handled her illness. 'She easily got tired – but we *all* got tired. I never really experienced any let up in her work and she never, ever complained.'[61] During the talks she was treated for pulling a muscle when swimming. She was walking round with an intravenous drip and she had physiotherapy, but she didn't complain then either.

She clearly regarded it as important not to do so. It would only give ammunition to her critics. She was determined to maintain her image of invincibility, even though it was evident what a devastating experience it was to be diagnosed with a brain tumour. After the former Conservative minister, Jean Denton, was found also to have a tumour, Mo was the first visitor to arrive at Charing Cross Hospital – even before Baroness Denton was out of the operating theatre. 'When I found I had a tumour I rang her because I didn't know anyone else who had had one and she rang me back within five minutes from her office,' said Jean Denton.[62] 'When I went into the intensive care unit, it was like the Mo Mowlam Fan Club and they couldn't believe we were friends because we came from different parties. She was very good.' She helped prepare her friend, who had been told her tumour was malignant, for the exigencies of radiotherapy and of steroid treatment. Mo advised her that the thing to do, when something horrid was going to happen, was to concentrate on an unconnected problem – and solve it. 'She must have more problems than me,' said Denton, 'because I'd always got them finished.' She warned Denton about the tiredness. 'She said she was Peter Mandelson's best candidate in the general election because she was too tired to go off message.' The two women met and compared their scars and scarves for a newspaper interview six months later. As Mo had given courage to Jean Denton, so Baroness Denton bravely spoke out to encourage others. 'It's not the end of the world. As long as you're above ground, you're all right,' she said stoically. 'You look at Mo, working through, and you think: "If she can do that, so can I".'63

One other significant change that Mo made during her period of office was to try to encourage civic social normality in Northern Ireland. She wanted people in Britain to know what life was really like there and she wanted the people of Northern Ireland no longer to feel that they were different and that Belfast was unlike other cities in the UK. She organised concerts. She arranged for Luciano Pavarotti to come and sing at Stormont. It was a great success. She also had Elton John perform at Stormont, famously provoking the hellfire-raising Ian Paisley to complain: 'And now she's bringing in the Sodomites!' There was always a rather stiff garden party every year at Hillsborough Castle, but Mo ran one for the children of Northern Ireland, inviting every school to send two children. There were bouncy castles and coke and burgers in the gardens of Hillsborough that afternoon. But no burghers. The *Blue Peter* programme came to Northern Ireland for the first time in twelve years. She opened up the gardens of Hillsborough on Saturday mornings and attempted to persuade the public that the park that surrounds Stormont was theirs and should be used.

Inside Hillsborough, when she was there for the weekend and it was feasible, she gave a succession of house parties such as the castle could never before have seen. She invited friends: MPs, journalists, actors. There was always an eclectic collection of people, old pals and celebs: Jeremy Irons and Sinead Cusack, Dawn French and Lenny Henry, Janet Street-Porter, Richard Wilson, Michael Cashman, Betty Boothroyd, Helena Kennedy. And everyone was always encouraged to bring their children. She loved having children there. She has always had a particular rapport with any child and has a particular empathy with children who have disabilities. The journalist Simon Walters wrote movingly about the unusual relationship Mo established with his daughter, Zara, who has Downs Syndrome and autism, when his family spent the weekend there.[64]

There was a similar pattern to the weekends: after arriving on Friday night, guests were invited to enjoy the place the next day. According to the season, there was tennis or croquet or badminton. You could play conkers or enjoy the gardens, depending on your age or aptitude. There would be a jolly session in The Hillside, the pub in the village, at lunchtime on Saturday and a meal in the evening cooked by Jon. The domestic staff were not on duty and everyone mucked in, peeling potatoes, doing the washing-up. After dinner they might play charades until the early hours – which must have been rather good, given some of the guests. There might be lunch on Sunday or Jon might cook bacon and eggs for everybody. The emphasis was on fun.

And it was fun, compared to the other things going on in her life. But for all that, she wanted to stay with the job, and said on a number of occasions that she hoped to remain there for another year. It was difficult for her politically but at the same time she was being canonised as a secular saint. She was popular with the party, with the public and with the press. Most of the newspapers were eating out of her hand, although, certainly with the Irish press corps, she could be very swift to turn against an individual who wrote something she didn't like. She could be ruthless then. The majority of political journalists at Westminster relished her candour and her humour. She passed through the press writing room at the Labour conference in Blackpool at the end of September, came up behind one journalist and when he turned round, she unexpectedly kissed him full on the lips. As he recovered from the surprise at this apparent touch of greatness she strode off, pausing only to call, laughing, over her shoulder: 'By the way, I've got 'flu!'

She was popular with the proprietors, particularly with David Montgomery, who remained as Chief Executive of the Mirror Group until January 1999. As a boy he had lived round the corner from David Trimble in Bangor, County Down, they went to the same school and Montgomery's brother had taught with Trimble at Queen's University, Belfast, for years. They had become close friends, and when Labour was still in Opposition, Montgomery had brought his former fellow pupil, David Trimble, as leader of the Official Unionists, to a Labour conference. His presence produced one of those anecdotes that illustrate Mo's sensitivities. Tony and Cherie Blair arrived at the Mirror Group party at the conference which Montgomery was hosting but he failed to escort the Labour leader among the guests. Blair was abandoned and immediately set upon by journalists. Mo Mowlam went up to one of the *Daily Mirror* hosts and detailed him 'to get over there and look after Tony'. She apologised when she bumped into the man, the *Mirror*'s leader writer, David Seymour, the next day in a lift. 'You know what David's like,' she said of Montgomery, 'the social skills of a snail.' But Blair appreciated Montgomery. At another private *Mirror* function, in Brighton in 1997, when Blair was Prime Minister, he told those present that the first thing he wanted to do was to thank David Montgomery for all that he had done in connection with the Irish issue.

It was Mo who got the public thanks the following year in Blackpool. It happened when, in the course of his speech as party leader, Tony Blair paid tribute to 'our one and only Mo'. She was accorded a standing ovation that lasted for 90 seconds and logged 110 decibels on the clapometer. There were many people who hinged the problems that she subsequently encountered upon that afternoon. She herself was discomforted. A friend told her on the Friday morning before they all left Blackpool: 'Don't you realise they're going to come gunning for you?' She said: 'I want to go away and think about it.' Then she added, in a characteristic phrase: 'It's a question of whether you want to be part of the dick-wavers or not.' The friend asked if she liked the adulation and she said: 'I'm not sure. I'm not sure.'[65]

Notes

Chapter 1: Belfast and London, 1998–2000

1. *Guardian*, 12 March 1999.
2. Interview with author.
3. *Time Out*, 20–27 October 1999.
4. *Independent*, 9 March 1999.
5. Interview with author.
6. Interview with author.
7. *Independent*, June 1998.
8. *Sunday Times*, 10 August 1997.
9. *Sunday Telegraph*, 27 July 1997.
10. *Daily Telegraph*, 1 May 1998.
11. These events occurred on 22 June 1999. See *Independent*, 'Unionists: Send for Mandelson', 23 June 1999.
12. *Sunday Express*, 18 July 1999.
13. *Mail on Sunday*, 29 August 1999.
14. Private information.
15. Private information.
16. Private information.

Chapter 2: Moulham, Watford and Southall 1066–1962

1. All references from Tina Mowlam taken from interview with author.
2. All references from Jean Hughes taken from interview with author.
3. Interview with author.
4. Mo Mowlam, 'First Person' interview. *Telegraph* magazine, 6 August 1994.
5. Ibid.
6. Interview with author.
7. Ibid. *Telegraph* magazine, 6 August 1994.

8.   Jean Jacques (née Mowlam), 'Relative Values', *Sunday Times*, 19 December 1993.
9.   Ibid.

Chapter 3: Coventry in the 1960s

1.   All references from Tina Mowlam taken from interview with author.
2.   Interview with author.
3.   Ibid.
4.   Interview with Lynda Lee-Potter, *Daily Mail*, 25 July 1998.
5.   Interview with author.
6.   Interview with author.
7.   *Life* magazine, *Observer*, 28 December 1997.
8.   Interview with author.
9.   Stephanie Oyama (née Ryan). Interview with author.
10. Anne Smith (née Bailey). Interview with author.
11. *Weekend* magazine, *Daily Mail*, 27 April 1996.
12. Profile of Mo Mowlam, Julia Langdon, *Guardian*, 16 May 1998.
13. *Parkinson* 1999.
14. Private information.
15. *Daily Mail*, op. cit.
16. *Weekend magazine*, *Daily Mail*, op. cit.
17. Interview with author.
18. Interview with author.
19. NACOA: Survey by Professor Martin Callingham, 1992.
20. *Addiction Today*. Vol. 10, No. 54 September/October 1998.
21. Confidential information.
22. NACOA: Information for professionals: introduction to codependency leaflet, January 1995.
23. Ibid.: 'It is the view of NACOA that whatever its validity in diagnostic terms, it is helpful to regard codependency as a general term used to describe the way in which family systems and individual psychology are affected by the presence of a chemically dependent or similarly dysfunctioning person.

     'Such families tend to produce children who may grow up with low self-esteem, diffuse sense of identity and a desperate need to control others in order to feel secure.

     'These symptoms are more often than not heavily disguised and the co-dependent person may appear to be happy, mature and successful.

    'The façade is most likely to crumble in mid-life through the development of addictions, compulsions and depression.'

24.   Interview with author.

25.   *Daily Telegraph*, 2 February 2000.

26.   Interview with author.

27.   Interview with author.

28.   Interview with author.

29.   Private information.

30.   *Telegraph* magazine, 6 August 1994.

31.   *You* magazine, 15 February 1998.

32.   Private information.

33.   Florence Foster retired from Coundon Court in 1972 and died in June 1998.

34.   Interview with author.

35.   Eileen Scholes, née Eileen Lennox, became a pupil in Marjorie's class at Coundon Court in 1964, two years after Marjorie.

36.   Interview with author.

37.   Interview with author.

38.   *Desert Island Discs*, 12 March 1999. The other records were David Byrne's 'Don't Fence Me In'; Frank Sinatra singing 'Chicago'; and The Jacksons' 'Blame it on the Boogie'.

39.   Private information.

40.   Interview with author.

41.   *Close Up North*: 'The Honourable Mo', BBC North-East, 24 September 1998.

42.   Private information.

43.   Coventry councillors voted unanimously to grant her Freedom of the City on 27 January 1999.

44.   *Coventry Evening Telegraph*, 14 November 1998.

Chapter 4: Coventry, Durham and London 1965–1972

1.   Fax to author.

2.   Julia Edwards. Interview with author.

3.   Chris Hutt. Interview with author.

4.   Tina Mowlam. Interview with author.

5.   *Telegraph* magazine, 6 August 1994.

6. Ibid.
7. Interview with author.
8. Interview with author.
9. *Telegraph* magazine, op. cit.
10. She meant the use of the word as an exclamation.
11. Warwick Avenue runs parallel to Styvechale Avenue and the gardens of the two roads backed on to each other.
12. Extracts from letter to Chris Hutt, dated 11 July 1966. All spellings and grammar original, uncorrected as written.
13. Extracts from letter to Chris Hutt, dated 20 July 1966.
14. Bridget Boardman, née Hughes, died of cancer in August 1991.
15. Extracts from letter to Chris Hutt, postmarked 5 August 1966.
16. Private information.
17. Now Heather Currie.
18. Chris Hutt. Letter to author, April 1999.
19. Letter to Chris Dammers, 19 August 1968.
20. Interview with author.
21. Profile in *House* magazine, 17 October 1988.
22. Ibid.
23. Interview with author.
24. Interview with author.
25. Now Bernadette McAliskey, former MP for Mid-Ulster.
26. Tony Benn. Interview with author.

Chapter 5: United States 1973–1979

1. Interview with author.
2. Interview with author.
3. Interview with author.
4. Interview with author.
5. Interview with author.
6. Interview with author.
7. Interview with author.
8. Interview with author.
9. Interview with author.
10. Interview in *House* magazine, 17 October 1988.
11. Interview with author.

12. Interview with author.
13. Interview with author.
14. It was entitled: 'The Dynamics of Eurocommunism: A Longitudinal Study of French and Italian Communist Party Supporters'.
15. Interview with author.
16. Interview with author.

Chapter 6: Newcastle-upon-Tyne 1979–1983

1. Interview with author.
2. Interview with author.
3. *Over Our Dead Bodies*, edited by D. Thompson, 1983.
4. Professor Michael Clarke is now the Director of the Centre for Defence Studies, King's College, London.
5. *Debate on Disarmament*, edited by Michael Clarke and Marjorie Mowlam, Routledge and Keegan Paul, 1982.
6. Interview with author.
7. Harry Cowans died in 1985.
8. Interview with author.
9. Interview with author. Major boundary changes between the 1979 and 1983 elections meant that the new constituency of Newcastle Central, while retaining the same name, was quite different in geographical terms and became a Conservative marginal.
10. Interview with author.
11. Interview with author.
12. The Labour Party keeps lists of potential candidates for local elections known as 'the local government panel'.
13. Interview with author.
14. Andy McSmith is now a distinguished political correspondent and author.
15. Interview with author.
16. Best known as a peace campaigner, member of the Institute of Workers' Control. Later MEP for Nottinghamshire North and Chesterfield.
17. Sir Laurence Martin was Director of the Royal Institute of International Affairs 1991–96.
18. Tim Gray. Interview with author.
19. Interview with author.

20. Supporters of Labour MP Tony Benn, who with other members of the Left was seeking democratic internal reforms of the Labour Party constitution in the early 1980s.
21. The Social Democratic Party was launched in March 1981 by a breakaway group of four former Labour Cabinet ministers: Roy Jenkins, Bill Rodgers, David Owen and Shirley Williams – all now members of the House of Lords.
22. Report of the National Executive Committee to the Eightieth Annual Conference of the Labour Party (Labour Party, 1981), quoted in *Faces of Labour* by Andy McSmith, Verso, 1996.
23. Joyce Quin, MEP for South Tyne and Wear 1979–89, became MP for Gateshead East in 1987.
24. In 1987 Hilary Armstrong became MP for Durham North-west, the seat held by her father, Ernest Armstrong, until his retirement.
25. Interview with author.
26. Ted Grant and four other members of the editorial board of the *Militant* newspaper were expelled from membership of the Labour Party after a long and bitter internal and legal wrangle.
27. Interview with author.
28. Interview with author.
29. He has twenty-one references to Mo Mowlam on CD Rom, detailing the occasion they met or had dealings.
30. Interview with author.
31. Interview with author.
32. Chris Dammers. Interview with author.
33. Interview with author.
34. Interview with author.
35. Jim Cousins won the seat for Labour in the 1987 election.
36. Private information.
37. Interview with author.

Chapter 7: Barnsley 1984–1987

1. Bob Fryer. Interview with author.
2. Tina Mowlam. Interview with author.
3. Interview with author.
4. Interview with author.
5. Bob Fryer. Interview with author. (Councillor Owen died in 1992.)

6. Private information.
7. Private information.
8. Interview with author.
9. Interview with author.
10. Private information.
11. Mowlam family.
12. Private information.
13. Now MP for Barnsley West and Penistone.
14. Interview with author.
15. Interview with author.
16. Private information.
17. Conversation with author.
18. Interview with author.
19. Interview with author.
20. The main source of disagreement was Scargill's refusal to allow a ballot on strike action. The Nottinghamshire miners stayed at work, defying pickets. The strike lasted over a year before collapsing and caused immense hardship to mining communities. Neil Kinnock attempted to distance the Labour Party from Scargill while sympathising with the families of the striking miners.
21. Interview with author.
22. Michael Clapham MP. Interview with author.
23. A system of checking whether individuals have voted on election day used widely in the Labour Party. It was developed by the late Labour MP Ian Mikardo in the town of Reading.
24. Interview with author.
25. Now Lord Mason of Barnsley.
26. Bob Fryer. Interview with author.
27. Hilary Armstrong. Interview with author.
28. Interview with author.
29. Private information.
30. Private information.
31. Now Lord Whitty.
32. Now Baroness Gould of Potternewton.
33. Richard Lewis. Interview with author.
34. Now Lord Burlison.
35. General Municipal and Boilermakers' Union.
36. The architect at the centre of a long-running scandal of local authority political corruption in north-east England, revealed in 1972.

37. Association of Scientific Technical and Managerial Staff, now part of the Manufacturing, Science and Finance Union.

Chapter 8: Westminster 1987–1991

1. *Independent*, 16 May 1988.
2. Private conversation with author.
3. Neil Kinnock. Interview with author.
4. *Independent*, op. cit.
5. *Observer*, 19 December 1993.
6. *Independent*, op. cit.
7. Julia Edwards, her friend from Coventry days, is also a constituency acquaintance of Ken Livingstone, in conversation with author.
8. *Life* magazine, *Observer*, 28 December 1997.
9. Conversation with author.
10. *House* magazine, 17 October 1988.
11. *You* magazine, *Mail on Sunday*, 15 February 1998.
12. Private information.
13. Interview with author.
14. The Government's attempt to prevent former MI5 agent Peter Wright from publishing his memoirs under the title 'Spycatcher'.
15. A Ten Minute Rule Bill enables a back-bench MP to raise an issue of public concern, but normally without much chance of any subsequent legislation.
16. 9 July 1987. Hansard cols 558–560.
17. *House* magazine, 17 October 1988.
18. Interview with author.
19. Interview with author.
20. *Daily Mail*, 27 April 1996.
21. *House* magazine, op. cit.
22. Ibid.
23. Private information.
24. Interview with author.
25. Private information.
26. Interview with author.
27. Interview with author.
28. *Mail on Sunday*, 12 November 1989.
29. *Financial Times*, 10 March 1992.

30. The system developed for provision of public money for financing Opposition parties negotiated by Lord Glenamara, formerly Edward (Ted) Short, Deputy Leader of the Labour Party and Leader of the House of Commons. In the 1987–92 Parliament Labour received £839,000 p.a. to run the Labour leader's office and to pay for Shadow Cabinet staff.

31. Private information.

32. *Mandelson*, Donald Macintyre, Harper Collins, 1998.

33. Nick Brown became Government Chief Whip in 1997 and later Minister of Agriculture.

34. Private information.

35. Private information.

36. Private information.

37. 'What's Wrong with Being Middle Class?' Marjorie Mowlam, Fabian Review, vol. 105, no. 1, January/February 1992.

Chapter 9: Redcar 1987–1995

1. Brian Roberts. Interview with author.

2. *Close Up North*: 'The Honourable Mo', BBC Newcastle, 24 September 1998.

3. 1987: Labour majority 7,735 on a turnout of 76.1 per cent; 1983: 3,104 on a turnout of 71.3 per cent. Conservative to Labour swing of 4.6 per cent. Source *The Times Guide to the House of Commons*, June 1987. Marjorie Mowlam continued to improve the size of the Labour majority. In 1992 the Labour majority was 11,414 (53.6 per cent of the vote on a 79 per cent turnout). In 1997 there was a 16.4 per cent change in the constituency boundaries, slightly to the disfavour of the Labour vote. Despite this the Labour majority was 21,664 (67.3 per cent of the vote on a 71 per cent turnout).

4. Interview with author.

5. Interview with author.

6. *Guardian*, 16 April 1997.

7. Interview with author.

8. Interview with author.

9. Ibid.

10. Clause Four of the Labour Party constitution, drafted by Sidney Webb in 1918, contained the politically significant commitment to the principle of public ownership. Tony Blair persuaded the Labour Party to replace it with a 'statement of aims and values'.

11. Interview with author.
12. Interview with author.
13. Jean McCourt later died of breast cancer.
14. Interview with author.
15. Interview with author.
16. Interview with author.
17. Barbara Follett became MP for Stevenage in 1997.
18. Private information.
19. Interview with author.
20. Private information
21. An error made by the author in a profile of Mo Mowlam, *Guardian*, 16 May 1998.
22. Private information.
23. Interview with author.
24. *Daily Mail*, 4 August 1992.
25. Private information.
26. Mo Mowlam had by this time bought her own flat in Dolphin Square.
27. Interview with author.
28. Interview with author.

Chapter 10: Westminster 1992–1994

1. Private information.
2. Pairing is the system by which individual members of opposing parties who have a formal arrangement with each other inform their pair of their intended absence from the Commons in order to balance the Government's nominal majority.
3. Michael Portillo, Conservative MP for Enfield Southgate 1984–97 and for Kensington from 1999.
4. Interview with author.
5. After a heart attack in 1988 John Smith started an exercise programme climbing the Munros – the 280 mountains in Scotland over 3,000 feet. Chris Smith, later Heritage Secretary, was the first MP to complete climbs of all 280.
6. *Women with X Appeal* by Lesley Abdela, Optima, 1989.
7. *The Times*; 24 July 1992.
8. *Mail on Sunday You* magazine, 15 February 1998.

9. *Independent*, 12 April 2000.
10. Interview with Alice Thomson, *Daily Telegraph*, 29 April 1997.
11. *Sunday Telegraph*, 16 January 2000.
12. Quoted in the Times, 17 January 2000.
13. Ibid.
14. Interview with author.
15. Private information.
16. Bryan Gould. Interview with author. The former Labour MP returned to his native New Zealand where he was appointed Vice-chancellor of Waikato University in 1994.
17. Private information.
18. Kath Taylor. Interview with author .
19. Private information.
20. *Faces of Labour. The Inside Story* by Andy McSmith, p. 26. Verso, 1996.
21. Bryan Gould. Interview with author.
22. Private information.
23. *Daily Mail*. 4 August 1992.
24. Interview with author.
25. Interview with author.
26. Interview with author.
27. Interview with author.
28. Interview with author.
29. Private information.
30. *Daily Mail*. 4, August 1992.
31. Interview with author.
32. Private information.
33. *Daily Mail*, 4 August 1992.
34. Interview with author.
35. Hansard col 1096. 17 June 1993.
36. *The Times*, 27 September 1997.
37. Interview with author.
38. Interview with author.
39. Later the Department of Culture Media and Sport.
40. *Guardian*, 15 November 1993.
41. *Observer*, 19 December 1993.
42. Quoted by Andrew Roth, *Parliamentary Profiles*, page 1,610: Marjorie Mowlam.
43. Private information.

44. Interview with author.
45. Interview with author.
46. Later Chief Executive Channel 5 Broadcasting.

Chapter 11: Westminster 1994–1997

1. Charles Clarke became MP for Norwich South in 1997. John Eatwell was created a Life Peer in 1992.
2. The author began preparing a profile that day of Tony Blair for the Sunday *Express*, published 15 May .
3. See, in particular *Mandelson. The Biography* by Donald Macintyre, Harper Collins.
4. *Tony Blair* by John Rentoul, Little, Brown, 1995.
5. Private information.
6. Private information.
7. Private information.
8. Quoted by John Rentoul, ibid. page 373.
9. Private information.
10. *Mail on Sunday* 7 August 1994.
11. *Daily Telegraph*, 17 August 1994. The journalist Martyn Harris died of a brain tumour in October 1996.
12. *The Unfinished Revolution* by Philip Gould, Little, Brown, 1998.
13. *Daily Telegraph*, 17 August 1994.
14. Charles Clarke was one of the few of the 1997 intake to become a Minister of State (for the Home Office) within two years.
15. Private information.
16. Private information.
17. Private information.
18. Private information.
19. *Tony Blair*, op. cit.
20. Private information.
21. 'Bobby' was the code name by which Mandelson had been known in the course of the campaign. It was widely thought to be a reference to 'Bobby' Kennedy, but Donald Macintyre entertainingly reveals in his biography of Mandelson that it was entirely random and was very nearly 'Terry'.
22. *New Statesman*, September 1994.
23. Private information.

24. Jim Prior, now Lord Prior, was Secretary of State for Northern Ireland 1981–84.
25. Private information.
26. 'The Honourable Mo', Close Up North, BBC Newcastle, broadcast 24 September 1998.
27. Ron Rose. Interview with author.
28. The National Union of Public Employees is now known as Unison.
29. Tom Sawyer retired as Labour's general secretary in 1998 and became Lord Sawyer.
30. She was sixth with 152 votes in 1995 and eighth with 206 votes in 1996.
31. Interview with author.
32. Interview with author.
33. Interview with author.
34. Private information.
35. *Evening Gazette*, Middlesbrough, 22 February 1997.
36. Interview with author.

Chapter 12: Northern Ireland 1997–99

1. Marigold Johnson. Interview with author.
2. Sir John Boyd, Master of Churchill College, Cambridge since 1996.
3. From unused text of interview for 'The Rise and Fall of Mo Mowlam', interview by Linda McDougall, May 2000.
4. Private information.
5. Private information.
6. Private information. Kevin McNamara was briefly appointed Shadow spokesman on the Civil Service in 1994 but resigned the following year.
7. Clive Soley. Interview with author. He became Chairman of the Parliamentary Labour Party in May 1997.
8. Clive Soley, 'Notes on Northern Ireland meetings', compiled 10 February 1998. Entry for 8 March 1994.
9. Ibid. Entry for 16 March 1994.
10. Private information.
11. Interview with author.
12. PIRA is the Provisional IRA.
13. The Social Democratic and Labour Party leader.
14. Ibid. Entry for 21 March 1994. John Hume negotiated with Gerry Adams in

what proved a successful attempt to kick-start the peace process. Hume was awarded the Nobel Peace Prize, jointly with David Trimble the leader of the Official Unionist Party, 10 December 1998.

15. Ibid. Entry for 22 July 1974. Viscount Whitelaw was the first Secretary of State for Northern Ireland after the reintroduction of direct rule in 1972.
16. Soley 'Notes'. Entry for 25 April 1994.
17. Ibid. Entry for 21 September 1994.
18. Ibid. Entry for 29 January 1995.
19. Peter Temple-Morris had chaired the British-Irish inter-parliamentary organisation and the Conservative backbench Northern Ireland committee.
20. Report by US Senator George Mitchell who chaired the peace negotiations at the invitation of the prime ministers of the UK and Ireland.
21. The Canary Wharf bomb on the Isle of Dogs brought an end to this phase.
22. Soley notes. Letter to Dr Marjorie Mowlam, 14 February 1996.
23. Clive Soley. Interview with author. Peter Temple-Morris was re-elected as a Conservative MP in 1997 and joined the Labour Party in 1998.
24. Baroness Blood became a member of the House of Lords in 1999. 'The Rise and Fall of Mo Mowlam', interview by Linda McDougall, Channel 4, May 2000.
25. Ibid.
26. On the anniversary of Labour's election on 1 May 1998, the Gallup poll in the *Daily Telegraph* gave Tony Blair a 72 per cent satisfaction rating. The same poll said that 86 per cent thought that Mo Mowlam was doing a good job (Bad job: 9 per cent; Don't Know: 6 per cent). In May 1998 the Guardian/ICM poll gave Mo Mowlam 74 per cent public approval compared to 60 per cent for Tony Blair.
27. Chris Patten, former Conservative Northern Ireland Minister, became Governor of Hong Kong and later European Commissioner.
28. Lord Dubs, a former Labour MP, was the spokesman in the House of Lords.
29. Sir Richard Needham, the former MP, was a minister in the NIO from 1985–92. An Irish peer, the 6th Earl of Kilmorey, he does not use the title. Interview with author.
30. Private information.
31. *New Statesman*, 31 October 1997.
32. Interview with author.
33. Private information.
34. *Sunday Times*, News Review 'Life With Mo', 3 May 1998.
35. Interview with author.

36. Private information.
37. Interview with author.
38. February 1999.
39. Private information.
40. She visited the Maze Prison on 9 January 1998. The official was quoted in *The Herald*, Glasgow, 30 June 1998.
41. Private information.
42. Tina Mowlam. Interview in the *Sunday Express*, 11 January 1998.
43. Interview with author.
44. Interview with author.
45. Interview with author.
46. Private information.
47. John Holmes was appointed Ambassador to Portugal in 1999 and was succeeded in this role by John Sawyers.
48. Private information.
49. Private information.
50. Private information.
51. Private information.
52. Private conversation with author.
53. *Ethnic NewsWatch*, 28 February 1998.
54. *Independent*, 24 May 1997.
55. 'The Boys' is a reference to the IRA.
56. Interview with author.
57. Chris Patten's wife.
58. Interview with author.
59. Private information.
60. Private information.
61. Interview with author. Paul Murphy was appointed Secretary of State for Wales in July 1999.
62. Baroness Denton was a minister in the NIO from 1994–97. Interview with author.
63. *Mail on Sunday*, 9 August 1998.
64. *Sunday Express*, May 10, 1998.
65. Private information.

Index

Index